CW00606957

EXPLORATIONS IN SOCIOLOGY
A series under the auspices of the British Sociological Association

Gareth Rees, Janet Bujra, Paul Littlewood, Howard Newby and Teresa L. Rees (editors)

19   *Political Action and Social Identity* *

Howard Newby, Janet Bujra, Paul Littlewood, Gareth Rees and Teresa L. Rees (editors)

20   *Restructuring Capital* *

*Published by Macmillan

Series Standing Order

If you would like to receive future titles in this series as they are published, you can make use of our standing order facility. To place a standing order please contact your bookseller or, in case of difficulty, write to us at the address below with your name and address and the name of the series. Please state with which title you wish to begin your standing order. (If you live outside the United Kingdom we may not have the rights for your area, in which case we will forward your order to the publisher concerned.)

Standing Order Service, Macmillan Distribution Ltd, Houndmills, Basingstoke, Hants, RG21 2XS, England.

RESTRUCTURING CAPITAL

Recession and Reorganization in Industrial Society

Edited by
Howard Newby, Janet Bujra, Paul Littlewood,
Gareth Rees and Teresa L. Rees

MACMILLAN

First published 1985

Published by
THE MACMILLAN PRESS LTD
Houndmills, Basingstoke, Hampshire RG21 2XS
and London
Companies and representatives
throughout the world

Printed in Hong Kong

British Library Cataloguing in Publication Data
Restructuring capital: recession and
reorganisation in industrial society.—
(BSA conference volumes series. Explorations
in sociology)
1. Industrial sociology
I. Newby, Howard, *1947–*   II. Series
306'.36   HD6955
ISBN 0–333–37334–0
ISBN 0–333–37335–9 Pbk

Contents

vi   *Contents*

List of Tables

List of Figures

Preface and Acknowledgements

The papers collected together in this book (and its companion, *Political Action and Social Identity: Class, Locality and Ideology*) were all presented at the 1983 British Sociological Association Conference, held at University College, Cardiff, on the theme 'The Periphery of Industrial Society'. The papers have been revised by their authors in the light of discussion at the conference and comments from ourselves.

In selecting rather a small number of papers we have found it impossible to be *representative* of the enormous diversity that was offered to the conference. We have been guided instead by considerations both of academic quality and the need to assemble a collection of papers with an acceptable degree of coherence and focusing upon the theme of economic and social restructuring. Within the broad rubric of recession and reorganization in industrial society the papers are grouped into three parts, underlining their thematic focus on the spatial aspects of the current restructuring process, its social consequences and the implications for gender relations. We hope that these papers are indicative of the great amount of research currently being undertaken on these issues in British sociology.

The selection of papers, and other matters associated with the production of this book, were a genuinely collaborative effort on the part of all the editors. We are happy to report that, despite the obvious problems involved in selection and our very scattered locations, this was achieved without difficulty or rancour. We found the process of co-operation to be a rewarding and stimulating one.

One of the more pleasant tasks in preparing this volume is to thank those who have assisted us. Anne Dix at the BSA office was at the centre of the successful organization which made the conference possible. Mike Milotte, also at the BSA, handled liaison with the publisher and tolerated the inevitable delays in production with kindness and good humour. Anne-Lucie Norton at Macmillan and Mary Girling and Jill Scott at the University of Essex expedited the preparation of the text for publication. We are grateful to all of them.

HOWARD NEWBY
JANET BUJRA
PAUL LITTLEWOOD
GARETH REES
TERESA L. REES

Notes on the Contributors

Frank Bechhofer is Reader in Sociology at the University of Edinburgh and Director of the Research Centre for the Social Sciences.

Janet Bujra is a Lecturer in the Department of Economic and Social History and Sociology at the University College of Wales, Aberystwyth.

Ralph Fevre is a Senior Research Assistant in the Department of Sociology and Social Anthropology, University College, Swansea.

Stephen Kendrick is a Research Officer in the Department of Sociology, University of Edinburgh.

Paul Littlewood is a Lecturer in Sociology at the University of Glasgow.

David McCrone is a Lecturer in Sociology at the University of Edinburgh.

Rosemary Mellor is a Lecturer in Sociology at the University of Manchester.

Glenn Morgan is a Lecturer in Sociology at Bradford and Ilkley Community College.

Lydia Morris is a Lecturer in Sociology at the University of Durham.

Peter Murray is a Research Assistant in the Department of Sociology, Trinity College, Dublin.

Howard Newby is Professor of Sociology at the University of Essex and Director of the ESRC Data Archive.

Gareth Rees is a Lecturer in the Department of Sociology at University College, Cardiff, and in the Department of Town Planning at the University of Wales Institute of Science and Technology, Cardiff.

Teresa L. Rees is a Research Fellow in the Sociological Research Unit at University College, Cardiff.

John Urry is Professor of Sociology at the University of Lancaster.

Alan Warde is a Lecturer in Sociology at the University of Lancaster.

James Wickham is a Lecturer in Sociology at Trinity College, Dublin.

Victoria Winckler is a graduate student in the Department of Town Planning, University of Wales Institute of Science and Technology, Cardiff.

1 Introduction: Recession and Reorganization in Industrial Society

HOWARD NEWBY

RESTRUCTURING SOCIETY AND RE-ORIENTING SOCIOLOGY

The implications of the current industrial restructuring for economic and social change provide the thematic focus of this book. It is now generally recognized that the 1980s have witnessed, and will continue to witness, a major transformation of the economic and social structure of all of the advanced capitalist societies. Moreover, this process is seen to be a fundamental *restructuring* of these societies and not – whatever the commonly-offered rhetoric on these matters – a simple recession. These are major changes, not temporary phenomena, and there will be no 'return to normal' should the general level of economic activity recover. In turn they have presented social scientists with a new research agenda, both theoretical and empirical. The chapters of this book go some way towards exploring this.

The recognition that the technologically-advanced industrial societies have been undergoing sectoral shifts in their industrial and occupational structures is not new. For more than twenty years some social scientists have turned their attention towards the long-term consequences of post-war economic and techno-logical innovation and have recognized the significance of the relative decline in employment opportunities in both the ex-tractive and manufacturing sectors and the commensurate growth in both public and private-sector service industries.

1

Debates over whether or not these changes herald the arrival
of the 'post-industrial' society have been around now for more
than a decade (see Bell, 1974; Kumar, 1978; Ellis and Kumar,
1983; and, from a very different perspective, Mandel, 1975;
Gorz, 1983). However, the 1980s have brought not only
'post-industrialism' but 'de-industrialization', a much less com-
forting interpretation. Structural change has not been effected
via the smooth and incremental transition which optimistic
interpretations written in the early 1970s suggested. Massive –
by post-war standards – structural unemployment has recently
accompanied this process and, in Britain in particular, the
major clear-out of manufacturing employment has occurred on
such a scale and with such swiftness that rising levels of unemployment could only ensue. At this very general level, then,
the overall outlines of this transformation are now becoming
clear. We are certainly in the presence of a recession, in the
sense of a reduction in rates of economic growth and a consequent rise in the rates of unemployment, but this recession is
also being accompanied by an economic and social reorganization which will produce long-term shifts in the economy and in
society. Together they represent a restructuring of social and
economic life: hence the title of this book.

Within the United Kingdom and Ireland – the two nations
on which the following chapters concentrate – the process of
social and economic restructuring has been far from uniform in
its effects. Different regions and different localities within
regions have been affected in very different ways. The process
of restructuring therefore exhibits a degree of complexity
which renders both empirical analysis and theoretical synthesis
extremely difficult. Just as the general processes at work have
not been applied evenly to all regions and localities, so in turn
there is no one 'typical' region or locality which can be investigated in detail in order to provide data from which these
general processes can be inferred. This becomes particularly
important where we wish to investigate the political, ideological and sub-cultural responses to the current restructuring,
which are thereby likely to vary considerably according to their
differential social and geographical impacts. (Many of these
issues are explored further in the companion volume to this –
Rees *et al.* 1985.) A further source of complexity is that the
analysis of the current restructuring is not one that sits happily

within the confines of any one social-science discipline, but transcends the boundaries between them. Although all the chapters in this volume are written by authors whose primary disciplinary affiliation is to sociology, it is clear that they do not regard the conventional apparatus of sociological theory to be in itself sufficient to provide an adequate analysis. There are clear signs here of the opening up of British sociology to new kinds of theoretical influences. It should be emphasized, however, that this is not simply a matter of picking up a few 'off-the-peg' theories from other social science disciplines and reworking them within a sociological framework. Quite apart from the arrogant assumptions which would lie behind such a proposal, such theories simply do not exist. All the social sciences are grappling in their various ways with the issues raised by the current restructuring process.

These comments apply particularly to attempts by economists to explain industrial decline in Britain, where the impact of recession has been particularly severe and the problems of restructuring thereby rendered that much more acute (see, for example, Gamble, 1981). There is some agreement over how the long-term historical factors associated with industrial decline can best be described, but there is much less consensus over how they can be analysed and explained. Thus most accounts of industrial decline begin by recognizing that Britain's industrial and imperial dominance during the nineteenth century was to be a mainspring of its weakness during the twentieth century. The system of economic relations between nation states which Britain promoted and sometimes forcibly imposed – namely free trade – also involved a specified role for Britain in the pattern of international trade. As the world's 'first industrial nation' Britain became the major centre of industrial manufacture, exporting both capital goods and consumer products and importing the necessary raw materials and cheap food for its industrial population. This international trade was financed through the City of London, which thereby became the world's commercial centre. For a time Britain's imperial power protected manufacturing industry from the threat of competition from subsequently industrializing nations by providing a captive market for British goods and a continuing exploitable supply of raw materials.

As Britain's imperial power waned and other nations

successfully accomplished the process of industrialization, so the conditions which underpinned British economic prosperity became threatened. A critical blow was supplied by the Second World War, from which Britain emerged not only weakened industrially by the exigencies of war, but faced with a total disruption of established international trading patterns, which now had to be reconstructed virtually anew. Britain's peculiar position in the international economy rapidly became transformed from a source of strength to a source of weakness. As both Scammell (1983) and Williams *et al.* (1983) have pointed out, a new international economic order was created, under American patronage, which was to promote both a massive increase in the trade in manufactured goods between the developed nations and – following on from this – a large increase of foreign direct investment in productive capital in each other's economies. The most highly developed industrial nations therefore became much more highly integrated with each other's economic activities, directly producing in each other's markets and establishing a highly complex pattern of both import and export of manufactured goods. The British economy, however, was trapped by its historical legacy, being more dependent on overseas banking and insurance and with a manufacturing base less capable of adapting to the new postwar circumstances. Moreover, the interests of domestic manufacture tended to be displaced by those of commercial and financial capital, the latter geared to maintaining Britain's traditional role in the international economic order (Longstreth, 1983). During the 1950s and 1960s the consequent failure to invest in British industry brought about a decline in economic performance relative to other advanced industrial societies. Continuing low rates of investment, output and productivity led to chronic problems of import penetration and a declining share of world trade. By the late 1970s these continuing difficulties manifested themselves in high rates of inflation, rising unemployment and the onset of deindustrialization. (These points are elaborated further in Rose *et al.*, 1984.)

Economists have disagreed sharply as to how this narrative historical description is to be interpreted and explained. They have focused on the notion of deindustrialization, which they interpret in a very different fashion from the optimistic discussions of many post-industrial theorists in sociology. There is a tendency, for example, to regard the manufacturing sector as the principal generator of economic growth, both directly and indirectly via the support it offers to the service sector. Job losses in manufacturing industry are therefore viewed as indicative not of rising productivity brought on by technological change, but of an absolute decline in manufacturing capacity. This trend is viewed as jeopardizing, rather than promoting, economic growth and rising living standards. The causes of deindustrialization continue to be greatly disputed among economists, however (see Blackaby, 1979). One thesis, generally associated with the work of Bacon and Eltis (1976), views deindustrialization as a consequence of constraints imposed by post-war growth in the state service sector. The non-market (primarily public service) sector has deprived manufacturing industry not only of labour, but, crucially, of the finance necessary for investment because of the level of taxation required to support it. Bacon and Eltis thus regard the long-term deindustrialization of Britain as a product of sectoral shifts in employment *within* Britain. An alternative explanation is associated with the Cambridge Economic Policy Group, and especially with the work of Singh (1977). In this perspective it is insufficient to understand deindustrialization in Britain in purely domestic terms. On the contrary deindustrialization is an indicator of the poor performance of the economy *vis-à-vis* its competitors. This explanation places a much greater emphasis on Britain's changing role in the *international* economy – its declining imperial power, loss of world markets, its high dependence on multinational corporations, etc.

These debates continue, but beyond the boundaries of economics there is some doubt as to whether 'deindustrialization' sufficiently encompasses the nature of the economic and social transformation which Britain is currently undergoing. Certainly no one would wish to deny the existence, or even the significance, of 'deindustrialization'. The absolute loss of jobs in industrial activities, and particularly in manufacturing industry, has been unparalleled anywhere in the world – 34.5 per cent between 1966 and 1983. Moreover half of this loss has occurred since 1979, representing one and a half million lost jobs in manufacturing industry. Beyond this, however, lies the question of whether 'deindustrialization' is sufficient to *explain*

very much at all. As Murgatroyd and Urry (1984) have recently
observed:

> to say that a local, regional or national economy has been
> 'deindustrialized' is . . . merely a way of *describing* certain
> shifts in the structure of employment – it does not provide any
> kind of explanation. Hence although Britain has experienced
> 'deindustrialization' in recent years, this in fact results from
> highly diverse processes, affecting different localities in differ-
> ent ways depending on their location within pre-existing and
> new forms of the spatial division of labour.

It is this *diversity* of processes and responses which recent
empirical research has been attempting to capture, though the
database remains somewhat thin. Not surprisingly, much of
this work has been conducted by geographers whose traditional concerns with location theory, the spatial divisions of
labour and the changing nature of the urban and regional
economic system have proved to be highly relevant to an
analysis of these issues.

Much of the work has consisted of a descriptive spatial
mapping of industrial restructuring, the production of a new
regional geography of Britain. This in itself has achieved a
great deal in creating an awareness of the sheer diversity of
impacts. We now recognize, for example, that while areas such
as the West Midlands have indeed been 'deindustrialized',
others, such as the less urban areas of the south-west, East
Anglia and the M4 corridor, have been subject to a considerable growth in manufacturing industry. Similarly inner-city
areas have suffered from a massive decline in manufacturing
employment, whereas it has remained buoyant in the rural
areas of the south and east. The axis of economic activity has
swung away from the London–Liverpool industrial corridor
towards a belt which runs from Bristol to the Wash. However
this *geographical* analysis of employment change has been
carried further forward by a recognition that 'space' is not
merely a passive surface onto which the world is mapped, but
also an active element in the processes of social and economic
restructuring which required a considerable reworking of conventional conceptualizations of spatial structure and the spatial
divisions of labour (see Massey, 1983; Cooke, 1983).

To sociological observers some of these reworkings look more satisfactory than others. Perhaps the most geographically-determinist *explanation* of restructuring is that of Fothergill and Gudgin (1982). On the basis of an examination of the changing pattern of location of manufacturing employment between 1959 and 1975 they concluded that the greatest decline in manufacturing employment had occurred in the most urban areas and especially in the conurbations, while in small towns and rural areas it had actually increased. Hence, given this pattern, differences *within* regions were greater than differences *between* regions. These findings have important implications for research strategy and methodology, as indicated at the beginning of this introduction. It is necessary to capture not only the character of the general processes at work, but the uniqueness and variety of the local effects. Fothergill and Gudgin's work sensitizes us to this, but then proceeds (arguably in a less satisfactory fashion) to explain this pattern via a theory of differential locational advantage. They argued that companies in city sites find their constrained locations do not allow them to expand their factory space, whereas in less urban areas, jobs are created in new factories and factory extensions where space constraints are less severe.

Massey and Meagan (1982) in their study of job losses, offered a much broader explanation. As Massey pointed out:

> These changes in the geographical organization of industry and employment within the country reflect national processes of recomposition of industrial structure and occupational structure. They reflect the changing national balance of different groups within the workforce: manufacturing /non-manufacturing, manual/non-manual, male/female, skilled/ unskilled. But precisely because these national changes are taking place integrally with geographical changes, different areas are experiencing them in different ways. In the 1980s different parts of the country are experiencing qualitatively different forms of economic and social restructuring, and consequently face often quite contrasting processes of adjustment. Places come from different histories, with the characteristics they inherit from them, and they are being inserted now into new places in a reworked national spatial division of labour. (1983, p. 8).

Massey and Meagan demonstrate that while some jobs have disappeared (as post-industrial theorists predicted they would) because of increasing productivity and others because of plant closures brought about by a lack of competitiveness, there is a third factor which is of increasing importance. This is the long-term increase in the importance of multiregional and multinational companies and the concomitant problems of branch plant economies and external control. Such companies have evolved new ways of organizing their activities between regions and nations. For example, at the regional level administrative functions have tended to remain centrally located in urban areas, while manufacturing and assembly have been transferred to small town and rural areas where more advantageous labour market conditions (cheaper, including more female, labour; weaker unionization, etc.) may exist. This pattern is repeated on a global scale by multinational corporations, which have transferred many of their labour intensive, semi- or unskilled manufacturing operations to Third World and newly industrializing countries, where supplies of cheap labour are plentiful.

At the local level, then, there is a broad range of 'shift effects' (cf. Newby *et al.*, 1984) which will have repercussions on the occupational structure, class structure, gender relations and social identities present. The nature of the social restructuring will be fragmented and diverse rather than homogeneous and uniform. In the older industrial areas the predominance of a male, manual working-class has been undermined as the occupational structure has become more differentiated by occupation, by industry and by gender. On the other hand in some rural areas the growth of manufacturing has increased the significance of the manual working-class, both male and female. The implications for political affiliation and action have yet to be fully explored, but some increase in sectional, rather than class-based, identities seem probable. Clearly the processes of restructuring will bring about changes in the social, as well as geographical, landscape of modern Britain.

Sociological interest in this restructuring process has only recently begun to emerge, partly because a resurgence of empirical research on British society is a relatively recent phenomenon. This interest has come from (at least) three rather different directions. The first is urban sociology, which during the 1970s, developed a greater theoretical understanding of the relationship between spatial structures and social structures whilst also adopting a greater concern for political economy. This has created closer affinities with regional economics and urban and regional geography which, as subsequent chapters in this volume demonstrate, have affected the nature of theoretical developments in sociology itself. In any case disciplinary boundaries have come to have less and less salience in the field of urban studies and this has, indeed, assisted in the early appreciation of the significance of the restructuring process in Britain during the 1980s (see, for example, Harloe, 1981).

A second relevant area has been that of social stratification, but this has been less sucessful in addressing the issues raised by the restructuring of British society during the 1980s. There are a number of reasons for this (these are elaborated in Newby, 1982) but perhaps two can be mentioned here. The first concerns the excess of what Goldthorpe (1979) has called 'wishful, rather than critical' thinking which has infected debates over the nature of the British class structure from the 1960s onwards – and particularly debates over the character and political role of the working class. Many sociologists continued to accept uncritically the salience of the manual/non-manual distinction and thereby to undervalue the significance of the 'shift effects' at work in contemporary Britain. This in itself derived from a second factor – namely that much of the study of social stratification in Britain was written within a frame of reference located in studies of 'affluence' in the 1960s – which was, in certain respects, ill-equipped to deal with the complexities of change in the 1980s. This is not to suggest that the research agenda developed from the 1960s onwards was totally irrelevant, but there was a lack of critical thinking about the links between class and the occupational structure and between class structure and class action which have only recently begun to be rectified (see, for example, Stewart *et al.*, 1982). Certainly the political reaction to conditions of recession and job loss has not been the one which many analysts of class might have predicted – and this in itself has led to some fundamental re-examinations (for further comments on this see Newby *et al.*, 1984; Marshall *et al.*, 1984). There is now,

however, a recognition of the need to undertake a new round
of empirical studies which do not take for granted conventional
conceptions of class, work, collective action and political behaviour, and these will certainly place at the centre of their
concern the effects of economic restructuring on the present
structure of rewards and life chances.

Research on the restructuring process has also emerged from
studies of gender. At the most basic descriptive level this has
derived from studies of increasing female participation in paid
employment and the associated recognition that the trend
towards increasing service sector employment is based disproportionately on female labour. This, in turn, has led to more
theoretically-laden studies of the relationship between gender,
occupation and class (for example, Garnsey, 1978; Murgatroyd, 1982; Allen, 1982; Stanworth, 1984). These concerns
with the 'public' sphere of work and employment have also
been related to the domestic sphere of relations within the
household (Siltanen and Stanworth, 1984). Consequently
those sociologists concerned with gender relations have become increasingly impatient with conventional definitions of
work and non-work and have sought to reconceptualize the
links between domestic labour and paid employment (see, for
example, the collections in Gamarnikow *et al.*, 1983a, b.), and
between productive and non-productive work (Gershuny,
1978, 1983). The current restructuring has therefore not only
created 'shift effects' in the occupational and class structures
and redrawn the regional geography of Britain, it has also been
associated with an increasing feminisation of the paid labour-
force, with implications for both gender and class relations
which have yet to be fully explored.

These brief introductory comments have sought to emphasize the extremely broad-ranging nature of the social and economic changes being undertaken under the rubric of 'restructuring'.
As Massey has commented:

It will have repercussions on the sectoral and occupational
structure of the workforce, on the social structure, the
balance of social strata within [an] area. It will have implications for social organization, for the labour movement, for
gender relations, and for the relation between paid work and
domestic labour. It may entail the reorganization of the

internal spatial structure of regions, and place changing demands on the social infrastructure. It will undoubtedly involve shifts in the relation between housing and labour markets and alter the composition and nature of unemployment. More widely, different regions will find that the ways in which they are linked into the international economy, and their degrees and type of vulnerability to it, are also altered. (Massey, 1983, p. 9.).

In their various ways the chapters of this book address different facets of these issues. They do so in the full awareness that the new economic and social conditions of the 1980s demand a new set of concepts and theories as well as a new empirical research agenda. Each of the authors would feel that they have done little more than scratch the surface of the problem (particularly in view of the constraint on length imposed by a collection of essays of this kind), but together they do constitute an exemplification of the kind of work which is required and which is now flourishing in British sociology.

THE CONTRIBUTIONS

A number of the themes outlined already in this introduction are addressed explicitly by the following chapters. The willingness of sociological analysts of the restructuring process to engage seriously with theoretical developments in other disciplines is well illustrated by Urry's paper which attempts to reconceptualize the relationship between time, space and the social structure. Within a realist philosophical framework he departs from those (few) sociological theorists who have seriously examined chronology and spatial structures in order to examine how they interact with social entities to promote or hinder the conditions for collective action. It is noteworthy that not merely does Urry attempt to incorporate into his analysis recent work in realist philosophy and political economy (a common feature of sociological writing in the past decade), but also the recent work of geographers who have attempted to theorize space – a much more innovative development of sociological theorizing.

The particular example of Urry's work represented here is

highly abstract and theoretical. It has been developed, however, not on the basis of speculative conceptualization, but
through his membership of a group of researchers at the
University of Lancaster who have been investigating the restructuring process in the north-west (Murgatroyd *et al.*, 1984).
Urry's theoretical work therefore emerges from a detailed
empirical study and his colleagues' attempts to make sense of
their findings. This notoriously difficult problem of relating
detailed, local studies to the broader, extra-local social and
economic processes at work is followed up in the chapter by
Warde, another member of the Lancaster group. Warde up-
holds the importance of detailed local studies in the analysis of
the changing spatial division of labour by challenging the
commonly-held, but unexamined, assumption among many
theorists of advanced industrial societies that there is a tendency towards an homogenisation of space. After reviewing a
number of contributions to the analysis of spatial change in
economics and economic history he concludes that there is no
strong overall trend in Britain during the twentieth century
towards either homogenization or differentiation of economic
activity. He then introduces some interesting evidence on
employment patterns in the North-West to support his 'speculative suggestions' that twentieth-century developments in
trade union organization and patriarchal relations in part explain a number of the manifest tendencies in the spatial division of labour and that together they represent powerful forces
promoting spatial homogeneity. That this process of homogenization remains limited and inconsistent signifies the
remaining effectiveness of other forces working towards differentiation.

Warde's chapter demonstrates that, whatever the trends at
the international level towards specialization and differentiation, the evidence for these processes occurring within nation-
states at the regional level is at best inconclusive. This point is
taken up by Kendrick, Bechhofer and McCrone in their analysis of industrial and occupational change in Scotland. It leads
them to be highly critical of those analysts who have attempted
to understand the pattern of social and economic development
in Scotland by an over-simplified application of 'dependency'
or 'core–periphery' theories of uneven development. Their
critique is primarily an empirical one: that the differences

between Scotland and the remainder of Britain which are often assumed by such theories simply do not exist. Rather, it is *within* Scotland that the most dramatic regional specialization has taken place, while many of the processes which account for this have little to do with Scotland's particular experience. These processes need to be examined in the complex interaction between the local, national (that is, British) and international factors which together produce different configurations of the restructuring process in different localities. The implications of both this chapter and Warde's is the need for a revival of locality studies where this complex interaction can be studied in detail on the ground.

Mellor's chapter on the history of urbanization in Manchester is one example of this, albeit in outline form. In this chapter she documents the nature of Manchester's industrial decline, and restructuring of non-industrial activities, in order to assess the extent of marginalization in the inner-city districts and the demands being made on the local state managers to administer the new 'periphery' – which, ironically, is now the inner city. Mellor stresses how the peripheralization of the inner city has been brought about by a combination of three different levels of restructuring – the deindustrialization of the region; the process of disinvestment in the inner core to the region; and the rationalization of the central area. Morgan pushes this multi-level analysis still further by arguing, on the basis of an initial focus on nineteenth-century Lancashire, that class relations both at the level of the labour process itself and at the level of political and ideological forms, were constituted in part by a much wider process of world development as well as through relations internal to the society under consideration. Sentiments of this kind have frequently been expressed in empirical studies of particular localities and industries, but have usually been pushed to one side in the actual analysis on the grounds of tractability or constraints on resources. Morgan demonstrates conclusively that such an analysis *is* feasible, ranging as he does literally 'from west to east and back again' by his careful mapping of the transnational character of class formation and recomposition in the wake of capitalist expansion in the textile trade. He begins from an account of the British class structure in the nineteenth century, concentrating on the cotton industry and its dependence on the Indian market. This leads to an analysis of the changes engendered in India and China by their integration into the British trading system and moves thence to the importation of Chinese labour into California from the 1860s onwards. His 'panoramic gaze' highlights the obsolescence of analyses of class-formation based solely within the confines of the nation-state. This point is echoed and emphasized in Fevre's study of the wool-textile industry in Bradford, with particular reference to fluctuating patterns of demand for Asian textile workers.

There are some interesting comparisons to be made between Fevre's chapter and that of Murray and Wickham. Both are concerned with industries which have required a substantial supply of cheap semi-skilled and unskilled labour and both demonstrate how employers have been prepared to draw upon hitherto relatively untapped sources of supply in order to obtain it. Fevre's paper concerns Asian workers in the Brad-ford wool-textile industry; Murray and Wickham analyse the employment of women in Irish electronics factories, both factories being branch plants of American multinational corpor-ations. Both chapters therefore address the relevance of 'dis-crimination' (racial, sexual) in understanding employment practices and local class relations, and both indicate that while discrimination is certainly present a more structural analysis of labour market conditions and the labour process offers a broader understanding of the industrial relations of the indus-tries concerned. Murray and Wickham's chapter also contains some echoes of points made by Kendrick *et al*. in their analysis of Scotland. Ireland, too, is commonly regarded as a 'periph-eral' economy, but Murray and Wickham show that this can be dangerously over-simplistic. In many respects the conditions to be found in the electronics factories studied by Murray and Wickham are those sometimes regarded as characteristic of 'core' sector industries in 'core' economies.

The final two chapters – by Morris and Winckler – concen-trate explicitly upon the relationship between industrial re-structuring and gender relations. Morris reports on her study of redundant steelworkers and their wives in Port Talbot in 1982. She is concerned with the sexual division of labour both inside and outside the household and how one interacts with the other. Her study is particularly significant in that it deals with a group of families drawn from an archetypal 'traditional proletarian' milieu (Lockwood, 1966). Insofar as this rested upon the existence of predominantly male, manual employment in the steel industry, large-scale redundancy from 1980 onwards provided Morris with the opportunity to investigate the effects of the removal of this employment base on the content of gender roles. Winckler's chapter, which is also based upon a Welsh case study, represents almost the obverse of this: the possibility of the renegotiation of traditional gender roles based upon the (planned) availability of considerable service-sector jobs for female workers. Notwithstanding the very different conditions in Cardiff and Port Talbot it is perhaps worth pointing out that in both cases local economic restructuring has served to exacerbate existing regional inequalities and done little, at least in the short term, to reduce sexual inequalities.

These comments serve to show the existence and complex ramifications of the current restructuring of the British economy and society. The papers presented here are indicative of the directions which current sociological research needs to take, even though each paper perforce offers a somewhat partial and preliminary consideration. In many respects their unity of thematic focus is complemented by their diversity of theoretical and empirical concerns, for no one research project can possibly encompass all the various aspects of the restructuring process. There is, however, plenty of evidence here that current sociological research in this area is both intellectually exciting and socially relevant. There is plenty of scope for interesting findings and lively debate in the years to come.

REFERENCES

Allen, S. (1982) 'Gender and Inequality and Class Formation' in Giddens, A. and Mackenzie, G. (eds) *Social Class and the Division of Labour* (Cambridge: Cambridge University Press).

Bacon, R. and Eltis, W. (1976) *Britain's Economic Problems: Too Few Producers* (London: Macmillan).

Bell, D. (1974) *The Coming of Post-Industrial Society* (London: Heinemann).

Blackaby, F. (ed.) (1979) *Deindustrialisation* (London: Heinemann).

Cooke, P. (1983) *Theories of Planning and Spatial Development* (London: Hutchinson).

Ellis, A. and Kumar, K. (1983) *Dilemmas of Liberal Democracies* (London: Tavistock).

Finnegan, R., Gallie, D. and Roberts, B. (eds) (1985) *New Approach to Economic Life: Economic Restructuring and the Social Division of Labour* (Manchester: Manchester University Press).

Fothergill, S. and Gudgin, G. (1982) *Unequal Growth* (London: Heinemann).

Gamarnikow, E., Morgan, D., Purvis, J. and Taylorson, D. (eds) (1983a) *The Public and the Private* (London: Heinemann).

Gamarnikow, E., Morgan, D., Purvis, J. and Taylorson, D. (eds) (1983b) *Gender, Class and Work* (London: Heinemann).

Gamble, A. (1981) *Britain in Decline* (London: Macmillan).

Garnsey, E. (1978) 'Women's Work and Theories of Class and Stratification', *Sociology*, vol. 12, pp. 223–43.

Gershuny, J. (1978) *After Industrial Society?* (London: Macmillan).

Gershuny, J. (1983) *Social Innovation and the Division of Labour* (Oxford: Oxford University Press).

Goldthorpe, J. (1979) 'Intellectuals and the Working Class in Modern Britain', Fuller Lecture, Department of Sociology, University of Essex.

Gorz, A. (1983) *Farewell to the Working Class* (London: Pluto Press).

Harloe, M. (ed.) (1981) *New Perspectives in Urban Change and Conflict* (London: Heinemann).

Kumar, K. (1978) *Prophecy and Progress* (Harmondsworth: Penguin).

Lockwood, D. (1966) 'The Sources of Variation in Working-class Images of Society', *Sociological Review*, vol. 14, pp. 248–63).

Longstreth, F. (1983) 'Financial Markets and the Political Business Cycle', Department of Sociology, University of Bath, mimeo.

Mandel, E. (1975) *Late Capitalism* (London: New Left Books).

Marshall, G., Newby, H., Rose, D. and Vogler, C. (1984) 'Fatalism, Familism and the Working Class', Department of Sociology, University of Essex, mimeo.

Massey, D. (1983) 'SSRC Industrial Location Fellowship: Report' (London: Social Science Research Council).

Massey, D. and Meegan, R. (1982) *The Anatomy of Job Loss* (London: Methuen).

Murgatroyd, L. (1982) 'Gender and Occupational Stratification', *Sociological Review*, vol. 30, pp. 574–602.

Murgatroyd, L. and Urry, J. (1984) 'The Class and Gender Restructuring of the Lancaster Economy, 1950–1980' in Murgatroyd, L. *et al.* (1984).

Murgatroyd, L. *et al.* (1984) *Localities, Class and Gender* (London: Pion Books).

Newby, H. (1982) 'The State of Research into Social Stratification in Britain' (London: Social Science Research Council).

Newby, H., Vogler, C., Rose, D. and Marshall, G. (1984) 'From Class Structure to Class Action: British Working Class Politics in the 1980s' in Finnegan, R., Gallie, D. and Roberts, B. (eds)

Rees, G., Bujra, J., Littlewood P., Newby, H., and Rees, T. (eds) (1985) *Political Action and Social Identity: Class Locality and Ideology* (London: Macmillan).

Rose, D., Vogler, C., Marshall, G. and Newby, H. (1984) 'Economic Restructuring: The British Experience', in *Annals of the American Academy of Political and Social Science*, September.
Scammell, W. M. (1983) *The International Economy Since 1945* (London: Macmillan).
Siltanen, J. and Stanworth, M. (eds) (1984) *Women and the Public Sphere* (London: Hutchinson).
Singh, A. (1977) 'UK Industry and the World Economy: A Case of Deindustrialization?' in *Cambridge Journal of Economics*, vol. 1, pp. 113–36.
Stanworth, M. (1984) 'Women and Class Analysis: A Reply to John Goldthorpe', in *Sociology*, vol. 18, pp. 159–70.
Stewart, A., Prandy, K. and Blackburn, R. M. (1982) *Social Stratification and Occupations* (London: Macmillan).
Williams, K. *et al.* (1983) *Why are the British Bad at Manufacturing?* (London: Routledge & Kegan Paul).

Part I
The Restructuring of Capital and Space

Part I
The Restructuring of
Capital and Space

2 Space, Time and the Study of the Social[1]

JOHN URRY

INTRODUCTION

In the physical sciences, Whitehead argued that:

> It is hardly more than a pardonable exaggeration to say that the determination of the meaning of nature reduces itself principally to the discussion of the character of time and the character of space (Whitehead, 1930, p. 33).

However, in the social sciences the incorporation of the temporal and the spatial aspects of social life have proved somewhat intractable. This is partly because most of the conventional distinctions between disciplines (especially those between economics, politics and sociology, on the one hand, and history and geography, on the other) make it difficult to relate time and space to the analysis of social relations which overlap these disciplinary boundaries. Specifically within sociology, it has proved difficult to specify the social in relationship to both the 'temporal' and the 'spatial'. In terms of the first, there has been a tendency to associate the temporal with social change, as though societies only exhibit temporality when they are experiencing change. If they are not changing, then they are taken to be, in a curious sense, atemporal. In respect of the spatial, sociology (apart from its urban specialism) has tended to pay insufficient and ineffective attention to the fact that social practices are spatially patterned, and that these patterns substantially affect these very social practices. Moreover, this particular deficiency is now more significant because of the major changes that are occurring within contemporary capitalist relations which undermine the coherence, unity and

21

wholeness of individual 'societies'. A crucial theoretical problem has been how to develop ways of understanding, not just how societies come into external relationships with each other, but the nature of these processes, especially of multiplant, multinational companies and international state structures, which transform the individual units of 'societies'.

It should be clear that most, if not all, theories in the social sciences contain implications about the patterning of human activity within time–space. Social activity necessarily involves passing through time and space. The passage of time involves movement through space. Pred, for example, wrote of social activity as 'a weaving dance through time–space' (Pred, 1977, p. 208). Changes in the temporal order of events generally involve changes in spatial patterning. Even the repetitions of everyday life involve both temporal and spatial regularities. However, most sociological theories of such activities do not draw out the temporal and spatial implications. They tend to remain at an implicit level. Indeed in many cases if the implications were fully specified they would be found to contradict other aspects of the theory in question. To illustrate this, consider Marx's famous, if controversial, discussion of the growth of revolutionary consciousness and organization amongst the working class (Marx, 1973b, pp. 283–9). I will take this discussion because he, unlike many other social and political scientists, was well aware of the importance of spatial relations. Indeed, it is a major element in his account that as capitalism develops there is an increasing concentration of workers within the progressively larger capitalist workplaces and cities. Hence the growth in the productive forces produces increases in the size, organization and effectiveness of the working class, a class which at least on some accounts is historically destined to revolt and overthrow capitalist relations of production. According to Marx, a necessary condition for this is the growth of the spatial proximity of workers within capitalist workplaces and cities. However, this account is not fully adequate, and there are two important spatial implications which run counter to this argument and which seriously undermine it. On the one hand, although each capitalist enterprise grows in size, this does not mean that workers within each of them are necessarily placed in ever-closer proximity to each other. Marx failed to demonstrate how class organization and consciousness can overcome this 'friction of distance' between spatially distinct capitalist enterprises. On the other hand, Marx did not sufficiently explore other important spatial foci within capitalist societies, namely neighbourhood, town, region and nation-state. Although these spatial foci are intimately related to the patterns of accumulation within the economy, they are not simply reducible to such patterns, nor are their political effects to be seen as necessarily subordinate to those within the economy. Capitalism dichotomizes home and work for wage-labourers; the spatial location of one's home, in a particular neighbourhood/town/region/nation-state, should not be viewed as politically irrelevant. Marx failed to show that these spatial foci will become less politically salient as capitalism develops.

So far then I have established some *prima facie* grounds for the significance of the 'spatial' to the analysis of the sociological. Incidentally I would not want to suggest that no sociologists have been aware of the importance of space, and of time, in examining social relations – see, for example, Goffman on front-stage and back-stage (Goffman, 1959), the symbolic interactionist analysis of the 'career' (McCall and Simmons, 1966), the recent investigations of the conditions for collective action (see Calhoun, 1982, and Giddens, 1981). However, I would argue that there has been relatively little attempt systematically to theorize space and time in relationship to the social. In the following I shall try to clear some of the ground necessary for such investigations. In particular, I have argued elsewhere for a theoretical realist conception of science – a project which involves the analysis of intransitive structures whose existence and effects are to be viewed as independent of the knowing subject and of the transitive concepts of science. It seems to be clear that if we are trying to give an account of these intransitive structures then it is crucial to recognize that these structures are necessarily structured, temporally and spatially. In what follows I shall try to elaborate provisionally the implications of a theoretical realist conception of science for the analysis of time and space within social relations (many of the contributors to Gregory and Urry, 1984, explore this further).

TIME, SPACE AND THEORETICAL REALISM

There is a long-established philosophical debate as to whether or not space and time are to be viewed as in some sense absolute entities, possessing their own natures or particularities. For example, is space something which is causally productive; is it to be distinguished from matter since it possesses its own structure? Or, on the contrary, is it merely a way of characterizing the relations *between* the constituents of the physical world? The latter view was articulated by Leibniz who argued that 'space is something merely relative' – it is 'an order of coexistences as time is an *order* of successions' (Körner, 1955, p. 33). According to this relational view the universe simply consists of pieces of matter, composed of various substances, and these pieces of matter exhibit spatial relationships between each other and between their own constitutive parts. Generally, relationists argue that if any statement do appear to assign properties to space it will be logically possible to reduce these properties to the relations *between* the objects concerned (see Leibniz, 1898; Hinkfuss, 1975).

The absolutist position has been maintained most strongly by Descartes and Newton (and in a rather different way by Kant) (see Garnett, 1939; Körner, 1955; Nerlich, 1976). Here it is argued that space and time do designate particulars, that space, for example, possesses distinctive properties, that it is continuous, quantitative, penetrable and immovably fixed. Absolutists, however, have disagreed about other properties which time–space may be said to possess, for example, whether there are three dimensions or four; whether space can be divided into intervals or is a continuum of infinitesimal points; and whether spatial relations are based on Euclidean geometrical principles or whether space is curved. Kant's absolutist position varied somewhat – and indeed his view that space is an *a priori* category has been seen as indicating that it is not a property of the things (*noumena*) themselves but is one category of the mind which makes knowledge possible.

I shall try to show that with respect to the social world neither of these positions, relationism or absolutism, can be sustained without qualification. This is because the social world (and by implication the physical world) is comprised of four-dimensional time–space entities, which bear complex and mutually modifying interrelations in time–space with each other. And these interrelations have the consequence of producing empirical distributions of social activities within time and space as a result of the partial and variable realization of the respective causal powers of these entities. Regarding the social world in this theoretical realist manner does however require what one might loosely describe as a Copernican revolution. This is because in our thinking, writing and experience of the social world it is common to believe that there is something epistemologically significant about the 'here and now' – that our knowledge is peculiarly constituted by and within the social relationships which *at present* surround us. Furthermore, Smart argued that our particular notions of past, present and future are normally taken by us to apply objectively to the universe rather than being significant only at the level of human thought and utterances (see Smart, 1963, pp. 132–5). The crucial point to note about both physical and social entities is that they endure: bodies extend in time as well as in space; and whether these exist in our past, our present or our future is simply contingent. Smart argued that we need a way of analyzing such matters 'tenselessly' since past, present and future are not real properties of the entities involved. Likewise, we also need a way of characterising such entities 'spacelessly', that is, that notions of space and time should be conceptualised non-anthropocentrically.

What I am going to argue here is that the contemporary theoretical claim that there has to be a decentring of the 'subject' within the human sciences is inadequate without further analysis of the subject's temporal and spatial structuring. According to Foucault it is particularly in the post-1800 period that the human sciences (plus biology) came to focus upon the concepts of 'man' and 'history' (see Foucault, 1970). Now however, it is argued that the human subject need not, and indeed should not, be placed at the centre of the human sciences. In particular the 'linguistic turn' means that all kinds of social practice should be viewed as linguistic, as systems of meaning and signification (see Coward and Ellis, 1977). It is these linguistic systems, especially their systematically arranged differences, which are held to be responsible for constituting the human subject as autonomous, self-conscious and self-willed. However, this decentring has not been sufficiently examined. In particular, it is necessary to examine further just how the individual subject is constructed in the 'here and now'. What are the processes which produce individuals as occupants and users of particular places, defined within a system of temporal and spatial differences? This means conceptualizing time and space outside the limitations of the 'here and now', in particular, by analogy with language identifying the four-dimensional social entities which, through their interrelations, are responsible for producing individual subjects as occupants and users of particular places. How does this leave the analysis of time and space?

First, neither space nor time are substances in the sense that matter is made of various substances, the existence of each being independent of all other entities. Space and time only exist when there are entities in some sense *in* space and time. Hence, they do not exist without at least two existent objects, which occupy a relationship within time–space. This means incidentally that if there are at least two such objects then there is never nothing – there is, as Kant argued, space – that is, the space between these two objects. Thus space is a set of *relations* between entities and is not a substance. As a result, therefore, there is likely to be a category mistake involved if we talk of 'society' and 'space' as interacting. 'Society' is in some sense at least a substance (as well as sets of relations) while 'space' is not. Likewise, we should avoid treating 'time' as itself productive – as producing effects as a simple consequence of its passage or of its 'flowing' (see Jacques, 1982, p. 33). There is no 'arrow of time' as though there were something concrete which could itself flow or fly or fall or pass us by.

Nevertheless, it does not follow because space and time are relational that spatial and temporal relations can be unproblematically *reduced* to the relations within and between social entities. However, to talk of entities and of their interrelations is to presuppose a particular conception of ontology and science which I have as yet left unjustified and which I shall now briefly discuss. I would argue against what is generally known as an event-ontology, namely, that the natural or social world is to be simply viewed as sets of discrete, atomistic events (actions, interactions, personality characteristics, social institutions, and so on) which happen to be distributed in time and space. I would follow Harré and Madden in arguing in favour of a thing-ontology, that there are persistent and enduring structures, located within time–space, and we do not have to give a special account of why such things persist (see Harré and Madden, 1975, as well as Harré, 1971, Bhaskar, 1975, 1979, Keat and Urry, 1982). They persist because of the causal powers which they possess and which are in part realized. However, I am not claiming that a particular class of events can and should be explained in terms of a single such entity. In other words, it is incorrect to maintain that a given entity possesses of *itself* the causal power to produce a whole class of empirical events. This is because of the need to investigate the conditions under which such causal powers are in fact *realized*. And when we do that we find that such conditions will on occasions consist of other social entities and at least the partial realization of *their* powers. This fundamental interdependence of such entities thus means that the causal powers of some entities constitute the conditions necessary for the realization of the powers of other entities. Hence, the empirical events generated (such as the spatial distribution of households or factories) are the product of highly complex *inter*dependent processes. I take it that this is roughly what Marx was alluding to when he stated that 'The concrete concept is concrete because it is a synthesis of many definitions, thus representing the unity of diverse aspects (1973a, p. 101; Sayer, 1979; Keat and Urry, 1982, postscript). For Marx the concrete object is concrete not because it exists or is 'empirical', but because it is the effect of the specific conjuncture of many diverse forces or processes, of (in my terms) entities with specific causal powers. Furthermore, these processes are not simply to be listed, or added up, but rather are *synthesized*. Their combination qualitatively modifies each constitutive entity. How does this discussion relate directly to the analysis of time and space?

First, as we have seen, empirical events are distributed *in* time–space. This is as true for the relatively routine features of everyday life, a weaving-dance through time–space, as it is for relatively distinct and unique social events. Indeed the idea that individuals occupy 'paths' through time–space highlights the 'physical indivisibility and finite time resources of the individual' – hence there is, as Pred put it, an 'intimate, intricate interconnectedness of different biographies that is an essential part of the everyday process of social reproduction' (Pred, 1981, p. 10).

Second, any given entity implies particular spatial relations and a specific structuring of time. Thus, for example, civil society, where labour-power is substantially produced, is partly constituted of relatively separated households with a distinct 'friction of distance' between them. The modern state, on the contrary, is highly centralized and contains spatially and temporally transformed means of surveillance (see Giddens, 1981, chap. 7). Capitalist relations themselves involve the commodification of both time and space as capital is systematically restructured. Capitalist relations are now less dependent upon the immediate presence or potential *presence* of controllers of those relations. The need for spatial proximity, which derived from the time taken to convey information or decisions, has been transformed by the development of electronically-transmitted information. The resulting functional and spatial splitting of offices from workplaces and of different workplaces from each other in terms of the different labour-forces and labour-processes employed, transforms the respective causal powers of different social classes which are themselves temporally–spatially structured.

Third, it is also necessary to consider the changing spatial–temporal relations *between* these different entities with their respective causal powers. There are varying relations existent between distinct entities which are spatially interdependent over time. One example here would relate to the development of the state as in some sense the manager of everyday life – a development which decreases the 'space' (literally and metaphorically) between it and civil society. Another example concerns the changing profile of capitalist relations of production, which are, as I argue elsewhere, increasingly deep but increasingly concentrated within certain first world economies (see Murgatroyd *et al.*, 1984, chap. 1). So although capitalist development involves the commodification of space, in that everyday life becomes progressively commodified, there is an increased distance between capitalist production *per se* and civil society within the emergent 'former industrial countries' of which the UK is the leading example. Capitalist production is progressively deepened yet is spatially concentrated. Many localities have become decapitalized and relatively separated and distant from direct capitalist relations of production *per se*.

Therefore, it is necessary to investigate the changing temporal–spatial relations between diverse determinate social entities, entities which are themselves temporally–spatially structured and which possess causal powers which may or may not be realized. Thus, empirical events in general, and the spatial patterning of such events in particular, are to be explained in terms of the complex, overlapping and temporally–spatially structured relations between such entities, relations which will involve the realization/part-realization/blocking of the causal powers of such entities. Thus, time and space occupy complex and variable relations in the analysis: they characterize 'empirical events'; the structuring of causally productive entities; and the interrelations between such entities.

RELATIONS BETWEEN TIME AND SPACE

Although I have argued that both temporal and spatial aspects of time–space have to be considered as comprising sets of relations, these relations are asymmetrical. In particular, relations within space must exhibit a constant sum, while relations within time are not so constrained. This is because if a given object occupies a given space another object cannot be in exactly that same point in space. Thus while two objects can occupy the same point in time (in different places) they *cannot* occupy the same point in space (see Harré, 1971, p. 241). Hence space is necessarily limited and there has to be competition and conflict over its organisation and control. Amongst other things, this means that if a causally powerful entity is to effect changes involving more than one object but at the same point in time, then these effects will have to be produced at more than one point in space.

However, it is not appropriate simply to distinguish between time or the temporal and space or the spatial. Time necessarily involves direction so that once some time has elapsed it is impossible to return to the original point in time. Lucas argued that 'Directionless time is not time at all . . . A uniform direction of time is . . . an essential condition of intersubjective experience' (quoted in Jacques, 1982, p. 28). Hence any finite movement through space must take time and hence the object concerned cannot move back to its temporal starting-point. Thus, spatial change necessarily involves temporal changes, but by contrast temporal change does not necessarily involve spatial change. Thus, we should distinguish between the 'temporal' and the 'spatial–temporal', rather than simply the temporal and the spatial.

Furthermore, it is the latter kind of change which will require more substantial powers to bring about and this is because such change must be effected at different points in space. Temporal change occurring at the same or at closely-related points in space, requires less power to bring about and hence is more likely to be initially implemented in any social process. *Spatial*–temporal changes will be likely to follow when at least some of the possibilities of temporal change have been implemented. This somewhat provisional argument can be partly supported by considering the processes of capitalist accumulation within the sphere of production.

There are three forms which involve different patterns of spatial change:

(1) absolute surplus-value production which does not involve any spatial transformation. Increases in surplus-value are obtained through lengthening the working day or intensifying the work done;
(2) relative surplus-value production where the spatial transformations involved occur within the sphere of circulation – that is, involving movements of *commodities* including that of labour-power but not of productive capital;
(3) relative surplus-value production where spatial transformations involved occur within the sphere of *production* – that new technologies, a heightened division of labour, the employment of new machinery, etc. all involve spatial relocations of productive capital and the construction of highly diverse and spatially-distinct circuits of capital.

Historically, there has been movement from (1) to (2) to (3), although this has not occurred at the same rate nor to the same degree within each sector of production. At any point in time each sector will exhibit a distinct spatial division of labour. Furthermore, movement from (1) to (2) to (3) is not something that develops automatically but depends upon both the temporal–spatial limitations implied by the existing form of surplus-value production and the specific social struggles and forms of state action occurring within and with regard to that sector. In broad terms, accumulation since the Second World War has been characterized by the increasingly pronounced emphasis upon (3), upon capitalist restructuring based on spatial–temporal transformations at the level of production rather than circulation. However, it is incorrect to argue that capital will simply seek the most appropriate forms of capitalist re-structuring, that *capital* will seek to move from (1) to (2) to (3). In this context Müller and Neusüss (1970) have interestingly discussed the development of the Factory Acts within Britain. These were important in preventing continued absolute surplus-value production based on extending the working day. Although these Acts stemmed from working-class resistance, they had the effect in certain industrial sectors of shifting the predominant form of surplus-value production from (1) to (2). Likewise the move from (2) to (3) has been partly produced *by* the struggles of labour, particularly within social democratic parties. There have been in Britain two especially distinctive developments, that of nationalization and that of encouraging the centralization of capital through the Industrial Reorganization Corporation in the late 1960s. Both aided the move from (2) to (3).

Another way of expressing this heightened significance of *spatial*–temporal transformations is to point to the contemporary *hypermobility* of at least certain forms of capital (see essays in Carney, Hudson, Lewis, 1980) and the contradiction between this and the existing practices within civil society. The latter revolve around and presuppose the constitution of individual subjects. It is through their social experience, through their position within various discourses, that individuals come to view themselves – and to act – as autonomous, whole and independent subjects. There are moreover two crucially important interpellations of the subject, those of spatio-temporal location and of gender (on gender, see Murgatroyd *et al.*, 1984). The effect of the former is that individuals are constituted who are aware of their presence as subjects residing within a particular spatial location (street, town or countryside, region, nation) at a given period of time (born of a particular generation defined by its place in relation to others). As Webber says:

The physical place becomes an extension of one's ego. The outer worlds of neighbourhood-based peer groups, neighbourhood-based family, and the *physical* neighbourhood place itself, seem to become internalized or inseparable aspects of one's inner perception of self . . . One's conception of himself [*sic*] and of his place in society is thus subtly merged with his conceptions of the spatially limited territory of limited social interaction' (Webber, 1964, p. 63; Cox, 1981).

Such subjects are necessarily spatially distributed (especially into households) and spatially constrained. Households cannot occupy the same point in space and the movement of individual household members is constrained by intervening patterns of land use, ownership, and access.

This contrast between capital and civil society is particularly significant since it is within the latter that wage labour is produced and reproduced. Indeed it is important to note how Marx's analysis of capitalist production is seriously deficient because he did not concern himself with the process of *producing* wage-labour (see Lebowitz, 1980; Urry, 1981). The text *Capital* is concerned with analyzing the production of capital, where labour-power is a mere presupposition of that process. Marx never completed the volume which would have involved analyzing the *production* of the commodity, labour-power. This obviously involves a process, not simply of consuming commodities produced within the sphere of capitalist production, but through human labour converting the articles for consumption into refreshed and energetic labour-power. This production of wage-labour is necessarily spatially located and constrained and attachment to 'place' is of particular significance. The key elements are those of spatio–temporal proximity, specificity and constraint (apart from gender-related issues, see Murgatroyd *et al.*, 1984). By contrast capital is progressively characterized by hypermobility, a functional rather than a spatial organization of different circuits distributed throughout the world and taking advantage of diverse variations within the conditions of production of wage-labour. Hypermobile capital has no need for spatial proximity nor indeed for any particular spatial location. It can be characterized by the principle of 'spatial indifference'. Hence, there is a contrast between the production of capital (apparently social but in fact structured through private appropriation) and the production of labour-power (that is, of individual subjects produced under conditions of relatively free, social but not socialised labour).

There are obviously many implications of the changing temporal–spatial relations between capital and civil society. Broadbent summarizes one such set relating to the *city*:

> The individual city appears less important because many processes which used to occur *within* the area, such as the different stages of production within a firm, or the circulation of funds from sales and profits back into investment in new building plant or equipment . . . now go on *outside* the area through the centralized industrial/financial and state concentration of power in London (Broadbent, 1977, p. 110).

Thus *spatial*–temporal changes have transformed the distribution of urban areas. As the economic processes (size of firms, growth of multiplant private and state enterprises, etc.) have spatially transcended each individual city, so each area is increasingly reduced to the status of a *labour pool*. The important linkages within the city are those which pass through the household, through civil society, not through the private or public enterprises located within that area. The other linkages, involving the sale and purchase of commodities between enterprises, occur across the urban boundary. Cities are thus increasingly crucially significant sites for the production of wage-labour, they are sites within which pools of labour-power are systematically created and reproduced. The urban area, as Broadbent emphasizes, is a system of *production*, a relatively closed system comprised of a large number of interdependent, relatively privatized households wherein wage-labour is produced. Cities are thus not so much an interlocking economy of producing and consuming enterprises but a *community of subjects* who produce, and who consume in order to produce. Moreover, this production is necessarily local, it is principally produced for the *local* market, subject to the constraints of time imposed by the particular relations between households and workplaces. Cities are thus to be viewed as 'relatively independent labour pools' (Broadbent, 1977, p. 115), each comprised of a large number of separately producing households, linked with each other and competing for urban space.

I have so far talked very generally of various spatial–temporal structures. I will now try to make this more specific by considering: (a) some of the different forms of the spatial division of labour which result from particular patterns of capitalist restructuring in which decisions about spatial location are to be seen as subordinate to the necessities implied by accumulation (see Massey, 1981; Massey and Meegan, 1982; Walker and Storper, 1981); and (b) some of the different ways in which a given civil society is spatially structured – such structurings not being viewed as simple emanations of the mode of production, as Aglietta seems to claim for the 'mode of consumption' (Aglietta, 1979: ch. 3).

(a) Six important forms of the spatial division of labour characterizing any particular industrial sector are:

  (i)   regional specialization;
 (ii)   regional dispersal;
(iii)   functional separation between management/research and development in the 'centre', skilled labour in old manufacturing centres, and unskilled labour in the 'periphery';
 (iv)   functional separation between management/research and development in the 'centre', and semi- and unskilled labour in the 'periphery';
  (v)   functional separation between management/research and development and skilled labour in a 'central' economy, and unskilled labour in a 'peripheral' economy;
 (vi)   division between one or more areas, which are characterized by investment, technical change and expansion and new products, and other areas where unchanged and progressively less competitive production continues with resulting job loss.

It is crucial to note that we should not analyze a given area as purely the product of a single form of the spatial division of labour. To do so is, as Sayer points out to 'collapse all the historical results of several interacting "spatial divisions of labour" into a rather misleading term which suggests some simple unitary empirical trend' (Sayer, 1982, p. 80). Rather any such area is 'economically' the overlapping and interdependent product of a number of these spatial divisions of labour and attendant forms of industrial restructuring.

(b) Civil societies can be characterized in terms of a number of different dimensions, each of which contains implications for its spatial structuring. The following are some relevant dimensions:

(i)   the degree to which the existing *built environment* can be reconstructed through new towns, suburbs, etc. (see Harvey, 1973; Walker and Storper, 1981, pp. 405–6);

(ii) the degree to which there is *integration* of the social relations of civil society into the wider capitalist economy, for example, whether the domestic property market assumes a 'capitalistic' or 'use-value' character (see Agnew, 1981);

(iii) the degree to which more generally the social relations of civil society are based on *community* rather than on commodity-relations (see Cox, 1981). Such a community-based civil society, premised upon mutuality and reciprocity, upon locally-derived criteria of power and status (such as patriarchy), and upon non-maximizing economic behaviour, provides a considerable insulation from the commodity relations of a capitalist economy, and from the 'capitalist production of a mode of consumption' (see Aglietta, 1979; Joyce, 1980, chs. 3 and 4);

(iv) the degree to which there is a *heterogeneity* of class experiences based upon the distinctive characteristics of particular communities, places of work, or kinship relations (see Cox, 1981, p. 435);

(v) the degree of *spatial concentration* of different social classes or other social forces (note the recent development in Britain of the shift of both employment and of the population out of the former heavily industrialized class-divided urban conurbations (see Urry, 1984);

(vi) the degree to which local or national civil societies are *vertically* organized, that is, where diverse social groupings and voluntary and informal associations are specific to particular classes and there is relatively little independent organization, or horizontally organized, where there are a large number of social practices which are non-class-specific and which generate relatively autonomous forms of organization and representation (see Urry, 1982);

(vii) the degree to which local civil societies are *long-established* with intergenerationally reproduced and sedimented patterns of life and cultural forms.

In the conclusion I shall briefly relate such issues to the analysis of classes as collective actors.

CONCLUSION

Marx seems to have believed that individual selfishness and calculation were the significant human characteristics generated by capitalist relations of production. As that production becomes more widespread so rational self-interest and utilitarian calculation would also become more common. However, as Olson and others have shown, this makes it *increasingly* difficult to organize classes to overthrow capitalist relations of production, a fact which Marx generally overlooked (see Olson, 1965; Calhoun, 1982; Lash and Urry, 1984). This analysis, though, concentrates upon the relations of production as the causally relevant entity. It is also necessary to consider the structuring of civil society and the interrelations between the two. Marx himself, as is well-known, devoted relatively little attention to such considerations, maintaining that since it was in workers' long-term interests to organize on a class basis in order to overthrow capitalist relations of production, this is indeed what they would ultimately do. However, we now know that this is not *simply* the case. A further crucial step in the analysis is to consider whether a given civil society is structured such that there are already established or potentially establishable bases for collective action which can in a sense dissipate the individual self-interest generated within the capitalist economy. Such collective bases are particularly important because, as Offe and Wiesenthal pointed out, the only way in which the organizations of labour can be systematically sustained is in fact through the existence of some kind of 'collective identity' which deflates the standards by which the costs of membership are assessed, and where the lack of immediate success is seen as being of relatively minor significance (Offe and Wiesenthal, 1979). Establishing and maintaining such identities depends upon the particular temporal and spatial structurings of civil society. Such structurings are crucial in potentially providing some non-public, non-collective benefits from collective organization.

I will now set out somewhat formally some conditions under which *class* may be the basis for collective action as opposed to either no such action or mobilisation in terms of some other organized grouping (also see Elster, 1978, pp. 134–50; Lash and Urry, 1984). Thus the actions of individual agents are more likely to take a class character the more:

(1) the spatially separated experiences of groups of individual agents can be interpreted as the experiences of a whole class – this depends upon particular 'local civil societies' being both class-divided and perceived as structured by class rather than by other significant social entities;
(2) that there is a high rate of participation and of concerted action within a range of spatially specific yet overlapping collective organizations;
(3) that other collectivities within civil societies are organized in forms consistent with that of class rather than being in conflict with it – this depends upon the organization of popular-democratic politics locally and nationally;
(4) other kinds of gains and benefit which could be attained through non-class actions (such as higher incomes, lower prices, better conditions of work, etc.) are perceived to be, and are, unavailable – this will be more likely to result where social inequalities are, and are believed to be, produced by antagonistically structured *national* classes;
(5) large numbers of individual agents located within different spatial locations conclude that class actions *can* be successful.

One implication of these points is that classes are rarely able to act as collective organizations. This is because collective action is normally *only* likely where the potential agents are involved in face-to-face contact within dense, multiplex relations and where there is a high certainty of the participation of others (see Calhoun, 1982, p. 231). The changing temporal–spatial relationships, between capitalist relations of production and civil society, entities which are themselves temporally–spatially structured, are obviously critical in analyzing the spatial structures wherein different and diverse forms of collective action may be contingently and precariously established.

I have thus made some suggestions as to how we should conceptualize social relations once we understand that such relations are both temporally and spatially structured in a number of different ways. I have argued that the social world is comprised of space–time entities having causal powers which may or may not be realized depending on the patterns of spatial/temporal interdependence between such entities. In particular, I have suggested how 'capitalist relations of production' and 'civil society' are spatially structured. I have not considered the spatial structurings of other social entities, especially the state. Nor have I provided more than a cursory analysis of the significance of the temporal and spatial interdependencies between the different entities in relationship to the conditions for collective action. Nevertheless I would argue that the kinds of issue considered here represent important advances on the typical anthropocentricism of epistemological studies and the analysis of an unreconstructed 'here and now'.

NOTE

1. I am very grateful for the comments of those present at the session at the BSA Conference (March 1983) where this was discussed. This chapter is a shortened version of 'Space, Time and Social Relations' which is to appear in Gregory and Urry, 1984.

REFERENCES

Aglietta, M. (1979) *A Theory of Capitalist Regulation* (London: New Left Books).

Agnew, J. A. (1981) 'Homeownership and the Capitalist Social Order', in Dear and Scott, pp. 457–80.

Bhaskar, R. (1975) *A Realist Theory of Science* (Leeds: Alma).

Bhaskar, R. (1979) *The Possibility of Naturalism* (Hassocks: Harvester).

Broadbent, T. A. (1977) *Planning and Profit in the Urban Economy* (London, Methuen).

Calhoun, C. (1982) *The Question of Class Struggle* (Oxford: Basil Blackwell).

Carney, J., Hudson, R. and Lewis, J. (eds) (1980) *Regions in Crisis* (London: Croom Helm).

Coward, R. and Ellis, J. (1977) *Language and Materialism* (London: Routledge & Kegan Paul).

Cox, K. R. (1981) 'Capitalism and Conflict around the Communal Living Space', in Dear and Scott, pp. 431–58.

Dear, M. and Scott, A. (eds) (1981) *Urbanization and Urban Planning in a Capitalist Society* (London: Methuen).

Elster, J. (1978) *Logic and Society* (Chichester: Wiley).

Foucault, M. (1970) *The Order of Things* (London: Tavistock).

Garnett, C. (1939) *The Kantian Philosophy of Space* (Port Washington: Kennikat Press).

Giddens, A. (1981) *A Contemporary Critique of Historical Materialism* (London: Macmillan).

Goffman, E. (1959) *The Presentation of Self in Everyday Life* (Hardmondsworth: Penguin).

Gregory, D. and Urry, J. (eds) (1984) *Social Relations and Spatial Structures* (London: Macmillan).

Harré, R. (1971) *The Principles of Scientific Thinking* (London: Macmillan).

Harré, R. and Madden, E. H. (1975) *Causal Powers* (Oxford: Basil Blackwell).

Harvey, D. (1973) *Social Justice and the City* (London: Edward Arnold, 1973) and R. Walker: 'A Theory of Suburbanization: Capitalism and the Construction of Urban Space in the United States', in Dear and Scott, pp. 383–430.

Hinkfuss, I. (1975) *The Existence of Space and Time* (Oxford: Clarendon).

Jacques, E. (1982) *The Forms of Life* (London: Heinemann) p. 33.

Joyce, P. (1980) *Work, Society and Politics: the Culture of the Factory in Later Victorian England* (Hassocks: Harvester).

Keat, R. and Urry, J. (1982) *Social Theory as Science* (London: Routtedge & Kegan Paul) 2nd edn.

Körner, S. (1955) *Kant* (Harmondsworth: Penguin) p. 33.

Lash, S. and Urry, J. (1984) 'The New Marxism of Collective Action: A Critical Analysis' in *Sociology*, 18.

Lebowitz, M. (1980) 'Capital as Finite', Marx Conference, University of Victoria, Canada.

Leibniz, G. W. (1898) *The Monadology and other Philosophical Writings* (Oxford: Clarendon).

McCall, G. J. and Simmons, J. L. (1966) *Identities and Interactions* (New York: Free Press).

Marx, K. (1973a) *Grundrisse* (Harmondsworth: Penguin).

Marx, K. (1973b) *Surveys from Exile*, ed. D. Fernbach (Harmondsworth: Penguin).

Massey, D. (1981) 'The UK Electrical Engineering and Electronics Industries: The Implications of the Crisis for the Restructuring of Capital and Locational Change', in Dear and Scott, pp. 199–230.

Massey, D. and Meegan, R. (1982) *The Anatomy of Job Loss* (London: Methuen).

Müller, W. and Neusüss, C. (1970) 'The Illusions of State Socialism and the

Contradictions Between Wage-Labour and Capital', *Telos*, 25, pp. 13–90.

Murgatroyd, L., Savage, M., Shapiro, D., Urry, J., Walby, S. and Warde, A. (1984) *Localities, Class and Gender* (New York: Pion).

Nerlich, G. (1976) *The Shape of Space* (Cambridge: Cambridge University Press).

Offe, C. and Wiesenthal, H. (1979) 'Two Logics of Collective Action: Theoretical Notes on Social Class and Organisational Form', in M. Zeitlin (ed.) *Political Power and Social Theory* (Greenwich: JAI) vol. 1, pp. 67–115.

Olson, M. (1965) *The Logic of Collective Action* (Harvard: Harvard University Press).

Pred, A. (1977) 'The Choreography of Existence: Comments on Hägerstrand's Time-Geography and its Usefulness', in *Economic Geography*, 53.

Pred, A. (1981) 'Social Reproduction and the Time-Geography of Everyday Life', in *Geografiska Annaler*, 63, pp. 5–22.

Sayer, A. (1982) 'Explanation in Economic Geography: Abstraction versus Generalisation', in *Human Geography*, 6, pp. 68–88.

Sayer, D. (1979) *Marx's Method, Ideology, Science, and Critique in 'Capital'* (Hassocks: Harvester).

Smart, J. J. C. (1963) *Philosophy and Scientific Realism* (London: Routledge & Kegan Paul).

Urry, J. (1981) *The Anatomy of Capitalist Societies* (London: Macmillan).

Urry, J. (1982) 'Some Themes in the Analysis of the Anatomy of Capitalist Societies', in *Acta Sociologica*, 25, pp. 405–18.

Urry, J. (1984) 'Capitalist Restructuring, Recomposition and the Regions', in Bradley, T. and Lowe, P. (eds) *Rurality and Locality: Economy and Society in Rural Regions* (Norwich: Geo-books).

Walker, R. and Storper, M. (1981) 'Capital and Industrial Location', *Progress in Human Geography*, 5, pp. 473–509.

Webber, M. M. (1964) 'Culture, Territoriality and the Elastic Mile', in *Papers and Proceedings of the Regional Science Association*, 13.

Whitehead, A. N. (1930) *The Concept of Nature* (Cambridge: Cambridge University Press).

3 The Homogenization of Space? Trends in the Spatial Division of Labour in Twentieth Century Britain[1]

ALAN WARDE

I SOCIOLOGY AND SPACE

Whilst most sociologists recognize the continued existence of spatial inequalities – that standards of housing provision, illness, income, unemployment, etc., vary between regions and towns within Britain – not much interest is shown in the degree to which these may change. This intellectual indifference is probably to be attributed to the dominance of the conception that there is a tendency in advanced societies towards the homogenization of space. Themes of modernization, mass society, convergence, decline of community, etc., which find classical inspiration in the *Gemeinschaft-Gesellschaft*, polarity, suggest that despite an increased division of labour in society there is a tendency toward economic, political and cultural homogenization. Where local-specific social characteristics are admitted they are attributed to differences in local class structures. The notable exceptions to these propositions have been community studies and urban sociology, both of which have been held in low esteem over the past couple of decades.

Currently issues have arisen which make it more important to understand processes of spatial change. The operation of local labour markets has begun to seem important. New, localized political effects have been identified. One of the more spectacular of these has been the puzzling phenomenon of neo-nationalism in the Celtic periphery. Another was the spatial distribution of the Labour vote in the 1983 general election. There has also been renewed concern with local and municipal politics, with the fact that some cities and regions have distinctive political traditions. The emergence of informal and self-service economies also puts at issue the extent of communal support and solidarity which may be expected in different local milieux: variation in community and household structures seems likely to become a critical aspect of social life in a deindustrializing Britain.

Sociological analyses of such questions of internal spatial distribution are in their infancy: sometimes theories of international comparative development are invoked (usually unsuccessfully); on other occasions attempts are made to adapt the insights of modern political economy to regional problems. Concerning spatial patterns sociologists are probably agreed upon one proposition – that the basis of spatial variation lies with the division of labour – but the connections between specialization of the division of labour and the spatial distribution of social relations remain obscure. This is partly because the reasoning of classical sociological texts is sparse on such subjects. It is also partly because it is unclear how and why the spatial division of labour has developed in capitalist economies. Before many of the most interesting sociological questions can be approached it is necessary to understand better the origins and development of the spatial division of labour.

Therefore, in this chapter I examine changes in the spatial division of labour, especially addressing the question of whether there is a tendency towards the homogenization of economic activity. By *homogenization* I mean a process whereby economic artefacts (for example, industries, occupational structures, incomes) become more evenly distributed throughout the areas of Britain with the passing of time. If homogenization occurs then economic activities will *diversify* across the UK, and the economic structures of different areas will tend to *converge*. The opposite trend, towards heterogeneity, is one whereby the economic structures of different areas tend to

differentiate, as activities become spatially *specialized* in particular areas of the UK. In an attempt to decide whether there is
a tendency towards convergence or differentiation I consider
some theoretical and historical materials. Section II looks at
some economic theories of regional change. Section III con-
siders accounts of British economic historians regarding spatial
change. Section IV explores some possible reasons for the
inadequacies of these theoretical and historical accounts. Section V offers some suggestions about how to explain the
historical evidence.

II ECONOMIC THEORIES AND SPATIAL CHANGE

Economic theories of spatial change are contradictory and
unpersuasive. One group of theories, of 'neo-classical' lineage,
anticipates (like the sociologists) spatial homogenization. The
market, because of its self-balancing propensities, will tend to
produce regional equilibrium. The archetypal empirical dem-
onstration of such a thesis is Williamson's essay which mobil-
izes an impressive array of international, comparative, time–
series data on incomes in support of the propositions that, 'in
the initial stages of national development regional inequality is
likely to increase all the more sharply due to a number of
disequilibrating effects', but that one should 'expect the elements which tend to cause divergence to diminish over time,
allowing the more classical equilibrating effects to make themselves felt' (Williamson, 1968, pp. 102 and 106). Despite his
impressive data, Williamson never explained the trends: a
cheerful faith in equilibrium substitutes for explanation. This is
perhaps inevitable since, as Holland documented at length in
Capital versus the Regions, the theoretical assumptions of
neo-classical accounts are unrealistic with respect to the twentieth-century geography of accumulation (Holland, 1976, pp.
1–35).
   Theoretically, it is more plausible to postulate tendencies to
spatial imbalance. Whether working from Marxist political
economy, or from more realistic assumptions about the inegali-
tarian effects of market mechanisms, there is a strong *a priori*
case for anticipating uneven spatial development. Yet even

among theorists who explicitly express attachment to a theory of 'uneven development', enormous disagreement exists as to the empirical manifestations of unevenness.

Prima facie, the concept of uneven development suggests the existence of a tendency towards economic specialization in particular areas, much as Marx in *Capital* diagnosed in the woollen industry. Certainly most theorists of uneven development would agree that international specialization is apparent. With respect to internal patterns within core states, however, the spatial effects anticipated are diverse: most project cumulative regional inequality, but some envisage the convergence of regions.

Mingione is one of the most uncompromising theorists of spatial differentiation. He has rejected convergence theories, like that of Williamson, as being based on the very distinctive experience of the USA and Canada. Elsewhere at least, the concentration and centralization of capital has tended to 'multiply territorial imbalances'. 'Contradictions and territorial imbalances tend to increase', he declared (Mingione, 1981, p. 127). This process entails the tendency for commercial and service activities to take the place of industry in congested metropolitan centres whilst three types of 'urban-industrial peripheral areas' are created. The first type contains specialized, but declining, industries – for example, textile and steel towns. The second type contains decentralized, unconcentrated and marginal industries. In both these types of area 'neo-dualist' characteristics may develop, the latter being particularly prone to depend upon informal or irregular economic transactions in order to 'get-by'. The third type contains decentralized, heavy industry, including some key-sector industries, which are moved from the metropolitan conurbations, but which have limited power to boost local economies because they employ few workers and have few local inter-linkages. Consequently the industrial areas of capitalist societies face bleak futures. Mingione has attributed these spatial trends to the general contradictions of capitalist accumulation and said that they become exacerbated in periods of crisis. Potential conflict, however, is contained, both by relieving congestion in the metropolis and by dispersing the working class into peripheral regions from which it is difficult to organize effectively.

Lipietz (1980) also argued that in the case of France regional specialization tends to increase over time, but he based his argument on the proposition that it is not so much the character of industries which is important in determining regional differences, but rather the skill-quotient associated with the occupations in particular production functions. What mattered to Lipietz is the proportion of senior staff, of professionals, and of skilled labourers in a regional labour force. Lipietz reckoned that the tendency for skill to be unequally distributed by region is increasing, both in the secondary and in the tertiary sectors. Thus business services (R & D, finance, etc.) and the more highly professionalized reproductive services (health, universities, etc.) tend to polarize by region; in the same way manufacturing employment concentrates regionally. Thus one finds in France the existence of four kinds of region, each distinctive by virtue of its labour force.

A partly-related argument has been advanced by Massey for Britain concerning manufacturing employment. She has presented a schematic view of how cycles of accumulation in a single country can, with reference to world economic conditions, be conceived as producing spatially uneven effects as a result of historically prior social uses of space. Her work, sometimes in co-operation with Richard Meegan, now constitutes a substantial body of empirically supported analysis of modern Britain's industrial geography (for example, Massey and Meegan, 1982). Increasingly, she has insisted on disaggregating production in terms of a spatialized hierarchy of functions within the firm (Massey, 1978 and 1979; Massey and Meegan, 1982). Her contention, like that of Lipietz, is that different functional levels require different qualities of labour, the activities of different branches within the same firm or sector become specialized by the proportions of different qualities of labour power required. In this respect she has distinguished three types of labour: professional-scientific engaged in control and development functions; skilled manual; and unskilled labour. These three different types of labour are not necessarily unevenly distributed between *regions*, though by implication the south-east must have increasingly attracted the first type. Labour may be *locally* specialized. On this basis Massey has argued that although some employment indicators may suggest a convergence between regions in the recent period, differentiation continues, but along new dimensions

(Massey and Meegan, 1982). The logic of Massey's account is that capital has come to use spatial differentiation as a resource in the competitive search for profit. There is a search for spatial advantage. Such advantage is most readily obtained by discriminating between available labour forces. This is to acknowledge that capital is nowadays highly mobile, and certainly more mobile than labour, thus implying that many constraints on location which pertained in previous epochs have been overcome (see Frobel *et al.*, 1980).

III ECONOMIC HISTORY AND REGIONAL CHANGE

A good many writers have attempted to resolve the problem of inconsistent theories of regional development by examining empirical trends in occupations, industries, incomes, etc. There is a rough orthodoxy about the British experience, though it conforms to no theory and is weak on the explanation of the processes concerned. It is also rather cavalier in its interpretation of trends, since the supporting evidence is fairly weak.

The orthodox account is the same one proferred by the *Report of the Royal Commission on the Distribution of the Industrial Population* (Barlow, 1940). Economic historians maintain that there was a period of regional specialization in the early industrial revolution when industry located in close proximity to its required natural resources: coal, iron ore, water, etc. This was the period when the north, north-west, Scotland and South Wales developed as industrial regions. Thereafter, at some unspecified time between 1880 and 1920, new industries – those destined to expand in the twentieth century – began to locate in the south-east and the Midlands. The Barlow Commission attributed this to a preference by industry for locations close to its *markets* rather than its *inputs*, since the transport of heavy and bulky raw materials had declined in both difficulty and cost. The inter-war regional problem, in this view, was the industrial structure of the declining regions: the staple industries of the industrial revolution lost their export markets on becoming internationally uncompetitive. Subsequently, post-war Keynesian intervention, especially in the form of regional planning, not only prevented the further decline of the depressed regions but even promoted some convergence. It is well to remember that in the mid-1970s some commentators were prone to say that the regional problem had been solved and that the real spatial problem of the 1980s was the deterioration of the inner-cities.

Such historical accounts can be found in the work of Pollard (1969, pp. 99–133); Lee (1971) and Hall (1975, pp. 81–98). The thesis is briefly summarized by Hobsbawm thus:

> Local and regional differentials were high and probably growing one hundred years ago; but have tended to diminish since 1900, though at times when some regions were relatively prosperous and others very depressed as between the wars, they could remain very large in practice because of unemployment. In theory the rise of state monopoly capitalism and employment in the public sector has also tended to even them out. In practice things are more complicated (Hobsbawm, 1981, p. 11).

The main defects of such accounts are two. First there is no clear explanation of one central change, that which Mandel enigmatically called 'regional role reversal' (Mandel, 1978, pp. 105–7) whereby the growth of the industrial regions halted and the centre of economic gravity moved to the south-east and the Midlands. Probably the most plausible maintains that the temporary prominence of the industrial areas was an aberration, the twentieth century merely witnessing a return to the predominance of London with its enormous population. But as Pollard observed, it was far from obvious that economically rational calculation would have resulted in the expansion of employment in the south in the early twentieth century (Pollard, 1969, pp. 130–1). Second, the evidence in support of the proposition that economic regions, and even more so localities, have converged since 1880 is tendentious.

If we examine available statistics, there is little evidence of any strong tendency toward homogenization. Commentators seem to have over-extrapolated trends toward regional convergence. Over the long term, Lee presented evidence concerning the localization of employment by industry in the British regions at the Censuses of 1881, 1921 and 1961. Coefficients of localization showed a marginal tendency toward specialization in the first period and a slightly stronger tendency towards convergence in the second period (Lee, 1971, pp. 227, 233, 239). The trends were weak.

Chisholm and Oeppèn (1973) set out directly to confront the question of whether or not there was spatial convergence or specialization. Surveying the sparse literature, they asserted that the work of Tress, Smith, Florence, etc., was presumptive evidence of convergence. The most comprehensive of such works, that of Florence, had calculated coefficients of localization for 140 employment categories in 1930, 1935 and 1951, by standard region. I quote Chisholm and Oeppèn:

> Of the 140 categories, a temporal comparison was not possible in some cases and in others there was no change in the coefficient of localisation; together, these amounted to forty-eight industries. Of the remaining ninety-two industries, fifty-eight showed a decline in the value of the coefficient and thirty-four an increase. *Though hardly cast-iron evidence*, this does indicate that the tendency toward a wider geographical dispersal of employment categories has been more common than the opposite trend, thus *confirming* the evidence advanced by other workers (Chisholm and Oeppèn, 1973, pp. 25–6) [my italics].

This is not to disparage the work of Chisholm and Oeppèn who were admirably explicit about the limits of their convergence thesis. They collected data for sixty-one sub-regions of the UK from 1959 to 1968 and were forced to admit that evidence for convergence was weak. The statistical technique which they had in principle preferred to use indicated that changes, by sub-region between 1959 and 1968, were in most cases statistically insignificant, and the technique which they used instead (Tress) showed a high degree of variation in the tendencies between different industries: employment opportunities in manufacturing industry tended to diversify, but in primary and service industries sub-regions tended to specialize.

If the evidence behind convergence theses is weak, that for differentiation theses is worse. Few indicators can be found to suggest an overall, long-term trend towards spatial differentiation. Of course regional differences in themselves corroborate some of the propositions of uneven development theory – the poorer UK regions are those which uneven development theory would expect to be poor. In Northern Ireland average income per head in 1979–80 was £38.30 whilst that of the south-east is £57.41 (*Regional Trends*, 1982, Table 8.3). In the south-east there are higher proportions of workers in professional occupations and financial services as compared to other regions, but the available evidence does not suggest that these proportionate differences are steadily increasing.

Considered generally, the historical evidence suggests that despite a great many spatial changes during the twentieth century there is no strong overall trend towards either homogenization or differentiation. Spatial inequalities have fluctuated over time, but with little cumulative effect.

IV THEORY AND EVIDENCE

The inconclusiveness of the evidence, or rather the poor fit between theories and evidence, may be accounted for in one of three ways. There may be technical reasons for disagreement; or, as some have contended, there may be no general theory or general tendency of spatial change; or else there may be some better explanation consistent with existing theory and empirical observations.

Technical and Methodological Problems

One source of chronic confusion derives from the difficulty of demarcating meaningful and comparable spatial areas. Whether one detects specialization or diversification depends to a degree upon which level of spatial disaggregation one chooses to use. Analyses variously refer to putative nations, regions, sub-regions, counties, urban systems, localities and neighbourhoods. Some of these are meaningful economic units, others are meaningful political units; but rarely is a single unit amenable to both political and economic analysis for any length of time. Nor is it necessarily the case that trends at each level move in the same direction: it has been suggested, for example, that statistical aggregation makes it appear that regions are converging, whilst component sub-regions remain as diverse as ever (for example, Fothergill and Gudgin, 1980).

Unsurprisingly, the level at which the most important spatial effects occur remains a matter of controversy among spatial theorists. These problems are compounded in international comparative studies.

A second problem arises from the apparent variety of national experiences. It seems likely that the American experience, of convergence, is not repeated elsewhere. Secchi, for example, having examined Italian patterns of regional development post-1945, concluded that the empirical evidence strongly corroborated a theory of regional specialization rather than convergence (Secchi, 1977). The British pattern appears to follow neither the Italian nor the American model.

A third associated problem arises over appropriate indicators for the economic tendencies at work in any given area. Keeble, for example, wrote with some conviction that British regional policy after 1965 had worked well because statistics on *per capita* income, unemployment, share of manufacturing employment, total employment and net migration, for the standard regions, had shown a noticeable tendency to converge over the subsequent decade (Keeble, 1977). Massey countered that although this might be so, it obscured a different set of regional inequalities, originating in the period of restructuring of British industry in the mid-1960s, which encouraged a change in the spatial hierarchy of the capitalist firm, such that the manufacturing employment which went to the regions was distinctive in being at best semi-skilled, whereas higher order functions were tending to concentrate in the south-east in particular (Massey, 1979). In other words, total quantities of employment change might be converging, but the quality of such work was diverging. Both authors may conceivably be correct, Keeble having picked up evidence of successful regional policy while Massey perceived a process whose effects have not yet fully developed. *Prima facie*, however, different indicators appear to be suggesting opposed conclusions. This might imply some deeper difficulties with the notion of homogenization.

Epistemological Problems

Some recent authors would contend that confusion necessarily arises from false expectations about the capacity of a positivist or empiricist social science to deliver generalizations about spatial patterns. Some would argue that space is simply an invalid object of study; others, more moderately, merely claim that the 'geometric' space which is the normal object of positivist geography is a 'chaotic abstraction' so that searching for empirical generalizations about space is futile (Sayer, 1982). Instead, it is often suggested that a realist conception of social science will direct attention toward rational abstractions, toward the uncovering of the unified mechanisms which generate phenomenal appearances. The promise is that the one feature of spatial change to which the existing evidence does bear witness – the uneven emergence and distribution of social artefacts in space – might be explained in terms of the effects and counter-effects of one or more underlying mechanism or contradiction. This appears a cogent enterprise, one which could make sense of the data on spatial change, but which is still more often invoked as a desirable project than put to explanatory use. In this context, one of the most provocative conclusions to be drawn from studies of spatial changes in economic activity was advanced by Walker:

> Recent evidence suggests that there is no imminent danger of a homogeneous geography of advanced capitalism, despite the efforts of fast-food outlets and tract home developers . . . It is important to see that there are two opposing tendencies constantly developing under capitalism, one toward spatial differentiation and one toward homogenization: they exist in uneasy juxtaposition. At any given stage of accumulation, the two forces are in a kind of stand off which may be called 'an equilibrium degree of homogenization/ differentiation' (Walker, 1978, fn.20).

As a description of the British experience, it seems to me that there is more truth in this, a footnote, than in most attempts to identify consistent trends, but of course the question remains 'what are the mechanisms which generate these two counter-tendencies, and what determines the outcome of their intersection?'. Whilst accepting that there is no space without social process and social action within it – that space, so to speak, is socially constructed and that spatial patterns may be considered a *mélange* of diverse effects of other social mechanisms –

it is still encumbent upon analysts to show *how* and *why* various mechanisms or contradictions generate manifest social patterns. In the next section I have some speculative suggestions as to the explanation of those patterns in terms of mechanisms which have offset tendencies towards spatial differentiation posited in uneven development theory.

V   TRENDS IN THE SPATIAL DIVISION OF LABOUR

I suggest that part of the explanation of the manifest tendencies in the spatial division of labour in twentieth-century Britain may be derived from considering the effects of two, often ignored, sources of homogenization: trade union organization at the national level, and patriarchal relations as indexed by the changing economic activity rates for women. In principle these factors are consistent with a theory of uneven development, identifying mechanisms which have constrained the tendency of capital accumulation to generate cumulative regional inequality.

The impact of labour organization on the spatial division of labour in Britain is relatively neglected. Recent American literature has devoted some time to trying to establish that labour resistance is a principal cause of the spatial division of labour. Some writers have attributed causal powers to struggles around the labour process, the outcome being a shifting of spatial forms at both regional and urban levels. Urban concentration, decentralization, the move to the 'Sunbelt', and the distribution of production in contemporary conurbations, have been seen as successive stages in the geography of industry determined by strategies of class struggle (Gordon, 1978). Another approach stresses the effects of national trade union organization.

Fox (1978) argued an interesting case concerning development in the USA. He claimed that regional differences within the US were declining significantly, but considered this quite consistent with uneven development theory. Two processes operate: the export of spatial underdevelopment to other parts of the globe through the world-system; and, internally, the intensification of 'metropolitan urbanization'. Concerning the first process, theorists would no doubt concur, since spatial inequality on the world scale is generally recognized. The metropolitan urbanization thesis contends that, whilst in the nineteenth century uneven development was promoted by uneven resources, in the twentieth century:

> the resource and manufacturing specialisation of regional development has been continually declining in favour of an increasingly similar form of development in all regions. The characteristic element of this form of development is the sales and service-oriented metropolitan area. The metropolitan approach concentrates on the fact that the mid-twentieth century population predominantly resides in two-to-three hundred similar metropolitan areas spread over all the eight major regions, and on the tendencies for both manufacturing and service production to become located in a corresponding pattern as a function of the location of people (Fox, 1978, p. 174).

The origins of this tendency is attributed largely to pressure from labour. Fox, like others (for example, Gordon, 1978), has attributed the new location of policies of monopoly capital in the USA to the pressure of labour in the big industrial cities at the end of the nineteenth century. First, manufacturers withdrew to the suburbs and hinterlands of the industrial cities, and later they left the industrial regions, because the territorial concentration of production and worker-residence increased the solidarity of labour. Capital thus turned to non-industrial labour forces but only initially could it obtain cheap, organized labour: 'Capital was thus able to draw upon a large supply of under-employed labour only in the initial stages of industrial development in the less developed regions' (Gordon, 1978, p. 82). Fox explained that the increasing spatial diversification of American industry derived from the capacity of trade unions to establish and enforce nation-wide wage-rates.

In Fox's view, once the last remaining rural reserves of labour had been incorporated into the industrial labour force in the 1930s it was no longer possible for capital to obtain spatial advantage from regional differences in wages. Thereafter, regional variations in income and occupational structures diminished.

If Fox was correct concerning the USA, with its relatively

sparsely unionized labour force, then it is even more likely that a similar effect occurred in the UK. Hunt's (1973) study of regional wage differentials in the nineteenth century concluded that probably the variable incidence of unionization had tended to *increase* regional wage differences until some time between 1890 and 1910. Subsequently, as a result of the increasing strength of the general unions and the tendency toward national rather than local or district bargaining, union practice tended to reduce regional differences. Turner (1952) attributed declining regional differentials from the First World War to the 1950s to the strategies of mass unions for maintaining solidarity among workers of different grades. Such unions preferred flat-rate wage rises which, over time, reduced both local and skill differentials. The period after the First World War was also one which saw some industries producing standardization agreements to reduce local wage differentials: railways and construction are examples of this (Rowe, 1928). *Prima facie*, there is some correlation between the strength of centralized mass unions and regional convergence. It seems likely that the principal impact of such a constraint on regional specialization would have been felt in the period between the First World War and the 1950s by which time local wage variations were relatively insignificant, regional income differentials being largely attributable to regional industrial structures.

At the same time, the role of the labour movements, and other social movements, in applying pressure to the state should be considered. Regional policy is not the only aspect of state intervention which tends to prevent regional polarization. Holland (1976) has pointed out that welfare payments tended to reduce inequalities of income between regions, but so too does the expansion of state-provided services of many kinds which has, for example, been part of the cause of the even regional expansion of professional and scientific employment. The general spatial impact of an interventionist state is too rarely considered in the literature.

Even more significant as offsetting tendencies towards regional differentiation from the mid-twentieth century in Britain have been changes in gender relations, as signified by the increased economic activity rates of women. This process, largely neglected in studies of regional development (though see Walby, 1984; Allin, 1982, and Bowers, 1970), shows probably the strongest tendency of any indicator towards regional and local homogenization. The range of variation in women's activity rates at the beginning of the century was enormous. Regional variations, shown in Figure 3.1, were considerable throughout the first half of the century: in 1911 the proportion of women employed in the north-west was twice that in the North. Convergence had scarcely begun in 1951, but was noticeable by 1961 and accelerated thereafter. Figure 3.2 shows the activity rates for all women in the County Boroughs of Lancashire, 1911–71; it shows a considerable evening out of activity rates by 1951, with an even more pronounced convergence between 1951 and 1971. By the 1970s where a woman lived still mattered in assessing her chances of employment – but to a much lesser extent than before. More dramatic still is the way in which the chances of a married woman being employed evened out over the country. Figure 3.3 shows the extent of variance in married women's activity rates in the Lancashire County Boroughs. In 1911 in St Helens only 4.1 per cent of married women were economically active as compared with 44.5 per cent in Blackburn. By 1971 the variance was much less, Southport having the lowest figure, 38.8 per cent, Burnley the highest, 54.6 per cent. The same trends can be observed in Table 3.1 which shows the proportion of married women workers among all women workers in Lancashire County Boroughs. In 1911, in some towns less than one woman worker in ten was married, whilst in others the proportion was more than one in three. The variance was still considerable in 1951, but had declined significantly by 1971. This evidence suggests the existence of a powerful mechanism tending toward spatial homogenization.

The origins and significance of this tendency toward homogenization in women's employment remains uncertain. My hypothesis is that once rural reserves of labour have been absorbed into the industrial labour force, and given the establishment of effective national trade unions for men, then the most easily available source of cheap labour, either for super-exploitation in advanced industrial sectors or for intensive exploitation in marginal enterprises, is female labour. To the present, female labour has been cheaper, more pliable and less well organized. That these attributes may make women attractive employees for capital is obvious: as Massey pointed out,

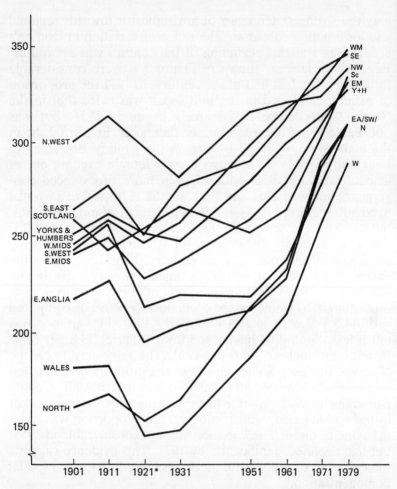

FIGURE 3.1 *Women's employment by region, 1901–79: women in work per 1000 females of all ages*

SOURCES C. H. Lee, *Regional Employment Statistics, 1841–1971*; S. Walby, 'Women's Unemployment: Some Spatial and Historical Variations' (1984).

* 1921 figures are unreliable. (Census contained 326 920 women 'place of work not specified' in England and Wales. This number is added as average of England and Wales total, i.e. 17 per thousand, to each region equally.)

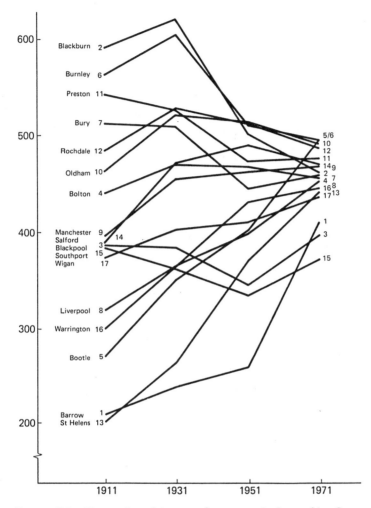

FIGURE 3.2 *Economic activity rates for women in Lancashire County*
Boroughs, 1911–71: numbers active per 1000 women over
school-leaving age

SOURCE *Census*, 1911, 1931, 1951, 1971.

firms restructuring since the mid-1960s have often preferred
women to men as a labour force. On the other hand, that
capital has not universally exploited such labour is also apparent. The reasons for this are contentious, but may be seen to
be grounded in the contradictory imperatives of patriarchal

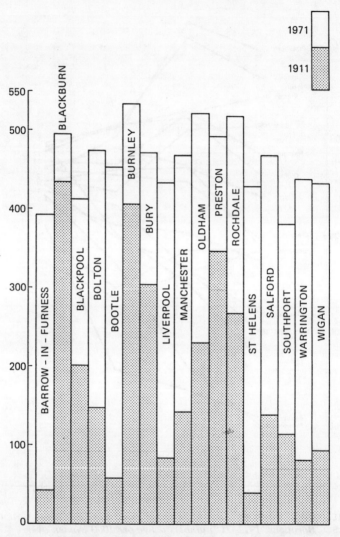

1971

1911

FIGURE 3.3   *Married women economically active per 1000 married women*
in Lancashire County Boroughs, 1911 and 1971.

domination and capital accumulation. There must be a limiting
case where the practices and legitimations which perpetuate
gender inequalities in paid work will be undermined by a high
proportion of (especially married) women no longer having a
primarily domestic role. In other words, to employers the

TABLE 3.1 *Married women as percentage of all women economically active in Lancashire County Boroughs, 1911, 1951 and 1971*

	1911	1951	1971
Barrow-in-Furness	10.4	31.3	63.7
Blackburn	33.2	56.2	66.9
Blackpool	22.0	42.9	62.3
Bolton	14.7	52.6	66.8
Bootle	9.9	36.8	56.7
Burnley	34.2	58.9	69.5
Bury	27.3	52.5	69.7
Liverpool	11.7	32.0	54.4
Manchester	16.2	45.9	57.3
Oldham	23.7	57.2	66.6
Preston	27.4	50.6	62.8
Rochdale	25.5	55.6	69.4
St Helens	9.8	38.9	64.0
Salford	16.2	49.1	58.4
Southport	10.5	33.4	58.1
Warrington	12.9	47.3	63.9
Wigan	11.0	43.1	66.3

SOURCE *Census*, 1911, 1951, 1971.

attractive conditions upon which they may buy female labour power depends upon deeper patriarchal structures which themselves become vulnerable the more frequently married women take paid employment. How exactly increased paid employment for women modifies patriarchal relations is still little explored, though the extent of local variation in the none-too-distant past makes comparative study relatively accessible.

The spatial impact of changing women's activity rates derives from the relative immobility of married women. That women are less geographically mobile at the local level is evidenced by the fact that local labour markets for women are much smaller in area than those for men (Ball, 1980), reflecting unequal access to private transport, low female wages and the inequitable burdens of domestic labour. With respect to longer distance migration it is also relatively unlikely that a move for a married couple will be precipitated by the wife's search for employment. In a situation where married women comprise a majority of the female labour force, capital is likely to have to move to find desirable pools of such labour. That pool will not necessarily be located in peripheral regions, though of course it may be. Rather it will be unevenly distributed through most regions as a function of localized variations in the prior sex-typing of occupations, industrial structure, patriarchal structures, trade union power, etc. The statistical effect of such a strategy on the part of capital would be towards the regional homogenization of income and occupational structures. The expansion of employment, especially in manufacture, in rural regions (Fothergill and Gudgin, 1982) where women's activity rates are typically lowest, is perhaps additional circumstantial evidence that capital has recently sought spatial advantage in such a fashion.

The logic of such a process seems consistent with Massey's propositions about the propensity of capital to seek spatial advantage by engaging cheaper, less skilled, unorganized and 'green' labour. Her studies (Massey 1978, and, Massey and Meegan, 1982) of the restructuring of capital in Britain in the 1970s identified strategies of reorganization, one of which was for firms to shed skilled labour in one location and replace it with unskilled jobs elsewhere. For example, premises in the inner cities, often employing workers who would resist deskilling, were closed down and the production process, perhaps with new technology, shifted to, or expanded in, other areas with more easily controlled workers. The evidence of women's activity rates suggests that the process described for job-loss in manufacturing industry has been of much more general applicability, with mobile employers systematically seeking pools of previously inactive female labour. The continual, rapid expansion of the female labour force since 1951 has offset any tendency towards regional polarization in Britain.

VI CONCLUSION

I have suggested that our understanding of changes in the spatial division of labour is limited and inconsistent. There has been little change over the twentieth century towards either homogenization or differentiation. Regional inequalities, overall, have neither increased nor decreased substantially. This apparent stasis, however, should be considered the resultant of various counteracting forces. I have identified two such forces, often neglected, which have been particularly important pressures towards spatial homogeneity: the capacity of trade unions to organize effectively on a national level, and the absorption of married women into the labour force. That these two pressures, enhanced also by the extended role of state intervention, have not had any substantial effect in creating homogeneity is testimony to the strength of the counter-forces which generate spatial differentiation. At the very least, this suggests that the mechanisms identified in theories of uneven development have persistent and pervasive effects. Accounting for spatial change generally requires more precise assessment of countervailing mechanisms.

NOTE

1. I would like to thank Jane Mark Lawson, Howard Newby, Michael Savage, Dan Shapiro, Sylvia Walby and John Urry for their comments in the preparation of this paper.

REFERENCES

Allin, P. (1982) 'Women's Activity Rates and Regional Employment Markets', in British Society for Population Studies, *Population Change and Regional Labour Markets*, OPCS Occasional Paper No 28, 67–81.

Ball, R. M. (1980) 'The Use and Definition of Travel-to-work-areas in Great Britain: Some Problems', *Regional Studies*, 14, pp. 125–39.

Barlow Commission (1940) *Report of the Royal Commission on the Distribution of the Industrial Population, 1940*, (London: HMSO) Cmd. 6153.

Bowers, J. (1970) 'The Anatomy of Regional Activity Rates', in *National Institute of Economic Social Research, Regional Paper* 1, (Cambridge: Cambridge University Press).

Chisholm M. and Oeppèn J. (1973) *The Changing Pattern of Employment: regional Specialisation and Industrial Localization in Britain* (London: Croom Helm).

Fothergill S. and Gudgin G. (1980) 'Regional Employment Change: a Sub-regional Analysis', in *Progress in Planning*, 12, pp. 155–219.

Fothergill, S. and Gudgin, G. (1982) *Unequal Growth: Urban and Regional Employment change in the UK* (London: Heinemann).

Fox, K. (1978) 'Uneven regional development in the US', in *Review of Radical Political Economy*, 10 (3) pp. 68–86.

Frobel, F., Heinrichs, J. and Kreye, O. (1980) *The New International Division of Labour: Structural Unemployment in Industrialized Countries and Industrialisation in Developing Countries* (Cambridge: Cambridge University Press).

62 *The Homogenization of Space?*

Gordon, D. (1978) 'Class Struggle and the Stages of Urban Development', in Perry, D. and Watkins, A. (eds) *The Rise of the Sunbelt Cities* (Beverly Hills: Sage) pp. 55–82.

Hall, P. (1975) *Urban and Regional Planning* (Harmondsworth: Penguin).

Hobsbawm, E. (1981) 'The Forward March of Labour Halted', in M. Jacques (ed.) *The Forward March of Labour Halted?*, (London: Verso, 1981).

Holland, S. (1976) *Capital versus the Regions* (London: Macmillan).

Hunt, E. H. (1973) *Regional Wage Variations in Britain 1850–1914* (Oxford: Clarendon).

Keeble, D. (1977) 'Spatial Policy in Britain: Regional or Urban?', in *Area*, 9, pp. 3–8.

Lee, C. H. (1971) *Regional Economic Growth in the UK since the 1880s* (Cambridge: Cambridge University Press).

Lee, C. H. (1979) *British Regional Employment Statistics, 1841–1971*, (Cambridge: Cambridge University Press).

Lipietz, A. (1980) 'Inter-regional Polarisation and the Tertiarisation of Society', in *Papers of the Regional Science Association*, 44, pp. 3–17.

Mandel, E. (1978) *Late Capitalism* (London: Verso).

Massey, D. (1978) 'Capital and Locational Change: The UK Electrical Engineering and Electronics Industry', in *Review of Radical Political Economy*, 10 (3) pp. 39–54.

Massey, D. (1979) 'In What Sense a Regional Problem', in *Regional Studies*, 13 (2) pp. 233–44.

Massey, D. and Meegan, R. (1982) *The Anatomy of Job Loss: The How, Why and Where of Employment Decline* (London: Methuen).

Mingione, E. (1981) *Social Conflict and the City* (Oxford: Blackwell).

Pollard, S. (1969) *The Development of the British Economy, 1914–1967* (London: Edward Arnold) 2nd edn.

Rowe, J. W. F. (1928) *Wages in Practice and Theory* (London: Routledge & Kegan Paul).

Sayer, A. (1982) 'Explanation in Economic Geography: Abstraction versus Generalisation', in *Progress in Human Geography* 6(1) pp. 68–88.

Secchi, B. (1977) 'Central and Peripheral Regions in a Process of Economic Development: The Italian Case', in Massey, D. B. and Batey, P. W. J., *Alternative Frameworks for Analysis*, London Papers in Regional Science no. 7 (London: Pion) pp. 36–51.

Turner, H. A. (1952) 'Trade Unions, Differentials and the Levelling of Wages', in *Manchester School of Economic and Social Studies*, 20 (3) pp. 227–82.

Walby, S. (1984) 'Some Spatial and Historical Variations in Women's Unemployment', in L. Murgatroyd *et al.*, *Localities, Class and Gender* (London: Pion).

Walker, R. A. (1978) 'Two Sources of Uneven Development under Advanced Capitalism: Spatial Differentiation and Capital Mobility', in *Review of Radical Political Economy*, 10 (3) pp. 28–37.

Williamson, J. G. (1968) 'Regional Inequality and the Process of National Development: A Description of Patterns', in Needleman, L. (ed.) *Regional Analysis*, (Harmondsworth: Penguin).

4 Is Scotland Different? Industrial and Occupational Change in Scotland and Britain[1]

STEPHEN KENDRICK, FRANK BECHHOFER AND DAVID McCRONE

An influential strand of argument concerning Scotland's economic, social and political development has in recent years been shaped by a set of framing assumptions centred on such terms as 'core' or 'centre' and 'periphery', and 'dependence' or even 'underdevelopment'.

It would be pushing it too far to call this set of assumptions as applied to Scotland a theoretical framework in the sense of a set of propositions which define what 'dependence' or 'peripherality' is and would allow an empirical check as to whether or not Scotland does in fact satisfy the criteria of 'dependence' or 'peripherality'. What has tended to happen instead is that Scotland is compared with England on a range of socio-economic indicators and whatever differences, or more precisely deficits, are found on the Scottish side are taken as evidence that Scotland is indeed peripheral to, or dependent on England.

A full understanding of why this set of assumptions became an 'obvious' framework within which to situate Scotland would involve a lengthy exercise in the sociology of knowledge. One source of the 'obviousness' of the core–periphery perspective as applied to Scotland is itself fairly obvious. That is Scotland's geographical position. Scotland is relatively far away from the economic and political centres of gravity of both the United

Kingdom and Europe. The spatial imagery implicit in the words 'core' or 'centre' and 'periphery' gives a great deal of leeway for conceptual slippage between geographic and economic applications.

However, the popularity of the framework for analyzing Scotland would seem to stem primarily from the coincident timing of the emergence of dependency and underdevelopment theory in a Third World context and the increasing success of neo-nationalist movements in Britain and other advanced industrial societies. During the late 1960s and 1970s, theories of underdevelopment and dependency seemed to provide a ready-made vocabulary for understanding the success of nationalist parties in Scotland and Wales. There were other vocabularies available but this one had the appropriate radical aura and chimed in beautifully with the prevailing political mood. Its popularity depended more on factors such as these than on any balanced assessment of Scotland's overall structural position within the world economy.

An early account which explicitly exemplified the logic involved was that of Buchanan in which a range of indicators were presented to show that Scotland and Wales (the lumping together of 'the Celtic nations' is a characteristic concomitant of the approach) have suffered from a 'satellite–metropolis relationship' with England 'of the type described by A. G. Frank' within which 'no real and balanced development of the satellite could take place' (Buchanan, 1968, p. 39).[2]

Much more theoretically ambitious and influential was Hechter's application to 'the Celtic fringe' of a variant of the internal colonialism thesis originally developed in a Latin American context. Of the three 'Celtic fringe' nations analyzed, Scotland was the most awkward customer in terms of empirically fitting Hechter's model yet he felt able to conclude that:

> Within their limitations, which are considerable, the findings tended to support the predictions of the internal colonial model, at least with respect to Wales, Scotland and Ireland (Hechter, 1975, p. 244).

Although Hechter has subsequently conceded that 'Scotland may not have experienced internal colonialism to any degree'

(Hechter, 1982, p. 10), his original analysis was a powerful intervention in cementing the conventional wisdom that the reverse was true.

Implicit in the core–periphery and dependence frameworks is what might be called an externalist perspective. Although the approach of Tom Nairn (1981) steers well clear of 'analytical Third Worldism' his approach does share this externalist perspective. In that Nairn's work shows nationalism in general and Scottish nationalism in particular as being comprehensible in terms of political response to the spatially uneven development of capitalism, his formulation too has helped cement the conviction that it is the *differentiæ* of Scottish economic and social development with respect to England which are of paramount importance.

We do not intend to spend time grappling with the theoretical will o' the wisp which is core–periphery or dependence or underdevelopment theory as applied to Scotland. One rather obvious point is worth making however.

To the extent that such formulations are derived directly or indirectly from neo-Marxist dependence theory developed in a Third World context, it should be remembered that according to these theories 'underdevelopment' or 'dependence' refers to the systematic blockage of the transition to *industrial* capitalism.[3] The adequacy of these theories in a Third World context is not at issue here. What is clear however is that Scotland, having made the transition to industrial capitalism along with the rest of Britain earlier than anywhere else, is, quite literally, the last place on earth to which to apply the term underdevelopment or any other terms which rely for their force on analogy with the current condition of the underdeveloped Third World.

This basic absurdity is perhaps the underlying reason why the application of underdevelopment and related terminology to Scotland so often remains at a rather vague and metaphorical level. As one commentator has pointed out in a wider context:

> The opposition of the centre and the periphery seems to belong more to the category of expressive images than to that of coherent theories. Many spatial mechanisms of power show a tension between the margins and the heart of the

system, but to lead everything back to that dialectic is unrealistic; it risks hiding the deeper causes of the lack of balance in the modern world (Claval, 1980, p. 70).

Such vagueness permits the defining characteristics of peripherality (or core) to be precisely those found in what is to be explained. Existing empirical disparities are used to identify areas which could potentially be regarded as core and periphery. The 'theory' is then used to explain how these disparities came about and why they persist.

More generally, assumptions of 'dependency' and 'peripherality' have tended to shape the interpretation of much *empirical* analysis of Scotland, and have generated lop-sided and misleading accounts, focussing over-much upon *differences* rather than *similarities* in the social and economic development of parts of the UK. In the context of the present analysis, it is the way in which such assumptions have weighted the interpretation of the development of the Scottish industrial and occupational structures which is of interest.[4] Two common themes can be taken as exemplifying the kind of accounts involved.

(a) Regional Specialization

It has often been claimed that the process of Scottish industrialization involved over-specialization in certain industrial sectors. The most common image of Scotland's industrial structure in the nineteenth century is that, as the economic historian, Lenman, has put it:

> By the 19th century, Scotland had developed a very specialised regional branch of the British economy, heavily oriented towards the manufacture and export of capital goods and coarse textiles (Lenman, 1977, p. 204).

As we shall see this is a debatable reading of the empirical data, but for the time being let us let that pass and follow the generally accepted argument. The specialization of the Scottish economy is seen as resulting from the subordinate relationship of Scottish to British capital. As one recent influential account put it:

In relation to Britain as a whole, what were to emerge in Scotland were *complementary* rather than *competitive* forms of capitalism, their interdependence being regularised under the political domination of Westminster. Such were the roots of the dependent or *client* status of the Scottish bourgeoisie (Dickson *et al.*, 1980, p. 90).

This argument, then, has similarities with that of Wallerstein, namely, that capitalist industrialization in Scotland was 'by invitation', or, at least, that capitalists permitted only the development of sectors of the Scottish economy which would complement, not compete with, English capital. It also suffers from a similar methodological problem to the core–periphery distinction discussed earlier. The answer to the question 'what is capitalism when it is not competitive?' appears to be 'complementary'. It is not easy to see by what process 'complementary' capitalism comes about. One would think that especially in the nineteenth century capital would flow into sectors where profits were to be made. To be sure individual capitalists or groups of capitalists might decide not to invest in certain sectors in Scotland because their interests elsewhere might be damaged. Such an argument, however, does not require the concept of complementary capitalism. Parsimony alone should make us wary of this notion. A similar problem arises with Hechter's use of 'cultural bias'; he posited that the ethnocentricity of 'core' investors inhibits investment in the periphery. As Cohn (1982) has recently shown, this thesis adds little to an orthodox economic model.

(b)   Proletarianization and De-skilling

This emphasis on the *specificities* – the peculiarities – of Scotland's economic and social development is also found in the analysis of contemporary Scotland. One assumption figures prominently, namely, that in recent years Scotland has undergone a highly specific process of 'proletarianization', whereby its 'working class' has grown in size relative to that south of the border, and has undergone a disproportionate degree of 'de-skilling'. This process is often linked to the increasing dominance of manufacturing industry in Scotland by foreign multinational companies. These elements are encapsulated nicely in the following:

> in importing production line branch plants requiring, in the main, semi-skilled workers and a disproportionately low number of technical and skilled workers as against indigenous employers, US firms reinforced the de-skilling processes already at work in the economy. This de-skilling led one writer to conclude that by the mid-1970s,[5] Scotland was 'more working class, and its population . . . less skilled, *vis-à-vis* England, than at any time since the First World War' (Dickson *et al.*, 1980, p. 246).

These are broad and influential assertions about Scottish society and its economy. It is beyond the scope of this chapter to examine them in detail, but our task will be to give an account of industrial and occupational change in Scotland which starts from the evidence available, and which is unencumbered by *a priori* assumptions as to the distinctiveness and peculiarity of Scotland. We shall in turn examine industrial change between 1851 and 1971; changes in sectoral employment, 1851–1981; and occupational change, 1921–71.

INDUSTRIAL CHANGE IN SCOTLAND, 1851–1971

A simple presentation of trends in the industrial structures of Scotland on the one hand, and England and Wales (or Britain) on the other, will not solve the debate about the precise nature of the structural articulations between the economies of these countries, and the mode of their insertion into the world economy. However, the work of C. H. Lee in attempting to reclassify the industrial and occupational data in the Censuses from 1841 to 1971 according to the 1968 Standard Industrial Classification provides an opportunity to come to a more precise estimation of differences between the industrial employment structures of Scotland and the rest of Britain.[6]

Most of the methodological pitfalls in constructing and using such a series have to do with changes in principles of enumeration and classification between successive censuses, to say nothing of the wider issues raised by real changes in the nature

of the industrial groups themselves – the textile industry in
1971, for example, is a far cry from that of 1841. However,
until someone attempts the task of constructing a series on the
basis of less time-bound and categories based on firmer theory
than are those of the 1968 Standard Industrial Classification,
Lee's series is the best we have, and is incomparably better
than what was available before. There are many fewer pitfalls,
however, in making inter-regional comparisons at a given point
in time. In this case, one is chiefly relying upon the use of the
same procedures by the census-takers in the different areas.
Although there may well have been some variation in practices, there seems little reason to believe that major inter-
regional distortions resulted. The problems raised by industrial
change remain, albeit in a much muted form, in that the textile
industry, for instance, in one region at a particular date may be
a somewhat different matter from that industry in another
region at that same date; such niceties are beyond the scope of
our analysis.

1851–1911

Let us look first at the sixty years following the 1851 Census.
Table 4.1 gives the structure of industrial employment (the
sixteen manufacturing orders plus mining and quarrying) for
Britain as a whole and for Scotland and Wales individually in
1851 and in 1911. Wales is included for comparative purposes
in view of the unfortunate practice of lumping together the
'Celtic peripheries' in many discussions. It can be clearly seen
that although there are differences between Britain and Scotland, they are not dramatic, and are dwarfed by those between
Britain and Wales. The simplest way of comparing industrial
employment structures is the positive percentage difference,
often simply described as the *index of dissimilarity*. For example, to calculate this index for the dissimilarity between the
industrial structures of Britain and Scotland in 1851, one
simply adds together the differences between the British and
Scottish percentages for those industries for which the British
figure is higher. If the structures were identical, the index
would be zero. If there were no overlap at all, the value would
be 100. The index thus has a nicely intuitive meaning in

TABLE 4.1   *Industrial orders as percentage of total industrial employment in Britain, Scotland and Wales, 1851 and 1911*

Industrial order	Britain		Scotland		Wales	
	1851	1911	1851	1911	1851	1911
2. Mining and quarrying	9.5	14.8	9.3	16.6	36.9	51.9
3. Food, drink and tobacco	10.0	13.6	9.0	13.2	8.1	10.2
5. Chemicals	1.2	2.1	0.9	1.9	0.6	1.1
6. Metal manufacture	7.2	7.1	6.3	9.3	17.3	11.9
7. Mechanical engineering	1.9	6.2	1.7	7.8	0.9	3.0
8. Instrument engineering	0.6	0.5	0.3	0.3	0.3	0.2
9. Electrical engineering	–	1.4	–	0.8	–	0.7
10. Ships and marine engineering	0.8	1.9	0.8	5.1	0.9	1.1
11. Vehicles	1.2	2.3	0.6	1.1	0.9	1.1
12. Other metal goods	2.4	3.9	1.0	1.9	1.0	1.5
13. Textiles	32.2	18.1	44.4	19.3	7.1	2.9
14. Leather, etc.	1.5	1.5	0.9	0.8	1.2	0.4
15. Clothing and footwear	22.3	15.0	18.3	11.0	20.3	9.7
16. Bricks, pottery, glass	2.4	2.2	1.0	1.3	0.8	1.1
17. Timber and furniture	4.7	3.8	3.5	3.8	3.1	1.6
18. Paper, printing, publishing	1.8	4.8	1.9	4.9	0.7	1.4
19. Other manufacturing	0.5	1.1	0.2	1.1	0.1	0.2

$$N = \begin{array}{ccc} 4\,022\,135 & 578\,974 & 181\,993 \\ 8\,350\,684 & 1\,008\,550 & 498\,484 \end{array}$$

percentage terms, although it is dependent on the categorization used and the number of categories. In 1851 the index of dissimilarity between Britain and Scotland was 12.3 and in 1911, 10.2. This may be compared with an index of dissimilarity between the industrial employment structures of Britain and Wales of 37.6 in 1851 and 41.9 in 1911. Wales is an extreme example in terms of the ten Standard Regions of Great Britain. However, if one calculates the indices of dissimilarity between the industrial structures of the ten Standard Regions and that of Britain as a whole, Scotland in both 1851 and 1911 was the *closest* to that overall British structure. In 1851 the mean value of the index between the regional structures and that of Britain as a whole was 25.4 compared with the figure for Scotland of 12.3, and in 1911 the mean was 25.7 compared with 10.2 for Scotland.

We can obtain a visual representation of Scotland's pattern of industrial specialization and industrial change relative to that of the other nine Standard Regions of Britain by means of multi-dimensional scaling.[7] The data upon which the scaling is based are the industrial employment distributions of the ten regions at four points in time (1851, 1871, 1891 and 1911). Positive percentage differences (dissimilarities) were calculated between all pairs of the forty industrial employment distributions. The multi-dimensional scaling programme tries to reproduce the rank ordering of the dissimilarities between the industrial structures in terms of distances between the corresponding data points in the plotted space. The result is that similar industrial structures will tend to be close together in the solution space.

The differences between the employment structures of the same region at different dates (or different regions at different dates) may be treated in exactly the same way as inter-regional differences at a given date.

Thus a spatial assessment can be made of the relative magnitude of shifts across time as compared with differences between regions at one point in time. Since the positive percentage differences on which the solution is based are generated by the distributions of the seventeen industrial orders which make up the industrial sector, different areas of the multi-dimensional scaling solution space will tend to correspond to specialization in particular industries or groups of industries with similar regional and temporal distributions. (See Table 4.2 for the contribution of selected industries to regional employment in 1851 and 1911.) The two-dimensional solution for the British regions at the four dates is given in Figure 4.1.

The four data points (1851, 1871, 1891 and 1911) for each region have been joined up to facilitate the tracking of the region's temporal trajectory through the 'industry space'. The group of regions at the top of the plot in Figure 4.1 consists of those whose industrial workforces in 1851 were most heavily concentrated into textiles. At the very top is the North-West of England with 60 per cent of its 1851 industrial workforce in textiles, followed by Yorkshire and Humberside with 55 per

TABLE 4.2 *British regions: selected industries as percentage of all industrial employment, 1851 and 1911*

	2 M+Q	5 MM	7,8,9 Eng	10 Sh+ME	12 MG	13 Text	15 C+F
1851							
South-East	1.4	5.3	2.9	1.1	2.0	10.8	34.4
East Anglia	1.5	7.1	1.7	0.7	1.0	13.6	37.9
South-West	16.0	6.5	1.4	1.1	1.1	16.7	34.1
West Midlands	12.6	16.2	3.8	0.1	9.6	11.2	18.7
East Midlands	6.5	4.4	1.3	0.1	1.2	42.9	25.1
North-West	5.6	3.8	3.2	0.5	1.1	59.6	12.7
Yorkshire/							
Humberside	6.9	6.6	2.1	0.2	3.9	54.7	12.6
North	27.7	9.6	2.5	3.4	1.4	10.9	21.0
Wales	36.9	17.3	1.2	0.9	1.0	7.1	20.3
Scotland	9.3	6.3	2.0	0.8	1.0	44.4	18.3
Britain	*9.5*	*7.2*	*2.5*	*0.8*	*2.4*	*32.2*	*22.3*
1911							
South-East	1.6	3.5	8.9	1.3	3.2	5.7	24.6
East Anglia	1.9	5.9	7.1	1.0	2.1	7.8	26.8
South-West	10.8	4.7	6.8	1.7	2.4	8.0	25.2
West Midlands	12.0	12.7	7.6	0.1	15.5	4.7	9.6
East Midlands	19.7	5.8	7.3	0.2	1.3	20.0	21.9
North-West	7.9	4.7	8.7	1.0	2.0	42.0	10.5
Yorkshire/							
Humberside	15.7	7.6	7.4	0.5	5.6	31.4	10.6
North	39.9	10.7	9.5	8.0	1.7	3.2	7.9
Wales	51.9	11.9	3.9	1.1	1.5	2.9	9.7
Scotland	16.6	9.3	8.9	5.1	1.9	19.3	11.0
Britain	*14.8*	*7.1*	*8.1*	*1.9*	*3.9*	*18.1*	*15.0*

cent. Scotland (44 per cent) and the East Midlands (43 per cent) showed a lower degree of specialization in textiles and this is reflected in their positions further down the plot. The distance which each of these four regions moves down towards the centre of the plot from 1851 to 1871 to 1891 to 1911 is a reflection of the extent to which they were moving away from specialization in textiles by these dates. The roughly similar total lengths of the tracks for Yorkshire and Humberside, the East Midlands and Scotland correspond to a shift of around 25 per cent of their total industrial workforces out of textiles. The

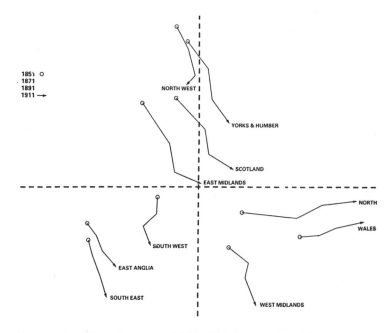

FIGURE 4.1 *Two-dimensional MINISSA scaling of positive percentage differences between Industrial employment structure (IOs 2–19) of ten British regions*

North-West of England experienced a much smaller shift out of textiles in this period reflected in a much shorter track towards the centre.

In the lower left-hand quadrant is another well-defined grouping marked in particular by a specialization in the manufacture of clothing and footwear combined with a low proportion of employment in the heavier industries. These geographically-contiguous regions – the South-East of England, East Anglia and the South-West of England – show a much smaller overall shift in the distribution of employment than does the previous group. What shift there is largely reflects the general move out of textiles and from clothing and footwear into engineering. The move of the South-West towards the South-East and East Anglia is primarily a reflection of the decline in the proportion of its workforce employed in mining and quarrying.

At the opposite extreme, on the far right of the plot are the two regions – Wales and the North of England – whose massive and increasing specialization in coalmining was the dominant feature of their employment shifts between 1851 and 1911, producing well-marked trajectories away from the other regions.

The West Midlands is the odd region out mainly because of its unique degree of specialization in metal goods and, by 1911, vehicles (7 per cent of total employment). In 1851, the West Midlands had formed a loose grouping with Wales and the North, the most important common factor then being metal manufacture.

There are then no grounds for saying that Scotland in the *nineteenth* century had an industrial structure which was particularly specialized with respect to the *British* economy. The significant specialization was that which was shared by Scotland and the rest of Britain, and that which took place, as we shall see, *within* Scotland. As Kirby put it:

> The distinctive nature of Britain's industrial structure was in fact one of the most outstanding features of the pre-1914 economy. In 1907 the old-established staple trades of textiles, coalmining, iron and steel, and general engineering accounted for approximately 50 per cent of net industrial output and employed 25 per cent of the working population. Most were heavily dependent upon an increasingly narrow range of export markets located mainly within the British Empire, South America and Asia, and coalmining, textiles and iron and steel alone contributed over 70 per cent of the country's export earnings (Kirby, 1981, p. 3).

If Kirby's characterization is compared with Table 4.2, it can be seen that while Scotland in 1911 had a slightly higher proportion of industrial employment in the four industries named by Kirby as *British* specialisms, reflecting Britain's control over Imperial markets, the striking feature is the closeness of the structure to Britain as a whole in this respect. Far from being as Lenman puts it 'a very specialised regional branch of the British economy', Scotland epitomized Britain's industrial structure and was 'more British' than the other regions. Scotland was simply especially well-adapted to take advantage of Britain's highly advantageous structural position within a world economy itself shaped around Britain's interests.

This rapid and thorough adaptation of Scottish industry to Britain's imperially guaranteed niche in the world economy is clearly brought out in Keith Burgess's contribution to *Scottish Capitalism* (Dickson *et al.*, 1980, chap. 5). However, intertwined with this account is the unsatisfactory characterization of Scottish capitalism as a client 'capitalism', and the associated ideas of 'exploitative' British capital, to which we have already referred. There is one category of English capital which might be said to have had an exploitative relationship with Scottish capital and that was finance capital centred on the City of London. Even here, however, Scottish capitalism, to the extent that it did have its own financial institutions, was in a better position than many English manufacturing regions. Paradoxically, to the extent that Scotland's financial network exhibited a greater tendency to channel investment funds abroad than to invest productively at home (Lenman, 1977, p. 192), it was precisely Scottish autonomy which contributed to a lack of investment in Scottish industry. This in turn made the post-First World War collapse of the international economy so much more of a catastrophe for Scotland. Even more ironically, through this greater tendency to invest abroad in search of higher profits, Scottish capitalism was more classically 'imperialist' in the sense introduced by Hilferding and Lenin than was the case south of the border. Yet again, the roots of Scotland's decline are to be found in a 'surfeit of imperialism' rather than, as is so often made out, in a position of clientage or dependence.

1911–31

To return to the rapid survey of the development of Scotland's industrial structure, the First World War and the brief post-war boom exacerbated the dependence of Scotland's and Britain's industrial structure on their imperial niches in a world economy of a particular form. The inevitable corollary was that when this international order collapsed, Scotland, locked firmly into it, suffered in the way experienced by Britain as a whole. The extreme localization of the effects of this collapse within Scotland in the 1920s and 1930s stemmed from the degree of regional specialization which had occurred *within* Scotland prior to the War. This process can be seen most simply in terms of Table 4.3.

Is Scotland Different?

TABLE 4.3 *Scottish industrial areas: selected industries as percentage of all industrial employment, 1851 and 1911*

	Industrial Order						
	2 M+Q	3 FDT	5 MM	7 ME	10 Sh+ME	13 Text	15 C+F
1851							
Ayrshire	17.2	5.1	3.5	0.7	0.4	53.1	15.0
Dunbarton	8.0	5.7	3.2	1.4	2.4	61.0	10.2
Lanarkshire	13.6	7.3	8.4	2.5	0.5	43.1	14.6
Renfrewshire	3.3	7.0	4.4	2.8	1.4	56.8	17.8
Midlothian	7.1	17.6	8.7	2.2	0.5	7.5	29.5
West Lothian	31.6	9.2	3.5	0.9	0.1	30.6	16.0
Clackmannan	20.6	7.7	5.2	1.2	0.6	44.2	12.2
Stirlingshire	14.0	7.6	10.5	0.9	0.3	42.7	12.7
Fife	12.4	6.9	4.1	1.3	0.3	58.0	11.5
Angus	1.3	6.2	3.1	1.4	1.0	72.1	10.2
Aberdeenshire	2.8	13.1	6.9	1.5	1.8	34.5	23.5
Borders	1.7	13.2	6.1	1.6	0.1	44.1	23.4
Scotland	*9.3*	*9.0*	*6.3*	*1.7*	*0.8*	*44.4*	*18.3*
1911							
Ayrshire	28.0	10.1	8.6	5.8	1.9	20.8	11.3
Dunbarton	7.4	7.3	8.1	20.6	26.1	14.3	5.1
Lanarkshire	18.0	12.2	14.4	10.4	5.4	9.5	11.6
Renfrewshire	2.4	9.5	7.9	13.8	17.8	30.2	6.1
Midlothian	13.8	19.2	4.7	4.8	1.3	6.6	14.7
West Lothian	57.0	7.8	6.3	2.9	0.4	1.6	4.9
Clackmannan	15.4	12.3	3.1	3.0	0.7	44.0	6.1
Stirlingshire	34.0	8.9	23.9	4.2	1.2	5.8	7.4
Fife	44.1	8.6	2.7	2.7	0.2	21.3	6.2
Angus	1.3	10.1	3.7	5.2	1.8	61.8	7.6
Aberdeenshire	7.6	20.5	5.2	5.2	3.2	14.6	15.9
Borders	1.0	12.3	2.8	1.8	0.1	60.2	12.2
Scotland	*16.6*	*13.2*	*9.3*	*7.8*	*5.1*	*19.3*	*11.0*

From a generally shared specialization in textiles in 1851, industrial specialization rapidly took place along two main axes (shown in the multi-dimensional scaling solution in Figure 4.2). The first shift, focussed in particular on Renfrewshire and Dumbartonshire (more correctly, on Clydeside) was into engineering and shipbuilding, represented by a move down towards the bottom of the plot. The second was into coal and steel, represented by those areas moving towards the top right-hand

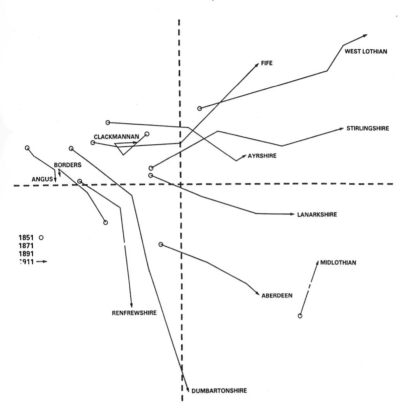

FIGURE 4.2   *Two-dimensional MINISSA scaling of positive percentage differences between industrial employment structures (IOs 2–19) of twelve Scottish industrial areas*

side of the plot. By 1911 there was thus a roughly tripartite pattern of regional industrial development formed by shifts along these two axes and the relatively unchanged position of those regions which had maintained their specialization in textiles – primarily around Paisley, Dundee and the Borders.

To anticipate somewhat, it has been this pattern of specialization – reflecting Scotland's rapid adaptation to the market opportunities resulting from the Empire – from which Scotland, and in particular certain regions of Scotland, have found it impossible to break in the course of the twentieth century.

Because of a switch in 1921 from an occupationally-based to an industrially-based classification in the Population Census, together with some deficiencies in the Census of that year, it is much more difficult to trace industrial employment changes over the crucial years from 1911 to 1931. Campbell (1980, pp. 198–200) has carried out calculations based on the Censuses of Production of 1907 and 1924 which cover roughly the same industries (with the addition of public utilities and construction). The general picture is one of stability, in that the industrial structures of Scotland and the UK both changed rather little and remained on the whole alike (the positive percentage difference between the Scottish and UK industrial employment structures moves from 12.0 to 10.5). However such differences as did exist in this period were to prove highly significant in the future. In 1907, 27 per cent of Scotland's industrial workforce were employed in the broad category of 'iron and steel, engineering and shipbuilding' compared with 22 per cent for the United Kingdom as a whole.

1931–71

Table 4.4 gives the pattern of industrial employment for Britain and Scotland from 1931 to 1971. Over this period, the industrial employment structure of Scotland appears to have been marginally more differentiated from that of Britain as a whole than was the case in the nineteenth century – at least to judge from the index of dissimilarity given in Table 4.5. This table also gives two versions of what could be called an index of specialization of the ten British Standard regions. The first is the mean index of dissimilarity between all pairs of regions. The second is the mean index of dissimilarity between the ten regions and the British structure. These suggest that there was a general process of convergence at a regional level. This must be seen in the context of the fact that in 1931 and 1951 Scotland was still the region with the industrial structure closest to the British mean and in 1961 and 1971 only the North-West of England was closer; the other regions can then in aggregate be seen as converging on Scotland.

Once again the multi-dimensional scaling plot (Figure 4.3) shows this tendency clearly. The temporal trajectories converge in such a way that the diameter of the circle needed to encompass the data points in 1971 is far smaller than that required in 1931.

TABLE 4.4 *Industrial orders as percentage of total industrial employment,*
Britain and Scotland – 1931, 1951, 1961, 1971

	Britain				Scotland			
	1931	*1951*	*1961*	*1971*	*1931*	*1951*	*1961*	*1971*
2. Mining + Q	14.9	9.5	7.9	4.6	16.4	11.4	10.8	5.0
3. FDT	9.1	8.4	7.7	8.7	11.6	11.1	10.4	13.7
4. C + P prods	0.4	0.5	0.6	0.7	0.6	0.5	0.5	0.4
5. Chemicals	2.8	4.5	4.8	5.4	2.1	3.9	3.9	4.2
6. Metal manufacturing	5.2	6.4	6.9	6.5	7.2	7.2	7.9	6.8
7. Mechanical engineering	6.4	10.5	12.4	13.2	8.0	12.2	14.6	14.0
8. Institute engineering	0.7	1.3	1.6	1.7	0.5	1.0	1.4	2.5
9. Electrical engineering	3.5	6.3	8.3	9.9	1.2	2.1	4.0	7.2
10. Sh & ME	2.2	3.1	2.6	2.1	4.9	8.8	7.9	5.6
11. Vehicles	5.8	8.3	9.2	9.3	3.3	4.2	4.0	5.1
12. Other manufacturing	4.6	5.7	5.8	6.9	2.2	3.4	2.8	4.1
13. Textiles	15.5	11.1	8.7	6.9	17.8	13.5	12.3	10.4
14. Leather, etc.	1.1	0.9	0.7	0.6	0.7	0.7	0.5	0.5
15. C + F	11.8	7.6	6.0	5.5	6.3	4.6	3.5	4.5
16. BPG	3.4	3.5	3.5	3.6	2.0	2.5	2.6	3.0
17. TF	3.9	3.7	3.3	3.5	5.5	4.5	3.5	3.8
18. PPP	6.2	5.8	6.7	7.2	6.8	6.0	7.1	7.3
19. Other manufacturing	2.5	3.0	3.2	3.8	2.7	2.4	2.4	2.2
	100.0	100.0	100.0	100.0	100.0	100.0	100.0	100.0

TABLE 4.5 *Indices of dissimilarity and specialization*

	Index of dissimilarity between Scottish and British industrial employment structures	*Indices of British regional specialization*	
		(I)	*(II)*
1931	15.4	29.1	30.2
1951	16.1	24.5	26.0
1961	18.2	24.1	24.9
1971	14.6	21.1	20.0

An idea of the relative pace of industrial transformation in
these years can be gained by simply calculating the positive
percentage difference between the industrial structures at successive Census dates:

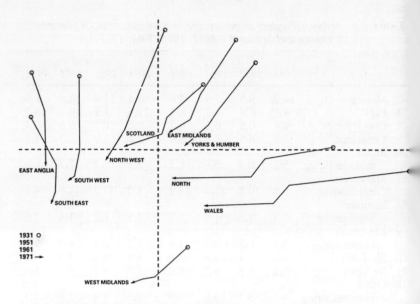

FIGURE 4.3   *Three-dimensional MINISSA scaling of positive percentage differences between industrial employment structures (IOs 2–19) of ten British regions*

Period	Britain	Scotland
1931–51	15.5	13.7
1951–61	7.4	6.6
1961–71	6.6	12.0

If we make the crude assumption that change was even within the twenty-year period 1931–51 and within the two following decades, these data give the interesting result that industrial change at this level of aggregation would appear to have proceeded at a relatively constant rate in Britain as a whole but to have shown a marked acceleration in Scotland in the 1960s.

A major aspect of this relatively accelerated rate of industrial change in Scotland in the 1960s was that Scotland caught up to some extent in terms of industrial order 8 – electrical engineering. Scotland's historically low proportion of employment in this order had long been held to be perhaps the major symptom of Scotland's failure to change over from the highly vulnerable traditional industries bequeathed by the nineteenth century to the 'next wave' of industries. The growth of vehicles, consumer goods and electrical engineering (with an increasing electronic component) in the English South and Midlands during the 1920s and 1930s had been the main factor behind these regions surviving the depression in much better shape than areas still reliant on the older, heavier industries. Table 4.4 shows the extent to which Scotland had indeed lagged behind Britain as a whole in this respect. By 1971, however, the gap was much smaller — particularly if one includes the closely related industrial order of instrument engineering. By then, 9.7 per cent of Scotland's industrial employment was in these two orders compared with 11.6 per cent of British. Most of the higher British figure can be accounted for in terms of the concentration of these two orders in the two regions of South-East England (18.3 per cent) and East Anglia (14.0 per cent) with all but two of the other British regions lying in a band between 8.9 per cent (Wales) and 11.4 per cent (South-West England).

The general process of convergence in the industrial structures of the British regions in the course of the twentieth century, is not mirrored – at least up to 1971 – *within* Scotland. The industrial employment structures of the main Scottish industrial areas, although they have tended to move away from some of the more extreme traditional specializations, have remained broadly within the main lines of specialization bequeathed by the high tide of Victorian industrial expansion.

Table 4.6 gives the structure of industrial employment for these major industrial areas from 1931 to 1971. The index of specialization for these areas (mean positive percentage difference between all pairs of these regions, over all industries) showed little change: 51.1 in 1931; 52.7 in 1951; 55.5 in 1961 and 49.4 in 1971. This stability seems to have been the result of two processes working in opposite directions. On the one hand, the decline in employment in some of the more localized traditional industries – in particular, mining and shipbuilding – see, for example, the massive decline in the share of employment in mining in West Lothian between 1961 and 1971 – has worked to reduce the degree of regional specialization. On the other hand, many of the newer industries – in particular chemicals and motor vehicles – have also been extremely localized and their growth has thus worked to increase specialization. Localization in the latter case has had less to do with

TABLE 4.6 Scottish industrial areas: selected industries as percentage of industrial employment, 1931–71

	2 M+Q	3 FDT	4,5 Chem	6 MM	7 ME	9 EE	10 Sh+ME	11 Veh	12 Text
1931									
Ayrshire	27.0	5.7	5.1	5.2	5.4	0.9	4.5	2.7	25.3
Dunbarton	7.4	3.9	0.6	4.2	30.6	0.5	33.3	1.9	9.5
Lanarkshire	15.9	10.2	2.0	13.4	10.0	1.4	9.9	5.1	6.5
Renfrew	0.5	6.9	1.7	2.3	14.4	0.7	26.6	1.2	30.3
Midlothian	16.4	18.4	4.0	1.7	5.3	2.5	2.7	2.7	4.8
W. Lothian	54.3	4.7	12.6	8.8	2.8	0.2	0.2	0.5	4.7
Clackmannan	18.7	14.1	0.1	1.9	4.1	3.7	1.1	2.0	38.9
Stirling	28.9	4.1	7.2	31.6	3.2	0.6	1.8	1.1	4.5
Fife	48.4	5.1	0.3	2.4	2.1	0.6	2.2	1.1	13.6
Angus	0.5	7.1	0.8	1.1	6.4	0.8	4.4	1.0	65.5
Aberdeen	1.7	23.4	3.0	1.0	5.3	0.9	8.0	3.8	13.1
Borders	1.0	6.4	0.2	0.7	2.0	0.5	0.2	2.0	71.4
Scotland	*16.4*	*10.5*	*2.5*	*7.9*	*8.4*	*1.2*	*8.8*	*3.3*	*17.3*
1951									
Ayrshire	21.6	5.3	15.3	3.6	7.8	0.2	3.6	4.0	22.0
Dunbarton	5.5	4.0	0.6	2.7	43.1	1.1	27.1	0.9	6.4
Lanarkshire	6.8	11.1	3.2	11.9	12.6	3.0	9.4	6.7	6.1
Renfrew	0.3	7.7	2.9	3.9	21.8	1.3	16.7	6.2	23.0
Midlothian	15.7	21.1	5.0	1.3	5.1	3.8	3.8	2.7	3.4
W. Lothian	49.4	3.5	9.1	10.4	1.4	7.2	0.4	0.2	5.0
Clackmannan	19.7	15.2	0.3	0.9	2.6	7.7	0.5	0.1	29.0
Stirling	15.5	5.4	11.4	34.4	4.4	0.2	2.7	1.8	2.5

Fife	39.3	5.8	2.8	1.4	3.0	0.1	12.2	3.1	9.4
Angus	0.5	9.6	1.7	0.2	16.4	2.5	4.7	0.5	44.3
Aberdeen	1.2	22.8	4.0	0.5	11.4	0.4	9.6	2.7	11.0
Borders	1.0	5.6	0.4	0.3	4.4	0.3	0.2	0.5	70.7
Scotland	*11.4*	*11.1*	*4.4*	*7.2*	*12.2*	*2.1*	*8.8*	*4.2*	*13.5*
1961									
Ayrshire	23.0	3.8	12.2	4.8	14.1	0.9	2.6	3.3	19.5
Dunbarton	5.0	4.8	0.6	4.3	51.7	4.0	1.6	0.6	2.5
Lanarkshire	5.3	10.4	2.8	12.8	14.7	5.8	8.8	5.6	5.6
Renfrew	0.3	7.1	3.9	3.5	23.1	2.2	13.8	13.2	17.0
Midlothian	17.7	21.5	4.1	2.5	5.2	8.4	3.0	1.1	3.4
West Lothian	47.6	4.7	5.9	11.4	1.8	8.9	1.0	0.4	5.7
Clackmannan	19.2	13.4	0.4	1.7	5.4	3.9	0.3	0.1	31.4
Stirling	9.8	5.1	20.7	31.2	2.3	0.5	2.3	2.0	2.1
Fife	41.7	5.1	0.5	3.9	2.8	0.6	13.5	0.5	7.5
Angus	0.5	9.8	1.8	1.8	19.5	4.4	3.0	0.4	39.5
Aberdeen	0.9	22.1	3.7	0.4	13.9	1.3	9.1	1.3	11.5
Borders	0.8	1.7	0.3	0.5	4.1	0.2	0.1	0.0	79.7
Scotland	*10.8*	*10.4*	*4.4*	*7.9*	*14.6*	*4.0*	*7.9*	*4.0*	*12.3*
1971									
Ayrshire	12.2	7.2	12.0	5.2	13.3	1.9	1.1	5.7	20.1
Dunbarton	0.4	12.3	2.3	4.2	39.2	3.9	13.9	1.7	2.4
Lanarkshire	1.7	13.0	2.5	12.5	15.7	9.6	5.6	4.3	3.8

continued on page 84

83

Table 4.6 continued

	2 M+Q	3 FDT	4,5 Chem	6 MM	7 ME	9 EE	10 Sh+ME	11 Veh	12 Text
Renfrew	0.1	8.9	4.2	2.4	15.6	6.7	13.3	19.5	12.2
Midlothian	12.0	22.2	4.4	1.7	6.2	11.5	3.0	1.9	3.2
West Loth.	19.0	10.1	0.6	9.5	4.6	14.0	0.1	22.4	2.4
Clackmannan	10.8	15.8	0.ᶟ	0.0	17.2	0.7	0.0	0.0	30.1
Stirling	5.1	5.9	22.2	19.7	4.0	2.0	1.5	3.0	1.5
Fife	17.3	7.8	1.4	2.6	9.5	12.7	10.3	1.0	8.0
Angus	0.2	8.9	1.9	1.7	23.0	5.2	2.3	0.3	27.8
Aberdeen	0.9	34.8	2.2	0.2	10.9	1.0	6.3	1.1	9.2
Borders	1.4	3.4	1.0	0.3	4.2	4.9	0.3	0.4	67.0
Scotland	5.0	13.7	4.5	6.8	14.0	7.2	5.6	5.1	10.4

ecological factors such as deep-water or raw materials and much more to do with the increase in the minimum size of individual production units. As the fate of Linwood and Bathgate motor vehicle plants has shown, much of this 'new' investment is just as vulnerable and has produced a new pattern of localized unemployment in its wake. The complexity of the regional pattern of industrial change and specialization in the mid-twentieth century is nicely reflected in Figures 4.4a, 4.4b, and 4.4c which represent a three-dimensional scaling solution of the positive percentage differences between the structures of the twelve regions over the five decades. In contrast to the clear-cut nineteenth-century pattern a two-dimensional solution is unacceptably stressed and three dimensions are required. The temporal trajectories suggest that the regions have retained in the twentieth century the relative positions bequeathed to them by the nineteenth.

The general message of this section on industrial change must be that in terms of industrial development what Scotland has shared with the rest of Britain far outweighs what has differentiated it. To make the point another way, far from being a specialized region of Britain, Scotland is a miniature, though highly internally-differentiated version of Britain as a whole. There are many parallels, one of the most obvious being that Edinburgh's employment structure in relation to the rest of Scotland is very similar to that of London as compared with the rest of England. The corollary of this is that in terms of industrial structure, Scotland is the 'wrong' unit. Industrial differentiation within Scotland has been of a higher order of magnitude than the industrial differentiation of Scotland from the rest of Britain.

CHANGE IN SECTORAL EMPLOYMENT IN SCOTLAND, 1851–1981

In terms of understanding occupational change, change at the broader sectoral level has been much more important than change in the industrial structure of mining and manufacturing. Table 4.7 shows the long-term trends in sectoral employment structure for Britain and Scotland from 1851 to 1981.[8] The overall trends can be fairly briefly outlined, although such a

86

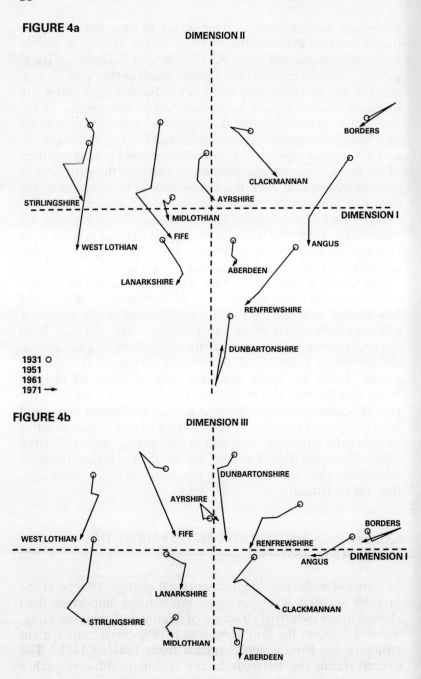

FIGURE 4a

DIMENSION II

BORDERS

CLACKMANNAN

AYRSHIRE

STIRLINGSHIRE

MIDLOTHIAN

DIMENSION I

FIFE

WEST LOTHIAN

ANGUS

ABERDEEN

LANARKSHIRE

RENFREWSHIRE

DUNBARTONSHIRE

1931 ○
1951
1961
1971 →

FIGURE 4b

DIMENSION III

DUNBARTONSHIRE

AYRSHIRE

FIFE

BORDERS

WEST LOTHIAN

RENFREWSHIRE

DIMENSION I

ANGUS

LANARKSHIRE

CLACKMANNAN

STIRLINGSHIRE

MIDLOTHIAN

ABERDEEN

FIGURE 4c

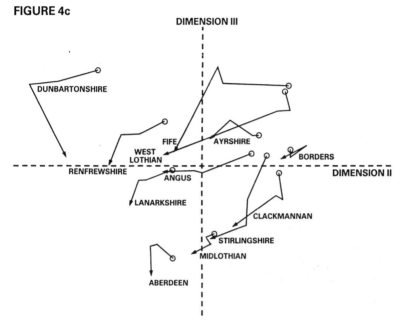

FIGURE 4.4   *Three-dimensional MINISSA scaling of positive percentage differences between industrial employment structures (IOs 2–19) of twelve Scottish industrial areas*

rapid survey will inevitably gloss over deviations due to cyclical factors (in particular the effects of the depressions of the 1870s and 1930s to say nothing of the present one–1984) and also some quite fundamental changes in the composition of the sectors themselves. The service sector for example has swung over from consisting predominantly of domestic-service categories to consisting predominantly of categories associated with the expansion of state functions, for example, the education and health sectors.

The long-term decline in the proportion of employment in agriculture, forestry and fisheries proceeded very much in parallel for Scotland and Britain. This decline has also reduced the contribution of this sector to the overall difference between the sectoral employment structures of Britain and Scotland. The long-term rise and fall of employment in mining and quarrying has also proceeded in parallel at the Scottish and British levels.

Is Scotland Different?

TABLE 4.7   *Sectors as percentage of total employment:* Scotland (top line), Britain (second line offset), 1851–1981.*

	AFF	M + Q	Manuf.	Const.	Inter.	Serv.	Index of dissimilarity
			Sector				
1851	26.0	4.4	43.2	5.5	5.0	15.9	5.2
	23.2	4.3	40.9	5.7	5.8	20.1	
1871	23.6	5.6	40.9	6.6	6.5	16.8	8.0
	16.7	5.1	40.3	6.8	7.0	24.2	
1891	15.3	6.3	43.2	6.4	9.3	19.6	6.5
	11.7	5.8	40.8	6.8	10.1	24.8	
1911A	11.4	8.7	43.9	6.0	10.3	19.8	6.8
	8.4	7.2	41.6	6.8	10.5	25.5	
1911B	11.8	8.0	36.5	5.9	18.5	19.3	7.5
	8.7	6.6	33.5	6.6	19.6	25.0	
1931	10.1	6.0	30.3	4.2	25.4	24.0	5.5
	6.4	5.6	32.1	5.0	24.0	26.8	
1951	7.4	4.5	35.1	6.9	21.9	24.1	4.3
	5.1	3.8	36.3	6.3	21.4	27.2	
1961	5.8	3.9	32.5	7.9	23.7	26.2	5.0
	3.7	3.1	36.1	6.9	22.6	27.7	
1971A	4.1	1.7	32.2	8.2	21.0	32.8	2.5
	2.7	1.7	34.6	7.1	21.0	33.0	
1971B	2.7	1.9	33.4	7.9	20.6	33.4	3.2
	1.9	1.8	36.4	5.6	20.6	33.5	
1981	2.3	1.9	25.4	7.5	19.8	43.1	4.3
	1.7	1.6	28.6	5.3	20.9	41.9	

* For sectoral definitions, see note 7.

The main explicit classificatory shift in the series occurred between Lee's Series A (up to 1911) and his Series B (1911 on). The major substantive recategorization involved at this date was the transfer of the employment categories now included in industrial order 23 (distributive trades) from the respective manufacturing orders to this order. At the sectoral level, this involves moving these categories from the manufacturing to the intermediate sector. As can be seen by comparing the Series A distribution for 1911 with the Series B distribution for the same year, this recategorization involved around 8 per cent of employment for both Scotland and Britain. Making allowance for this reclassification (either by adding on 8 per cent to the figures for manufacturing for the years after 1911 or subtracting 8 per cent for the years before) what stands out is the quite remarkable stability in the share of manufacturing employment, for both Britain as a whole and Scotland, in the hundred years from 1851 to 1951.

Up to 1911, Scotland's proportion of manufacturing employment was around 3 percentage points higher than that for Britain as a whole. The greater impact of the depression in Scotland, however, pushed its share below that for Britain, where it has since remained.

The main implication of the hundred-year stability in the share of manufacturing employment is that, contrary to the most commonly-held image of long-term sectoral change, the decline in employment in agriculture, forestry and fisheries was accompanied not by an increase in the share of manufacturing employment, but by a growth in the shares of the intermediate and service sectors, plus, in the nineteenth century, mining and quarrying.

In the second half of the nineteenth century, the corollary of Britain's lower share of employment in agriculture, forestry and fisheries was a higher share of employment in the service sector than was the case in Scotland. This imbalance was the largest component of the difference between Scotland and Britain's sectoral employment structures in the years up to 1911. This difference in service employment between Scotland and England was almost entirely due to the contribution of South-East England to the British figure. In 1851, the percentage employed in the service sector in England and Wales outside the South-East was 17 per cent – just 1 per cent above the Scottish figure – compared with 31 per cent in the South-East itself. In 1911, again, the figure for England and Wales outside the South-East was just one percentage point higher, at 21 per cent, than that for Scotland, compared with a figure for the South-East of 38 per cent.

To put the degree of differentiation of the Scottish sectoral employment structure from the British into perspective, in both 1851 and 1911, of all the ten standard regions, Scotland's structure was the closest to the British – as we saw was the case for industrial employment above.

In comparison with the relatively clear-cut trends and differentiations fo the late nineteenth and early twentieth centuries, the patterns from 1931 on are somewhat more complex, although there is a slight trend towards a convergence of sectoral employment structures both between Scotland and Britain and between the standard regions in general.

It is only from 1951 onwards (at least in terms of Census dates) that what is usually regarded as the dominant trend of the 'occupational transition' in advanced industrial societies – the switch in employment from the manufacturing (secondary) sector to the service (tertiary) sector – can be said to have gathered steam. Even by the 1960s however, the by now rapid relative expansion in the service sector was accompanied by an uneven pattern of decline across all the other sectors rather than by a decline in the share of manufacturing alone. Only in the 1970s was the pattern predominantly one of a straight switch from manufacturing to services under the impact of an ominous combination of processes common to other advanced industrial societies, as well as Britain's specific loss of industrial competitiveness.

As can be seen from the indices of dissimilarity listed in Table 4.7, by 1971 Scotland's sectoral structure of employment was extremely close to that of Britain as a whole. This can be seen as an aspect of a general process of convergence between the sectoral employment structures of the British regions. By 1981, only three of the standard regions had an index of dissimilarity from the British sectoral structure greater than 6. The South-East (8.1) had a disproportionate share of service employment (though by no means to the extent that this was true of the nineteenth century), the East Midlands (10.7) and West Midlands (11.1) had managed to hold out longer against the drop in the share of manufacturing employment.

Regional differences in sectoral employment structure, as in industrial employment structure, were much greater within Scotland. Without going into the trends in detail, Table 4.8 gives an idea of the degree of unevenness involved at the two widely-separated dates of 1851 and 1971 – with little apparent change in the degree of regional differentiation over the whole period.

However, to return to the Scottish level (see Table 4.7) the accelerating increase in the share of the service sector, from 24 per cent in 1951 to 26 per cent in 1961 to 33 per cent in 1971 and finally to 43 per cent in 1981 – a jump of 19 percentage

TABLE 4.8   *Scottish regions: sectors as percentage of total employment, 1851 and 1971*

	Agr.	M + Q	Man.	Const.	Inter	Service	*
Sector							
1851							
Ayrshire	21.8	10.4	50.1	3.9	4.4	9.3	(12.9)
Dunbarton	17.8	4.6	52.7	7.2	6.0	11.8	(12.4)
Lan. + Renf.	7.1	7.5	60.1	5.4	6.5	13.5	(21.5)
Dumf + Gall	42.0	2.0	27.3	6.0	4.2	18.5	(19.1)
Borders	43.4	0.7	30.0	7.3	2.9	15.7	(19.2)
Mid/E. Lothian	14.4	3.3	37.2	7.1	7.6	30.5	(18.8)
Central	20.1	10.4	45.5	6.5	4.6	12.9	(9.3)
Fife	21.2	6.9	51.8	5.3	4.6	10.2	(11.1)
Angus	14.8	0.9	63.5	5.0	4.9	10.9	(20.3)
North East	45.3	0.8	27.0	4.9	3.8	18.4	(21.8)
Highlands	49.2	1.1	24.7	5.2	3.3	16.4	(23.7)
Far North	56.5	0.9	21.5	3.8	3.6	13.7	(30.5)
Scotland	*26.0*	*4.4*	*43.2*	*5.5*	*5.0*	*15.9*	*(18.4)* (mean)
1971							
Ayrshire	3.7	5.1	36.8	8.6	19.0	26.8	(8.4)
Dunbarton	0.9	0.2	43.1	8.5	15.6	31.8	(11.2)
Lan + Renf	0.7	0.5	38.8	7.7	22.6	29.7	(8.2)
Dumf & Gal.	16.6	0.5	23.6	8.0	20.6	30.7	(12.5)
Borders	13.8	0.5	33.3	7.1	16.7	28.7	(10.8)
Mid/E. Lothian	1.8	2.9	21.9	8.1	23.2	42.3	(12.9)
Central	2.0	4.4	37.9	8.9	17.9	29.0	(9.1)
Fife	4.0	7.0	30.0	8.3	18.3	32.5	(5.4)
Angus	4.1	0.1	38.4	7.8	18.9	30.8	(6.2)
North East	11.9	0.2	23.5	8.0	20.5	36.0	(11.0)
Highlands	12.1	0.5	13.4	11.0	21.7	41.3	(20.0)
Far North	19.4	0.0	12.1	9.2	20.2	39.2	(21.7)
Scotland	*5.8*	*3.9*	*32.5*	*7.9*	*23.7*	*26.2*	*(15.7)* (mean)

* Final column: index of dissimilarity between regional sectoral structure and Scottish sectoral structure. For sectoral definitions see Note 7.

points in thirty years, or 17 percentage points in twenty years – has been by far the greatest single shift in sectoral employment which Scotland has experienced in a comparable time-span, certainly in the period covered by the data, and probably ever.

Compared with the sheer brute fact of this shift, the specificities of Scotland's pattern of change – even the fact that the comparable shift at the British level was only 15 percentage points compared with Scotland's shift of 19, so that Scotland moved from having a lower to a higher share of service employment – pale into relative insignificance.

The growth of the service sector has been by far the greatest single identifiable motor of social change in Scotland since the Second World War. The changes in occupational structure, patterns of female employment and social mobility right through to household structure, demographic behaviour and political orientations can be traced to a greater or lesser degree back to this single transformation.

OCCUPATIONAL CHANGE IN SCOTLAND, 1921 TO 1971

The problems involved in constructing a long-term series based on the Census, showing changes in the occupational structure, are even more daunting than those involved in constructing an industrial series, so much have the bases of occupational categorization changed in this century alone. However, as background work to the Scottish Mobility Study, an attempt was made to reclassify the occupational distributions published in the reports of the 1921, 1931 and 1951 Censuses of Scotland according to the socio-economic group classification used in the 1961 and 1971 Censuses.[9] No detailed description of the reclassification procedures used is available and the status, or even the possibility, of such a series has been the subject of controversy. If two provisos are kept in mind, however, one methodological and one of a more epistemological nature, the series can be accepted as giving, in broad outline, a sketch of the evolution of the Scottish occupational structure between 1921 and 1971.

The methodological proviso is that a system of categories constructed on the basis of one set of criteria – for example, the occupational classification used in the 1921 Census – can never be precisely translated into a system of categories constructed on the basis of a different set of criteria, such as the socio-economic group classification used in the 1971 Census. Without access to the original data, however, such a translation is the only basis for comparing the two different occupational structures. All that one has to go on in performing the translation are common-sense assumptions of continuity between the meanings, the concrete referents, of the component occupational titles of the two classifications.

At an epistemological level, a series such as this depends upon some degree of acceptance of the proposition that applying a category such as 'skilled' to the 1921 distribution of occupational titles means the same as applying the same term to the 1971 set. Industrial change, as well as influencing the numbers doing particular jobs, changes the nature of the jobs themselves. The mention of such considerations does nothing more than signal the existence of a vast area of methodological debate. Nothing short of a full-scale historical investigation of changes in the precise characteristics of all the jobs involved, and probably not even that, would satisfy the sceptic as to the possibility of such a long-term series.

Bearing these difficulties in mind we shall examine the data nevertheless (see Table 4.9). Over the period as a whole, two marked uni-directional trends stand out. First, the continuous decline in skilled manual workers (socio-economic group 9) as a proportion of the non-farm workforce – from 35.3 per cent in 1921 to 24.3 per cent in 1971. Second, the continuous rise in non-manual employment (socio-economic groups 1 to 6). The precise temporal expression of these two underlying trends can be seen to be largely dependent upon the rhythms of industrial change and upon fluctuations in the level of economic activity. It is equally important to remember that many of the socio-economic groups have shown no long-term trend. Furthermore, no single non-manual socio-economic group shows an increased share for all four intercensal periods.

This last point is a particular instance of the general circumstance that the trends do not display as much regularity as theorizations of the development of occupational structures in industrial society might lead one to expect. It would seem that twentieth century Scotland is too old and complex an industrial society for its occupational trends to be encompassed by a small number of generalizations. Accounting for many of the individual changes in the shares of these aggregate socio-economic groups would involve at the very least their disaggregation into component sex and occupational sub-groups. One

TABLE 4.9   *Socio-economic groups 1 to 12 (non-farm, non-armed forces) as percentage of total in socio-economic groups 1 to 12; Scotland, England and Wales, 1921-71*

Socio-economic group		1921	1931	1951	1961	1971
1 and 2. employers	Scot	6.1	5.6	6.2	6.8	8.0
and managers	E+W	7.2	6.3	7.3	8.2	9.7
3. Professional	Scot	0.6	0.4	0.4	0.7	0.7
self-employed	E+W	0.5	0.6	0.4	0.6	0.6
4. Professional	Scot	1.3	1.1	1.6	1.8	2.8
employees	E+W	1.0	0.8	1.6	2.4	3.2
5. Intermediate	Scot	3.1	3.1	4.4	6.1	8.2
non-manual	E+W	3.2	2.9	4.0	6.2	8.1
6. Junior	Scot	14.7	15.9	19.5	21.9	21.6
non-manual	E+W	12.9	15.3	19.6	21.8	22.6
7. Personal	Scot	7.7	8.9	5.7	4.7	5.7
service	E+W	8.8	9.7	5.8	5.0	5.5
8. Foremen and	Scot	1.4	1.5	1.9	2.5	2.6
supervisors	E+W	1.4	1.3	1.8	2.5	2.6
9. Skilled	Scot	35.3	31.3	29.0	28.2	24.3
manual	E+W	33.6	30.1	28.3	25.5	22.4
10. Semi-skilled	Scot	15.4	14.1	14.9	15.8	13.9
manual	E+W	16.7	14.4	14.8	16.1	13.5
11. Unskilled	Scot	10.3	13.9	13.8	9.6	10.3
manual	E+W	9.1	13.2	12.1	8.4	7.8
12. Own account	Scot	3.9	4.2	2.5	1.9	2.0
workers	E+W	5.6	5.4	4.4	3.4	3.9
p.p.d. between structures		5.1	3.2	3.0	4.1	5.2

SOURCE   Payne, 1977

could then explore the diverse social processes which, comprehensible in themselves, combine to produce resultants which at this level of aggregation are too complex to pin down.

A crude measure of the pace of occupational change is the positive percentage difference between the socio-economic group distributions of the successive censuses, as follows:

1921-31	6.2
1931-51	7.3
1951-61	6.6
1961-71	6.1

With the exception of the two decades between 1931 and 1951, the pace of decadal change can be seen to be relatively even. There was no consistency, however, in the nature of these changes. From 1921 to 1931 the main component was the decline in the skilled manual group and the increase in the unskilled manual group. From 1931 to 1951 the main factors were the increase in non-manual groups, especially the junior non-manual, and the decline in personal service and skilled manual groups. In the 1950s the decline in unskilled work was the single most dominant factor, but this was followed by a faster decline in skilled work in the 1960s. Finally, since many of these changes were not uni-directional, some assessment should be made of the change over the whole period. The positive percentage difference between the socio-economic group distribution of the non-farm, non-armed forces population in 1921 and that in 1971 is 16.4. To change the 1921 structure into the 1971 structure, in aggregate one in six of the non-farm, non-armed forces population would have had to change socio-economic group, 11 per cent of the total leaving the skilled manual group and 15.5 per cent entering the non-manual groups (socio-economic groups 1–6).

The general impression given by Table 4.9 of the relation of the Scottish socio-economic group structure to that of England and Wales is again one of parallel development. The positive percentage difference between the two non-farm structures showed some convergence from 5.1 in 1921 to 3.0 in 1951 followed by some divergence back to 5.2 by 1971. England and Wales have tended to move ahead in terms of the proportion of non-manual workers; Scotland has maintained its relative preponderance of skilled manual workers. By 1971, however, the biggest discrepancy was Scotland's larger proportion of unskilled manual workers. Aggregate socio-economic group differences between two areas can arise typically in two ways. Thus, for instance, a larger proportion of unskilled manual workers might arise from a preponderance of the kind of industries which employ large proportions of such workers, *or* from a greater tendency in one of the two areas to employ such workers in a given industry. Trevor Jones (1977, p. 405) performed calculations on the 1971 industry by socio-economic group matrices, and showed that Scotland's higher proportion of unskilled manual workers was not the result of characteristics of its industrial structure, but reflected a higher proportion of unskilled manual workers *within* industries. The same was true, however, of Scotland's higher proportion in the skilled manual category.

What light, then, do these data throw on the assumptions about 'de-skilling' and proletarianization in Scotland relative to England which we have discussed? First, there appears to be some analytic confusion involved. Given the reference to semi-skilled workers, what the earlier citation from Dickson *et al.* is presumably referring to is de-skilling *within* the manual labour force, principally in the form of a swing away from skilled manual work towards semi-skilled manual work. What Payne meant by Scotland's population being less skilled *vis-à-vis* England and Wales, however, was a change in the relative balance between non-manual (more skilled) and manual (less skilled but *including skilled manual*) employment in Scotland as compared with England and Wales. In other words Dickson *et al.* see a relative diminution of skilled manual workers as a proportion of the *manual* workforce as evidence of de-skilling whereas Payne is actually referring to the fact that Scotland has relatively more skilled and unskilled manual workers as a proportion of the *total* workforce. Such inconsistency suggests that Payne's conclusion is not being used analytically but as convenient confirmation of conventional wisdom (cf note 5).

Additional light is shed on the significance of these differences between the socio-economic group structures of Scotland and England and Wales in Table 4.10 which gives the socio-economic group structures (for males only) of the other nine British regions, together with the positive percentage differences between their structures and that of Great Britain as a whole. As one would have expected from the closeness of its industrial structure to the British mean, Scotland's socio-economic group structure is also relatively similar to that of Great Britain – only that of the North-West of England is closer to the British mean. Scotland's own closest neighbour in terms of socio-economic group structure is the North of England, with the other 'non-Southern' industrial regions fairly equidistant from Scotland. Scotland's proportion in most socio-economic groups occupies a fairly median position with respect to the other regions.

However, Scotland does have the highest proportion of unskilled workers as well as the lowest proportion of the two socio-economic groups which have a 'petty bourgeois' tinge – socio-economic group 2, employers and managers in small

TABLE 4.10 *British regions: socio-economic groups as percentage of all economically active men, 1971*

Socio-economic group	Great Britain	England and Wales	Scotland	South-east	East Anglia	South-west	West Midlands	East Midlands	North-west	Yorkshire and Humberside	North	Wales
1.	3.8	3.9	3.6	4.5	3.1	3.3	4.0	3.5	3.7	3.5	3.3	2.7
2.	7.9	8.1	6.2	10.0	7.7	8.4	6.7	6.7	7.4	6.8	5.6	6.6
3.	0.9	0.9	0.9	1.1	0.9	1.0	0.7	0.7	0.8	0.7	0.7	0.9
4.	4.2	4.3	3.7	5.6	3.5	3.8	3.8	3.6	3.8	3.0	3.2	3.1
5.	5.7	5.8	5.0	6.9	5.0	5.8	4.9	5.0	5.3	4.6	5.0	5.2
6.	12.2	12.3	11.1	14.9	10.1	11.5	10.2	10.6	11.9	10.5	10.5	9.6
7.	1.0	1.0	1.1	1.4	1.0	1.1	0.6	0.6	0.9	0.8	0.8	0.8
8.	3.6	3.6	3.5	3.2	2.9	3.0	4.0	4.1	3.9	4.3	4.1	4.1
9.	30.6	30.3	33.1	25.4	27.1	26.7	35.4	36.4	31.7	35.1	36.1	32.5
10.	13.0	13.0	13.1	11.4	11.7	11.8	15.6	13.1	14.8	14.3	13.1	14.2
11.	7.8	7.6	10.2	6.4	6.8	6.6	7.1	6.7	9.6	8.7	10.1	9.8
12.	4.6	4.8	2.5	5.6	5.3	6.1	3.8	4.1	4.5	4.0	2.6	4.4
13.	0.8	0.8	1.1	0.4	2.1	1.8	0.7	0.9	0.4	0.7	1.0	1.1
14.	0.8	0.8	1.0	0.3	1.7	2.1	0.8	0.9	0.5	0.7	1.2	2.8
15.	1.6	1.4	2.7	1.0	6.3	2.7	1.2	1.9	0.5	1.4	1.6	1.4
16.	1.5	1.6	1.3	1.9	5.0	4.1	0.7	1.2	0.3	1.0	1.2	1.0
p.p.d. from Great Britain			6.6	10.2	11.1	8.3	7.9	6.9	5.1	7.3	9.0	8.3

SOURCE 1971 Census; Great Britain Regional Economic Activity, Pt IV, Table 31 establishments, and group 12, own account workers. Jones' calculations show, however, that Scotland does not lack those industries which in Britain as a whole contain a large number of small or one-man businesses. In Scotland socio-economic groups 2 and 12 are under-represented within these industries.

In terms of white-collar employment, the divide is not between Scotland and the rest but between the South-East of England and the rest, with East Anglia and the South-West also having relatively high proportions of white-collar employment. This will be partly a reflection of the fact that the service sector makes up a high proportion of employment in these regions. For all the white-collar groups, Scotland occupies a fairly median position. In terms of skilled and semi-skilled workers, the division is again between the three 'southern' regions – this time with low proportions – and the rest. In terms of the proportion of unskilled workers, the three southern regions are joined by the two Midlands regions with low proportions. This is the only socio-economic group in terms of which Scotland occupies an extreme position – its proportion being marginally the highest of the group formed by Scotland, Wales and the three northern regions.

The overall message of this section on occupational structure is analogous to the conclusion of the section on industrial structure. Just as it was then concluded that in terms of the impact on the overall process of social change in Scotland, the expansion of the service sector was by far the single most important transformation, so in terms of occupational change, the expansion of white-collar employment has been by far the single most important transformation since the Second World War.

CONCLUSION

We suggested at the beginning of this chapter that an intellectual atmosphere pervaded by the notions of core–periphery, dependence and the like had led to an over-emphasis on the differences between the pattern of social development in Scotland and that in the rest of Britain. In a form of circular reasoning, the existence of such differences is seen either as evidence for the operation of mechanisms akin to dependence or as demanding that such mechanisms be invoked to explain them. The message of the present chapter is that in terms of industrial and occupational structure, differences sufficient to justify the invocation of such mechanisms do not exist. Or, in other words, the differences which do exist are sufficiently small to make the circular process of argument not only wrong but superfluous.

In terms of the pattern of industrial employment, the most striking aspect of the Scottish distribution has been its similarity to that of Britain as a whole. Contrary to conventional wisdom, Scotland as a whole ranks among the least specialized regions of Britain, and in many respects its industrial structure is the most diversified of them all. Rather, it has been *within* Scotland that the most dramatic regional specialization has taken place.

Similarly an examination of sectoral employment change only confirms how close the Scottish structure has been to that of Britain over the whole of our period. Scotland like Britain as a whole has experienced a massive shift into service employment, first in terms of a slow move from agriculture, forestry and fisheries, with manufacture retaining its share for the best part of a hundred years; then in terms of a rapidly accelerating shift mainly (though by no means exclusively) at the expense of manufacturing. The implications of this shift go far beyond the scope of this paper and are a major focus of our current research project on social change in Scotland between 1971 and 1981.

As we concluded at the end of the previous section, no dramatically different conclusion can be drawn from the occupational data. The Scottish structure looks remarkably like that of Britain as a whole, and since the Second World War the expansion of white-collar employment has been the most salient trend. The rise of non-manual employment has been accompanied by a long-term decline in skilled employment, though in 1971 Scotland still had a somewhat higher proportion of skilled manual workers than England and Wales, as well as a higher proportion of unskilled manual workers. In both cases this appears to be the result of the way in which labour is used within industries rather than a function of differing industrial structure.

In this chapter then, we have been critical of attempts to

explain industrial and occupational change in Scotland by exaggerating certain distributional differences, and by linking these to some version of 'dependency' theory. The tendency has been to focus on those aspects of the Scottish social and economic structure which are different, in order to explain Scottish phenomena (such as the rise of the Scottish National Party). Thus factors which are specific to Scotland (and these often include cultural specificities) or which express Scotland's differential position in a wider structure tend to be given greater prominence than they analytically deserve. It is important to stress in contrast that there are processes operating which are nothing to do with Scotland's particular experience, but more to do with the fact that Scotland is a part of Britain. In a wider sense processes are at work within Scotland which are to some extent common to all industrial societies – the shift in the balance of the working population from the primary to the secondary to the tertiary, from the extractive to the manufacturing to the service sector.

The point is not to try to account for Scotland's industrial and occupational structure either in terms of Scotland's position in the world economy, or in terms of an 'occupational transition' common to all industrial societies, but to recognize that they both emphasize different aspects of the structuring process at a global level, and that the interaction between them is likely to be complex.

NOTES

1. This paper is a revised version of the paper presented to the British Sociological Association Conference at Cardiff, 5–8 April 1983. We gratefully acknowledge the assistance of the SSRC, whose grant, No HR6948, funded much of the research on which this paper is based. Much of the empirical material appeared in Working Paper 2, *Industrial and Occupational Structure*, of the *Social Structure of Modern Scotland Project* and some was used in Kendrick (1983).
2. More recently Bryden (1979) applied the dependency framework to the Scottish case – or more precisely to the industrial West of Scotland and the Highlands – but was unable to confirm its usefulness.
3. See for example Frank, 1967, p. 53, and Amin, 1974, p. 38. The fact that much of the imagery employed by early neo-Marxist dependence theorists derives from Marx's analysis of the preconditions for the genesis of industrial capitalism only strengthens the case against the application of these theories to the Scottish case. See Kendrick, 1983, pp. 78–80.

4. There are, we should say at once, some dissident voices. See for instance Keating and Bleiman (1979); Webb and Hall (1978). The latter also make the point emphasized later on the similarity of the occupational structures of Scotland and England.
5. The writer mentioned is Geoff Payne. Payne's (1977) analysis of trends in occupational structure is a classic instance of the stress on difference under the influence of core–periphery and internal colonialism models. For other examples of Payne's conclusions being taken up by subsequent authors as the most significant characterization of the Scottish occupational structure see Watson, 1980, p. 154, and Watt, 1982, p. 222.
6. We are grateful to Clive Lee for allowing us to re-analyze his data and for making available data at Scottish county level. Data at English county and Scottish regional level is published in Lee, 1979.
7. The program used was MINISSA, originated by E. E. Roskam, as implemented in the MDS(X) Series by the Program Library Unit at Edinburgh University. For further details see Coxon, 1982.
8. The allocation of the Industrial Orders of the 1968 Standard Industrial Classification to the sectors used in Tables 4.7 and 4.8 follows fairly commonsense lines:
   AFF: Agriculture, Forestry and Fisheries – IO 1
   M + Q: Mining and quarrying – IO 2
   Manuf: Manufacturing – IOs 3–19
   Const: Construction – IO 20
   Inter: Intermediate – IOs 21 (Utilities), 22
       (Transport and Communication), 23 (Distribution)
   Serv: Services – IOs 24–7
9. The data discussed hereafter and reworked in Table 4.9 are presented in Payne (1977).
10. In this paper we are concerned primarily with the implications of patterns of industrial and occupational structure for the appropriateness of imputing mechanisms akin to dependence to the Scottish case. Although his primary concern was with Wales, Phil Cooke (1982) did assess the extent to which Scotland satisfied a range of criteria of dependence derived from more recent versions of dependence theory. Only on isolated indicators (such as the openness of the economy) did Scotland appear 'dependent'. The results fell far short of justifying the application of any 'strongly structural' dependency theory to Scotland.

REFERENCES

Amin, S. (1974) *Accumulation on a World Scale* (Sussex: Harvester Press).
Bryden, J. (1979) 'Core-Periphery Problems – the Scottish case', in Seers, D. *et al.* (eds.), *Underdeveloped Europe: Studies in Core-periphery Relations* (Sussex: Harvester Press).
Buchanan, K. (1968) 'The Revolt against Satellisation in Scotland and Wales', *Monthly Review*, 19.
Campbell, R. H. (1980) *The Rise and Fall of Scottish Industry* (Edinburgh: John Donald).

Claval, P. (1980) 'Centre/Periphery and Space: Models of Political Geography', in Gottman (ed.).

Cohn, S. (1982) 'Hechter's Theory of Regional Underdevelopment: A Test using Victorian Railways', *American Sociological Review*, 47(4).

Cooke, P. (1982) 'Dependency, supply factors and uneven development in Wales and other problem regions', *Regional Studies*, vol. 16, no 3.

Coxon, A. P. M. (1982) *The User's Guide to Multi-dimensional Scaling* (London: Heinemann).

Dickson, T., *et al.* (1980) *Scottish Capitalism* (London: Lawrence & Wishart).

Frank, A. G. (1967) *Capitalism and Underdevelopment in Latin America*, (New York: Monthly Review Press).

Gottman, J. (ed.) (1980) *Centre and Periphery: Spatial Variations in Politics* (London: Sage Publications).

Hechter, M. (1975) *Internal Colonialism: the Celtic Fringe in British National Development, 1536–1966* (London: Routledge & Kegan Paul).

Hechter, M. (1982) ' "Internal Colonialism" Revisited', *Cencrastus*, (Autumn).

Jones, T. (1977) 'Occupational Transition in Advanced Industrial Societies – a Reply', *Sociological Review*, 25(2) Table 5.

Keating, M. and Bleiman, D. (1979) *Labour and Scottish Nationalism* (London: Macmillan).

Kendrick, S. W. (1983) *Social Change and Nationalism in Modern Scotland*, (Ph.D. thesis, University of Edinburgh).

Kirby, M. W. (1981) *The Decline of British Economic Power since 1870* (London: Allen & Unwin).

Lee, C. H. (1979) *British Regional Employment Statistics, 1841–1971* (Cambridge: Cambridge University Press).

Lenman, B. (1977) *An Economic History of Modern Scotland* (London: Batsford).

Nairn, T. (1981) *The Break-Up of Britain: Crisis and Neo-Nationalism* (London: Verso).

Payne, G. (1977) 'Understanding Occupational Transition', in *Sociological Review*, 25 (2).

Watson, T. J. (1980) *Sociology, Work and Industry*, (London: Routledge & Kegan Paul).

Watt, I. (1982) 'Occupational Stratification and the Sexual Division of Labour', in Dickson, T. (ed.), *Capital and Class in Scotland* (Edinburgh: John Donald).

Webb, K. and Hall, E. (1978) 'Explanations of the Rise of Political Nationalism in Scotland', in *Studies in Public Policy No. 15* (University of Strathclyde: Centre for the Study of Public Policy).

Part II
The Restructuring of Capital and Social Transformation

Part II

5 Manchester's Inner City: The Management of the Periphery

ROSEMARY MELLOR

The history of urbanization in the capitalist industrial societies is marked by the decentralization of economic activity and the deconcentration of population. Therefore the idea of the city as a distinctive unit of economic and social analysis was early replaced by that of the city region in recognition of the centrifugal pattern of development. Yet the residual position of the central city within the city region, and the peripheralization of the inner-city neighbourhoods, did not attract attention until the black ghetto (US) and the inner city (UK) came to the fore as issues requiring policy resolution.[1] In both cases the trigger to state policy initiative was racial conflict, and the structural weakness of the central city as a periphery within the modern economy was underestimated.

The core–periphery model uses a spatial analogy to indicate a political relationship, between states (as used by Wallerstein), or within states to denote the political activation of ethnicity with uneven development (see Hechter, 1975). In this context 'peripheralization' refers to a political relationship. It has also been used to describe the polarization of labour markets between a 'core' and a 'peripheral' labour force (Friedman 1977, Byrne, 1982). The terms 'marginality' and 'marginalization' derive from studies of urbanization in developing societies, and have increasingly been used in discussions of the inner city (see Friend and Metcalfe, 1981, Harrison, 1983). There is a tendency to use 'peripherality' and 'marginality' interchangeably (see Cross, 1982), though they come from opposed conceptual models in development studies. Marginality relates the situation of the urban poor to culture, that is, to be marginal is not to have the capacity to change the terms of this poverty (Roberts, 1978a, pp. 160–74), whereas peripherality relates their situation to the structural locking of dependent economies and cultures into those of the core, so denying participation on equal terms. As concepts, peripherality and marginality sit uneasily in the class vocabulary of British sociology and politics, but they do point up the frailty of that class vocabulary in face of polarization in labour markets, differentiation of subcultures within British society, and the regionalization of party political support. In this chapter, peripherality is used to refer to structural categories, marginality to conditions of individuals. Therefore, inner-city Manchester, the place as mediated by image and reputation, may be judged socially peripheral; the people, estimated in everyday convention by housing, style of life, or family composition, may be socially marginal.

It can be argued that cities like Manchester have entered a new phase in urban development in that urban land is becoming derelict. Manchester has its particular interest in that it retains some of its historical significance as a core city, while experiencing extreme industrial decline. Consequently, élite activities in the city centre have been revived and enhanced, so that prestigious building and conservation schemes are juxtaposed with the blight and remedial landscaping of the peripheralized areas outside the redefined city centre. There results a townscape, and a social profile, for the central city which is more often associated with the 'political' cities of underdeveloped societies than those of industrialized societies.

In the following sections are set out some of the dimensions of Manchester's core/peripheral status, in the context of (i) its urbanization history; and (ii) its industrial decline, and restructuring of non-industrial activities, to assess (iii) the extent of marginality in the inner city districts, and (iv) the demands on the local state establishment in its management of the new periphery. At this stage the intention is to document a situation: further implications of the situation for sociological orthodoxy need to be thought through.

URBANIZATION HISTORY

Convention has it that 'Manchester is primarily an industrial city' (Nicholas, 1945, p. 97). However, the city's exceptional wealth came first from its position as a centre for the international trade in finished cotton goods, and then as the business centre for the industrial North. Manchester and its partner city, Liverpool, were the first world cities, with perhaps the most total command over a commodity market there has ever been (see Sharpless, 1978; Roberts, 1978b). The city as a 'vast cotton metropolis' therefore had a reputation as a bastion of middle-class culture and politics, and an occupational profile in which factory employment was under-represented in comparison with the surrounding region.

By 1901 Manchester seems to have developed some of the features of a metropolitan labour market as outlined by Jones for London: large plants being state-financed or public utilities; otherwise seasonal irregular work, small plant size, low rates of investment, intensive use of labour, low unionization, and fragmentation in a labour force divided between artisans and casual labourers, with – as a sub-stratum – an 'urban residuum' in the central area slums (Jones, 1972). There was certainly evidence of under-employment in inner Manchester and Salford in 1894, when there were demonstrations against the Manchester Ship Canal Company importing dock labour (Grant, 1978, p. 143). The difference, of course, was that Manchester retained a tradition of factory work that London had never had, but there is every indication that inner Manchester's poverty and poor living conditions were of a different kind to those of the more stably employed, soundly housed and better drained factory townships.

The political impact of the nineteenth century development is less clear than the legacy of the slums. The city's political life was characterized by an absence of the paternalism evident in many of the smaller towns, and by a distancing between the mass of the population and the few that were politically active. It is conspicuous that early initiatives by the local authority in housing, planning and educational policies came from these middle classes and were carried out with support across party lines. The subsequent determination shown by the local authority in the rebuilding of the inner city neighbourhoods without heed to local community structure, may be one legacy of the original core status of the city in the world economy. There was a secure progressive political establishment acting on the living conditions of a population many of whom lacked the political affiliation given by the security and organization of industrial employment.

THE INNER CITY ECONOMY

The collapse of the inner city economy has three components: (i) deindustrialization of the region; (ii) disinvestment in the inner core to the region; (iii) rationalization in the central area.[2]

(i) Deindustrialization of the Region

Despite the investment of the inter-war years which allowed Greater Manchester to retain its image as a growth pole in the British economy it has been in absolute decline (in terms of employment) for the past thirty years (Law, 1980, pp. 37–40).

After 1966 the loss of jobs in manufacturing industry accelerated so that there was a net loss of 136 000 jobs, (25 per cent) between 1966 and 1975. All sectors of production were affected. Lloyd attributed this decline to the vulnerability of the textiles–clothing–engineering complex, the restructuring by major firms so as to displace jobs, and 'the growing inability of a locally significant community of small business enterprises to maintain themselves against an increasingly hostile external environment' (Lloyd, 1980, p. 65). Although 48 per cent of manufacturing jobs were still controlled by local interests in 1975 (as compared with only 14.2 per cent of those of Merseyside) there was 'an across the board' let-down 'of manufacturing industry' (ibid, p. 71). By 1980 investment in manufacturing industry amounted to £77 per head of the Greater Manchester industrial workforce, £152 for that of Wales, and £186 for that of the northern region.

Neither the range of industries present in the region, nor their ownership, can explain the severity of this disinvestment. The collapse of the local textile industry (with employment in 1980 only 10 per cent of that in 1951) is only the extreme aspect of the sequence of falling profitability and plant closure. Regional policy might have been another source of weakness, for regional aid policies directed investment away from the region. Between 1945 and 1967, for example, it is estimated that the Manchester region attracted only 9000 of the 108 000 manufacturing jobs created by enterprises entering the region; conversely of the 26 000 jobs lost to the region by relocation, 17 000 were supplied by Manchester (Rodgers, 1980). The apparent buoyancy of service activities, particulary conspicuous in the public sector, masked the weaknesses of the industrial economy so that Manchester did not assume the state-assessed profile of a region in distress. In the absence of a strongly-determining history of narrow specialization in production and regional dependency there can only be agreement with the statement that Manchester is 'perhaps the weakest large industrial city in a weak industrial nation' (Rodgers, 1980, p. 35) though this ignores Glasgow.

(ii) Inner City Disinvestment

The inner industrial core to the region (the inner districts of Manchester and Salford) was encountering massive absolute decline throughout the period. The information as to components of this decline is particularly full for the period 1966–75 (Dickens and Lloyd, 1977; Lloyd and Mason, 1978; Mason, 1980; Lloyd, 1980). It can be summarized as follows:

1. industrial employment declined by 43.4 per cent (some 30 per cent of the job-loss for Greater Manchester). This decline was experienced by all sectors of production;
2. the greater part (89 per cent) of this loss is accounted for by closure of plant;[5]
3. closures were spread across all size of plant. Small firms (employing less than 50) were twice as likely to close, and accounted for half the job loss, but closure of eleven large plants accounted for 20 per cent of job losses;
4. fewer jobs were locally controlled at the end of the period (62 per cent against 27 per cent) but key sectors were still Manchester-controlled (clothing, and mechanical engineering for example);
5. all ownership categories experienced loss, more or less

equally. There was no distinction between local and external ownership, single or multiplant firms;
6. closure and job-loss could be related to change of ownership. Acquired firms were twice as likely to close down;
7. The clearance programme which caused 13 per cent of plant closures involving 2600 jobs (40 per cent of which were reinstated elsewhere) was a small element. (Lloyd and Mason, 1978). The effects on local labour markets, however, can only be surmized.

It can be concluded that the weakness of the inner core was a double one: it failed to retain the larger establishments, and/or attract similar plant, and the small-plant–small-firm sector which had characterized the core districts since the nineteenth century was collapsing.

For the area administered by Manchester City Council (hereafter referred to as Manchester, as distinct from the Manchester region) estimates based on a survey of 1981 (Manchester City Council, 1981) indicated that there had been a further decline of 20.3 per cent in manufacturing jobs between 1976 and 1981. In numerical terms, there had been a movement from 108 000 jobs in 1971 to 69 000 in 1981; in monetary terms, a mere 8.6 per cent of the city's rates (2.8 per cent of its income) now comes from local industry. By 1976 72 per cent of Manchester's employed population were in the service sector, more than a quarter of these in the 'professional and scientific' category (12 per cent of total employment). Health, education and public administration had been the growth areas in the previous ten years. However, after 1979 there were redundancies reported in all categories of the service sector, increasing particularly in the categories of public administration and insurance, business and banking where the effects of new technology, work-efficiency schemes, and the cuts in local authority revenues had cumulative impact.

(iii) Rationalization in the Central Area

Much of this description of the Manchester region could have been made of London. Both cities have experienced a displacement of new investment far beyond the recognized regional boundaries. In fact the Manchester region shed industrial employment at a slightly lower rate than London (GLC, 1966–74, −27 per cent; GMC, 1966–75, −25 per cent, see Mason, 1980, p. 173). It is the strength or weakness of the area central to the city region that distinguishes the two. Manchester still has a significant financial quarter, a concentration of office-floor space second to London, a network of newspaper, radio and television offices, the largest higher educational complex in the UK, a large, diverse, and specialized shopping centre, and a full range of entertainment outlets. For all this, shops and offices new and old, stand empty or under-occupied, and it is only a matter of time before other urban landmarks fall into disuse. Central Manchester does not have the power of central London to command investment nor does it have the crowd appeal of a world city, and despite substantial investment its share of regional economic activity has contracted.

In 1976 there were 25 per cent fewer journeys to work in the city centre than in 1966 (Manchester City Council, 1980, Table 19). Industry, warehousing, retail activities, financial services, and general administration had all diminished employment needs in the city centre, though for different reasons. Office employment was affected by rationalization within the firm, movement out of the city centre, and diversion of new investment to the suburban ring; warehouse employment by the shrinkage in the textile and clothing industry as well as by changing patterns of food distribution. The shopping centre was affected by an absolute decline of one-third in the immediate catchment population over twenty years as well as by high rents and rates, changing patterns of shopping, and the proximity of alternative shopping centres in the outer ring to the region. For none of these activities was a central location sufficient to compensate for the high acquisition and maintenance costs of city centre property and poor accessibility. The central area was therefore highly vulnerable to relocation ensuing from the reappraisal of property assets triggered by high rates of inflation.

However, there is apparent just a touch of a 'reconquest of the central city' (Castells, 1978, p. 104). Private capital has rehabilitated some of the monumental buildings of the grand decades in Manchester's history, state agencies are subsidising élite services (notably theatre), and facilities for the corporate business sector (hotels, exhibition centre, apartments), so as to retain the central city's image and appeal as a dominant centre.

Planning is directed to furthering its appeal as perhaps the major cultural venue outside London, and this subsidy is seen as an antidote to the 'desert for unemployment'.

The effect of these employment changes has been the generation of demand for specialized skills in, for instance, entertainment and the state welfare sectors, as well as for auxiliary manual labour. A service economy such as that of Manchester now, implies one that is polarized on the dimensions of skill and bargaining power. The contraction of manufacturing employment, continuing at a rate three times that of service employment, removes the opportunity to use skills with status in the local community. Areas such as Beswick in East Manchester, with a tradition of lifetime jobs and craft skill, have lost their reason for being. Closure of industrial plant has been succeeded by a rapid programme of land reclamation, and despite considerable out-migration, the unemployment rate for men (September 1983) was 34 per cent. Other areas such as Moss-Side, with a history as transitional areas, find that new entrants to the labour market must accept long-term unemployment or the blind-alley jobs implied by an unemployment rate of 40 per cent. (In 1951 the unemployment rate for men in Manchester had been 2.3 per cent, with an economic activity rate of 89.6 per cent. By 1981 it had risen to 18.5 per cent, and the economic activity rate was 74.3 per cent. By 1983 it was 28.9 per cent.) Selective migration meant that increasingly there was concentrated a no-skill, never to be skilled peripheral labour force in the inner city districts.

The Inner Core of Manchester's Inner City

The fall in population for Manchester (and also Salford) amounted to one third in the two decades 1961–81. In aggregate the fall can be accounted for by the clearance programmes (which in Manchester alone reduced the stock of dwellings by 40 000), falling household size, and vacancy rates which are probably underestimated. Although there are more than the average number of large households in the city, small households predominate. The census enumeration also indicates a polarization by age in that there are more young people (aged 16–24 years) in Manchester, and more middle-aged and elderly than the national average, and a marked under-representation of adults in the child-rearing age groups (Manchester City Council, 1982b). The birth rate, however, is above the national average, and rising. Housing conditions, by the standards of twenty years ago, are good, in that overcrowding is minimal, and only 4.2 per cent of households did not have exclusive use of a bath. The problems of living in Manchester are not those of sanitation and overcrowding.

The aggregate data masks the migration flows, investment decisions and housing allocation policies which have brought about this demographic profile. It also masks the differentiation within Manchester, in particular the distinctive inner city identified readily by its appearance (modern, with half the dwellings in multi-storey blocks), tenure (87 per cent owned by the local authority), and clustering of demand for welfare services (Manchester City Council, 1975). It occupies a zone of approximately three-quarters of a mile radius outside the central area, and has 59 000 residents. The population has fallen by 75 per cent from that in 1951. This is an area with a socially peripheral status within both Manchester and the Manchester region. Its image is that of poverty, fecklessness, youth, and unconventionality. Parts are thought of as ghetto areas. Its population may be distinguished on the following dimensions of marginality within British society, (i) position in the labour market; (ii) ownership of housing and transport; (iii) youth and ethnic background; and (iv) marital status and household composition.

(i)

TABLE 5.1   *Position in the labour market, selected areas of Greater Manchester, 1981*

	GMC	'core'	Central	Moss-Side	Didsbury*
% men unemployed	14.0	31.4	33.3	36.4	8.2
% households headed by unskilled	6.6	19.1	21.7	16.0	3.2
% 16–59/64 yrs temporarily or permanently sick	3.6	7.2	7.9	5.2	2.2

* The 'core' refers to the six innermost wards of the city among which are Central to the north-east of the centre, and Moss-Side on the south. Didsbury, the most affluent ward is included for comparison.

SOURCE: 1981 census

Health can be taken to be a measure of opportunity over a life-time. In these core wards the standardized mortality ratio (for all causes of death) on the north side of the city centre (1975–9) was 155, for the south 141. (Manchester City Council, 1982a).

(ii)

TABLE 5.2   *Ownership of housing and transport, selected areas of Greater Manchester, 1981*

	GMC	'core'	Central	Moss-Side	Didsbury
% local authority tenants	33.0	86.0	90.2	32.8	4.6
% households with car	52.8	14.6	16.0	27.8	65.5

In fact the common denominator of the 'core' population is its lack of property. In other respects – age, household type, ethnicity, education – the population is markedly heterogeneous. A typology worth remembering is that derived by Seeley for an American slum (Seeley, 1959) in which the 'opportunists' are distinguished from the 'necessitarians', and those whose stay is intended to be 'permanent', from those whose affiliation is 'temporary'. In Manchester's inner-core wards there is a large body of students and other young people quite distinct from either the long-stay poor or young families accepting tenancies on a 'temporary' basis. This heterogeneity means that there is no one dimension of marginality distinguishing the population of peripheral neighbourhoods. Youth and ethnicity are both marked characteristics, but by no means preponderant.

(iii)

TABLE 5.3   *Youth and Ethnic Background, selected areas of Greater Manchester, 1981*

	GMC	'core'	Central	Moss-Side	Didsbury
% residents aged 16–24 years	14.5	22.1	17.4	17.4	13.6
% NCWP households*	5.8	16.0	2.7	28.7	4.2

* households where the head was born in the New Commonwealth or West Pakistan.

Perhaps more unexpected is the frequency of non-marital status. Even excluding the student age-groups, the adult population is less likely to be married, and children more likely to be brought up by one parent than the national average.

(iv)

TABLE 5.4 *Marital status and Household Composition, selected areas of Greater Manchester, 1981*

	GMC	'core'	Central	Moss-Side	Didsbury
% married 30–44 yrs					
Men	80.6	57.5	56.8	66.1	74.2
Women	84.9	64.5	66.4	66.0	78.1
% households with dependent children with at least one-parent family	16.4	39.5	40.1	40.5	12.5
lone adults' households with children as % of all those with dependent children	7.2	16.1	17.9	18.7	5.1
illegitimate births as % of all births* (1976–80)		41.0	35.4	52.1	7.2

SOURCE   Manchester Area Health Authority

In the 'core' just half the population lived in a household headed by a married man; one third in woman-headed households. There may be some scepticism as to the validity of using household-organisation and marriage practices as dimensions of marginality. However, given the strength of the family-and-marriage ideology in British society this measure indicates a non-conventionality in everyday life. It also indicates poverty and social exclusion. The concentration of such households in the lowest-status local authority estates goes far to explain the poverty ratings for the inner city. It also confirms its reputation as an area which is peripheral to the social mainstream.

In some respects this social profile confirms the old stereotypes of an urban population living 'outside civil society', of a community culture seemingly immune to the normalization of social disciplinary agencies. Many of the reforms of the nineteenth century had as their intent the regularization of the lives of the labouring population. The marginality of the urban residuum in particular posed the need to instil conventional standards of decency in private life. (The night-time raids of ticketed houses in Glasgow was one of the more extreme forms of this regularization visited on the urban masses by a zealous urban bourgeoisie (Damer, 1976). For inner Manchester now it is tempting to draw the analogy with that urban culture that so offended Victorian morality. Then of course, it was the absence of deference to middle-class *mores* – church-going, regulated marriage, protection of children from exposure to sexuality, street life, or untimely death – that shocked the domestic missionary. There is something of the same evidence of social marginality in this census data. An urban culture, seizing on the scale of the city as giving distance from official morality, is a taken-for-granted element in the way of life of the inner city.

PLANNING FOR DECLINE

The collapse of the inner-city economy, the fading attraction of the city centre and the polarization in the city region's social structure, the components of the inner-city 'crisis', are a threat to the standing of the local authority as a political entity, and to the central state. Historically, the legitimacy of the central state in the provinces has rested on the collaboration of local élites in the governmental process. Incorporation of the towns brought in first the urban bourgeoisie, typically those with *rentier* interests, and subsequently the labour aristocracy of trades councils and labour parties. On the municipal socialism of the latter rested much of the respect for the modern welfare state. The superimposition of a metropolitan tier of administration, together with city decay and declining revenues, has meant the emasculation of the big city authorities, the strongholds of the 'labourism' that had ensured working-class support. With awareness that the investment policies enforced by this town-hall machine have intensified the crisis by enlarging the contradictions between investment goals and living outcome, then there can only be a redefinition of that local political establishment's claim to authority.

The argument of the 1970s was that any capitalist state has

two conflicting needs: 'efficiency and legitimacy' (Kraushaar, 1981, p. 109). Now that the legitimacy of welfare spending is questioned, and at local level checked by central government (there was a fall of 24.6 per cent in the Rate Support Grant for Manchester between 1980–81 and 1982–3), the retention of legitimacy has come to depend on skill in maintaining and maximizing the efficiency, that is, profitability, of private capital. There is nothing concealed in this function, for the city's survival as an economic entity has come to depend on the assiduity of local state agencies in blotting out the effects of economic decline and modernizing the city's infrastructure to enhance its appeal to investors. The emphasis of Offe 'the existence of a capitalist state presupposes that systematic denial of its nature as a capitalist state' would seem to be a false one in a situation of decline. It is instead the contradiction between welfare and efficiency that will be central to the politics of decline.

'Deroutinization' is the first symptom of a new claim to loyalty. The urban political establishment will take unanticipated initiatives to justify a claim to competence so that the unthinkable is overnight the only rational policy. There is evident, as there is for the central state, a redefinition of the claim to legitimacy, a sense that the power of the state no longer resides in 'uneventful routine rather than in conscious and active purpose of will' (Westergaard and Resler, 1975, p. 144). The political establishment will therefore move from the mediatory to the initiatory position. The recent housing and planning record for Manchester offers several examples of state professional initiative: notably the plan for revitalizing the central area, and the introduction of a more open system of housing allocation.

The role of the state professional[3] in urban change has been of concern to urban sociologists (Pahl, 1977; Cockburn, 1977; Lambert *et al.*, 1978; and Elliott and McCrone, 1982). From an initial concern with the state professional as manager mediating between the conflicting demands of state and capital, central state and local population, and in their control of the everyday routine of administration exercising a considerable autonomy in the 'who–where' decisions, the emphasis shifted to planning (and by inference other state functions) as 'ideological discourse and negotiating instrument' (Castells, 1978,

p. 82). Managerial style might have 'potential ideological force' (Lambert *et al.*, 1978, p. 169), but this interpretation generally reflected officials' own representation of their limited discretion. Subsequently, there has come a stronger reading of their power 'to create the broader constraints and actively formulate central and local state policy' (Dickens and Gray, 1982, p. 15). So, in the 'rehabilitate Manchester programme', state professionals have been instrumental in devising new approaches and moderating the constraints set by the local political community. The political–professional institution has taken on a development agency function novel to local government.

Further, there is evident a redefinition of the relationship between the state and local community in the initiative of the planning profession in setting a policy of open information on all aspects of development process. In this way public opinion can be mobilized in support of Manchester as a place, and that support can be called on in negotiations with central government. Ahead of more general demands for open government, accountability, or decentralization, the profession worked for a redefinition of managerial style in development policies so altering the public image and standing of the local authority. It is the development decisions that catch the media eye: if these are seen to be open to public debate, then the authenticity of the state is enhanced. As the welfare function of the state retracts, so this appeal to the public, by-passing the political representatives, will have an efficiency legitimation.

MANAGEMENT OF THE 'PERIPHERAL'

Modern capitalist society has seen the 'penetration of the state into everyday life'. A life cycle is subject to intervention and surveillance by professional groups acting on the basis of legal powers conferred by the state, and with the authority of state bureaucratic institutions. The medicalization that affects birth, death, and sexuality, the superimposition of 'education' on household culture and the intervention of social-work agencies in family life, all indicate a subordination to 'management'. Marxist writers have tended to emphasize the functional fit of the welfare state with the requirements of the capitalist mode of production, as ensuring 'the reproduction of the social relations of capital'. Recently, Byrne has argued:

> Increasingly a function of the local state is the management of local populations who have been rendered peripheral by capitalist development. These groups can be considered to represent a contemporary form of the stagnant reserve army of labour and are a potentially destabilizing force in late capitalism. Ghettoized through housing policy, managed personally through social work, accultured through education, maintained through supplementary benefits, they are the objects of the local state and the local agencies of the national state (Byrne, 1982, p. 75).

It is indeed tempting to see inner Manchester this way – as one resident called it, an 'open concentration camp'. The local authority's approach to clearance was total – the planned, state-owned and managed environment is all-encompassing. It is a client society. A common feature of the heterogeneous population of the inner core is its reliance on state benefits: such that only a minority will not be reliant on the goodwill of some part of the state bureaucratic machinery. This is not an autonomous population, free to move about, to decide its own future, but one where 'getting on' requires expertise in manipulating the allocative institutions.

However, there is a tendency to overestimate the capacity of state agencies, especially the local authorities, to manage. Social work is often targeted here as an 'apparatus of investigation, control and regulation' (Friend and Metcalfe, 1981, p. 136). In Manchester, at least the ratio of case-workers to the relevant client population is absurdly low: for example, a city average of 2.18 case-workers per 1000 aged 0–19 years. Nor is there marked weighting in staffing for the 'stagnant reserve army' of the inner-city. Similarly, housing: the monopoly ownership of the inner-core districts would seem to place its population in conditions of state management, but the relationship between local authority and tenant is a strictly pecuniary one, no less distant than that of the building society and its mortgagee. For planning it is the same: the participation initiatives may seek to bring the politically marginal into the investment decisions affecting the neighbourhood (as in Moss-Side's 'front line') but such activity is spasmodic and of limited impact.

Inner-city neighbourhoods are segmented, and urban location confers impersonality and freedom to pass from one neighbourhood to another; local state agencies are internally fragmented, each operational empire within them too large to exercise that persistent personal control conjured by the phrase the 'management of the peripheral'. The inherent scarcity of welfare resources means that state agencies cannot penetrate that barrier between the core labour-force and that rendered peripheral, between the socially conventional and the non-conventional, between those amenable to professionally-defined codes of family and household life, and those that bitterly resent their incursion. The more fruitful stabilization strategy would be the co-optation of protest organizations. But in conditions of economic and social marginality, it is by no means axiomatic that deprivation will lead to such organizations. The riots of 1981 gave an edge to the local authority's demand for investment incentives for the city, and more resources from the central state, but the divided inner-city population remained a weak political force. Its social composition and housing history left it without community identity, and there has been effective mobilization only on single issues (housing allocation, and policing) which have been answered, largely, by a 'deroutinization' of the state-professional bureaucracy.

CONCLUSION

Manchester is one of the most accessible places in Britain. In historical terms it had a world metropolitan role and a position as the counter-core to London. As a regional city, with its public administration, media establishment and training institutions, it remains a controlling centre. Its 'peripherality' is common to all such centres, subordinate to the initiative of centralizing state institutions. In that respect, peripherality is a dimension of 'being local'. In Manchester, however, there is a population that is marginal to the life of the city, living in areas judged as peripheral locations on economic and social criteria, near, but far from, the state agencies charged with its management. These conditions of economic and social marginality cannot be bundled into the rubric of class: the population is poor, but so are other neighbourhoods; the majority are manual workers and local-authority tenants, but so is the majority of the population of Manchester. Nor can race serve as the analytical category, for the white population shares the same conditions of peripherality as the black. The situation in the inner-core districts of Manchester is an urbanization phenomenon: urbanization history, over the past thirty years state-history, has concentrated marginal groups in the urban periphery – the inner-city.

NOTES

1. The 'inner-city problematic' can be dated to about 1968. There was then a battery of policy initiatives and new state powers, chiefly the designation of the educational priority areas after the Plowden Report (1967), improved funding of house improvement (Housing Act 1969), the direction of extra resources to the big city authorities (Urban Aid Act 1968), the instigation of research by the Home Office with the Community Development Projects (1969), and the legislation against racial discrimination (Race Relations Act 1968).
2. The 'Manchester region' relates to the area administered by the Greater Manchester Council; the 'inner industrial core' to the Manchester–Salford inner-city partnership area. The 'central area' here refers to the regional business district administered by Manchester City Council.
3. The term 'state professional' is used in preference to the more general 'managers' (Pahl, 1977) or the more restrictive 'bureaucratised intelligentsia' (Elliot and McCrone, 1982). There is a group of state officials that draw a double authority, first from their position in the hierarchy of state command with a legitimacy derived from law and the practice of administration; second, from their position as certified professionals with a knowledge base and technical competence that carries its own authority in the making of legal and administrative codes, as well as with the lay public.

REFERENCES

Byrne, D. (1982) 'Class and the Local State', in *International Journal of Urban and Regional Research*, vol. 6, no. 1.
Castells, M. (1978) *City, Class and Power* (London: Macmillan).
Cockburn, C. (1977) *The Local State* (London: Pluto Press).
Cross, M. (1982) 'The Manufacture of Marginality', in Troyna, B. and Cashmore, E., *Black Youth in Crisis* (London: Allen & Unwin).

Damer, S. (1976) 'Property Relations and Class Relations in Victorian Glasgow', University of Glasgow, Department of Economic and Social Research, Discussion Paper no. 16.

Dennis, R. (1978) 'The Decline of Manufacturing Employment in Greater London', in *Urban Studies*, vol. 15, no. 1, pp. 63–74.

Dickens, P. and Lloyd, P. (1977) 'Inner Manchester: Components of Industrial Change', Manchester School of Geography Working Paper, no. 5.

Dickens, P. and Gray, I. (1982) 'Professionals and the Management of Social Relations', unpublished paper, BSA Study Group.

Elliott, B. and McCrone, D. (1982) *The City, Patterns of Domination and Conflict* (London: Macmillan).

Flynn, R. (1981) 'Managing Consensus: Strategies and Rationale', in Harloe, M. (ed.) *New Perspectives in Urban Change and Conflict* (London: Heinemann) pp. 50–62.

Friedman, A. L. (1977) *Industry and Labour* (London: Macmillan).

Friend, A. and Metcalfe, A. (1981) *Slump City: The Politics of Mass Unemployment* (London: Pluto Press).

Grant, R. (1978) *The Great Canal* (London: Gordon & Cremonesi).

Hamnett, C. (1983) 'The Conditions in England's Inner Cities on the Eve of the 1981 Riots', *Area*, 15, No. 1.

Hechter, M. (1975) *Internal Colonialism* (London: Routledge).

HMSO (1977a) *Policy for the Inner Cities*, Cmnd 6845 (London).

HMSO (1977b), *Inner Area Studies: Summaries of Consultants' Final Reports* (London).

Jones, G. S. (1972) *Outcast London* (Cambridge: Cambridge University Press).

Kraushaar, R. (1981) 'Policy Without Protest', in Harloe, M. (ed.), *New Perspectives in Urban Change and Conflict* (London: Heinemann), pp. 101–21.

Lambert, J., Paris, C. and Blackaby, B. (1978) *Housing Policy and the State* (London: Macmillan).

Law, C. M. (1980) 'Post-war Employment Changes', in White, H. P. (ed.) *The Continuing Conurbation* (Farnborough: Gower Press, for British Association).

Lloyd, P. (1980) 'Manchester: A Study in Industrial Decline and Economic Restructuring', in White, *The Continuing Conurbation*.

Lloyd, P. and Mason, C. (1978) 'Manufacturing Industry in the Inner City', Transactions of the Institute of British Geographers, no. 3 pp. 66–90.

Manchester City Council (1975) *Social Information Study*, Social Services Department.

Manchester City Council (1980) *City Centre Local Plan Consultation Document*, Planning Department.

Manchester City Council (1981) *Employment in the City of Manchester*, Planning Department.

Manchester City Council (1982a) *Manchester's Inner Area*, Planning Department.

Manchester City Council (1982b) *1981 Census Digest*, Planning Department.

Mason, C. M. (1980) 'Industrial Decline in Greater Manchester', in *Urban Studies*, vol. 17, pp. 173–4.

Nicholas, (1945), *City of Manchester Plan 1945*, Manchester.

Pahl, R. (1977) 'Managers, Technical Experts and the State', in Harloe, M. (ed.) *Captive Cities* (London: Heinemann).

Roberts, B. (1978a) *Cities of Peasants* (London: Edward Arnold).

Roberts, B. (1978b) 'Agrarian Organization and Urban Development', in Wirth, J. D. and Jones, R. L. *Manchester and Sao Paulo* (California: Stanford).

Rodgers, H. B. (1980) Manchester Revisited', in White, *The Continuing Conurbation*.

Seeley, J. (1959) 'The Slum: Its Nature, Use and Users', in *Journal of American Institute of Planners*, vol. 25, pp. 7–14.

Sharpless, J. B. (1978) 'Intercity Development and Dependency: Liverpool and Manchester', in Wirth and Jones, *Manchester and Sao Paolo*.

Westergaard, J. and Resler, H. (1975) *Class in a Capitalist Society* (Harmondsworth: Penguin).

6 From West to East and Back Again: Capitalist Expansion and Class Formation in the Nineteenth Century

GLENN MORGAN

INTRODUCTION

One of the clearest trends in recent sociological theorizing has been the dawning recognition that for too long sociologists have unproblematically taken for granted the centrality of national boundaries in their discussions of social structure. The concept of society has drawn in its trail a whole set of assumptions that the nation–state is the basic framework for sociological analysis (cf. Urry, 1981). Such an approach has involved bracketing off both anthropology and history as well as themes from a number of earlier sociologists. Thus the findings of anthropologists on the shifting geographical boundaries and decentralized political forms of tribal and nomadic societies as well as historical analysis of pre-capitalist empires have been dismissed as irrelevant to the dynamics of class in capitalist nation–states. Instead analyses of class structure and the state have tended to occur as though one can abstract one 'society' from a set and analyze it individually without reference to the other members of the set. In doing so, the state and class structure become, as it were, phenomena determined internally to a set of geographical boundaries; they enter into a set of external relations – with other states – as preconstituted by their internal relations. The objective of this paper is to show that such a view is untenable; the state and class structure are constituted just as much in terms of their external as of their internal relations.

Such an approach is undoubtedly gaining in strength within current sociological analysis. In a recent paper for example, John Rex has argued:

> The appropriate unit for any sociologist concerned with serious macro-sociological problems is something like the British Empire over four hundred years (Rex, 1980, p. 4).

On a wider front, the writings of Wallerstein have done much to emphasize the importance of seeing capitalism as a world economic system, though here the attempt to define capitalism in primarily market terms has tended to minimize the attention paid to the relations of production and the labour process as constitutive of class relations (Wallerstein, 1979; Brenner, 1977). In his recent work, Giddens has pushed this emphasis on the interrelationship between societies (whether tribal, imperial or capitalist) even further: 'I want to emphasize the generic shortcomings of treating any type of society as an isolated entity'. (Giddens, 1981, p. 24). He goes on to argue that:

> The approach upon which this book is based recognizes that there are both endogenous and exogenous sources of change in human societies (where what a 'society' *is* assumes widely differing forms) but that neither has a generalised primacy over the other (Giddens, 1981, pp. 166–7).

Like Wallerstein, however, Giddens accepts that the advent of capitalism brought a qualitative change in the nature of these interrelationships between societies: 'Crucially, capitalism for the first time in human history initiates the creation of an inter-social system that is truly global in its scope' (Giddens 1981, p. 168). The development of these theoretical perspectives on world systems provides the potential for a new look at issues of class. In particular, it becomes less than valid to analyze the process of class formation as though it occurs solely within the confines of the nation–state. There is a need to examine again the interpenetration of societies, class structures and states.

In this chapter I wish to apply these theoretical insights to certain processes of class formation in the nineteenth century. In particular, I wish to show how class relationships that developed in certain parts of Britain and America are only understandable through the connections that were developed between these societies and India and China. Thus the class relations that came into being in Lancashire and California were only part of a wider series of changes which were altering the distribution of political and economic power throughout much of the world. As a part of this wider process, these class relations in their totality can only be understood from a world perspective. Thus I will argue that class relations both at the level of the labour process itself and at the level of political and ideological forms were constituted in part by this wider process of world development as well as through relations internal to the society under consideration.

The chapter will therefore consist of the following sections:

1. an analysis of British class structure in the early–mid-nineteenth century concentrating particularly on the cotton industry and its dependence on the Indian market that is, 'Capitalist expansion and class formation in Britain';
2. the changes brought about in India and China by their integration into the British trading system under the heading 'China trade and India';
3. an analysis of Chinese labour in California in the mid-nineteenth century, under the heading 'The Chinese in California'.

While the analysis is dependent on secondary sources and therefore necessarily somewhat limited and tentative, its main purpose will be to show the importance to analysis of class formation of a world perspective.

CAPITALIST EXPANSION AND CLASS FORMATION IN BRITAIN

The idea that class formation must be considered from an international perspective is not new. It was in fact first developed by Lenin in *Imperialism*. In that work, Lenin wrote:

It must be observed that in Great Britain the tendency of imperialism to split the workers, to strengthen opportunism among them and to cause temporary decay in the working class revealed itself much earlier than the end of the 19th century and the beginning of the 20th century . . . The causes are: 1) Exploration of the whole world by this country (Britain); 2) Its monopolist position in the world market; 3) Its colonial monopoly. The effects are: 1) A section of the British proletariat becomes bourgeois; 2) A section of the proletariat allows itself to be led by men bought by or at least paid by the bourgeoisie (Lenin, 1969, p. 247).

Lenin's argument links formation of the labour aristocracy quite clearly with the processes of monopoly and imperialism. Later authors however have tended to be drawn into a much more gradational approach, that is, defining labour aristocrats by, for example, their higher standards of living than the rest of the working class. Hobsbawm (1966) for example, in the most widely quoted paper on the subject attempted to identify the labour aristocracy on the basis of wage differentials. His argument has been effectively challenged by Pelling (1968) who argued that it is impossible to distinguish a small group of labour aristocrats on this basis. Instead, according to Pelling, there exists a larger group of workers who, by virtue of long hours, hard effort and the pooling of wage from all the family managed to maintain a 'respectable' standard even though this could be severely threatened by trade depression and the vicissitudes of illness, injury and old age. A number of other authors have tried to salvage the concept. Gray, for example, in his study of class structure in Edinburgh has sought to demonstrate the existence within the working class of a 'separate upper stratum, marked off from other working-class groups by a particular style of life and to some extent conscious of its distinctive position' (Gray, 1975, p. 19). In his later work, however, Gray (1981) seems to have moved back from such positive statements towards arguing that:

The labour aristocracy thesis has helped historians to get beyond a view of the working class as a homogeneity and encouraged them to investigate the experience and activity of different groups. (Gray 1981, p. 63).

As Moorhouse said in his discussion of the labour aristocracy thesis:

> What is raised here is the relation of any labour aristocracy to much more general sectionalism and division within the workforce, for such sectionalism is much more prevalent and multi-fissured thàn simply the detachment of some small élite at the apex of the class (Moorhouse, 1978, p. 69).

The desire to hold to one particular division between the aristocracy of labour and the rest of labour as particularly crucial in explaining reformism in the British labour movement characterizes a number of other authors (for example, Foster, 1974; Jones 1975; Burgess 1975. See also the debate in Social History between Moorhouse, 1978; Reid, 1978; Musson, 1976; Moorhouse, 1979; McLennan, 1981, and Moorhouse, 1981). Given, as is generally accepted, that the British working class (like most other working classes) has been internally differentiated along skill, status, sex, income, ethnic lines, what is the point of emphasizing the labour aristocracy segment above all others even supposing, which seems doubtful, that one could identify such a segment?

Rather than continuing to pursue this strand of the labour aristocracy debate, I wish to look at the element linking British workers to the expansion of British capitalism in the nineteenth century. Now one of the reasons for neglecting this aspect of Lenin's argument has been the emphasis he placed on the export of capital. Thus Musson attacked Foster's attempt to provide a Leninist basis for the emergence of a labour aristocracy in the mid-nineteenth century by locating there a major switch to capital export:

> There was (Foster) maintains, 'a massive switch to capital export . . .' In fact, however, capital exports had been growing strongly in the previous period . . . They continued, of course, to grow thereafter . . . but there was no 'discontinuity' at mid-century . . . there was no 'decisive shift within the economy from the export of commodities to the export of capital'. Cotton exports alone, in fact, continued to dwarf both machinery exports and annual overseas investment (Musson, 1976, pp. 348–9).

Musson's argument against Foster is however double-edged. Foster may have been wrong to emphasize capital exports but, as Musson himself suggested, cotton exports were extremely important.

Let us examine the role of cotton and its exports in more detail. As has often been noted, cotton was the moving force of British industrialization. Cotton it was that moulded the first British industry society in Lancashire. The proportion of the population directly employed in cotton manufacture in Lancashire was high. For much of the first third of the century it was nearly one-third of the labour force. In the second third of the century, it fell somewhat to around one-fifth and during the last third was around one-sixth to one-seventh. Even as a proportion of the labour force of the UK as a whole, cotton was between 4 and 5 per cent. If one could include the ancillary industries which were directly dependent on cotton, that is, the engineering firms concerned with the manufacture of textile machinery, the figures would be even higher (see Farnie, 1979).

The cotton industry, however, was in no sense an indigenous industry. In terms of its raw material, the industry was from the first dependent on imports of raw cotton. Even in terms of its sales, the cotton industry was inevitably export-oriented. For one thing the climate of Britain meant that cotton cloth was only really wearable during part of the year. The rest of the time the population would be dependent on the heavier cloths of woollen and worsted. For another thing, internal demand during the early stages of the industrialization was not great. As a result then the cotton industry looked to exports to broaden its market. Cotton exports reached their all-time peak proportion of total exports in 1830 when they were 51 per cent. From 1831 to 1850 they were 45.4 per cent and for the latter half of the century when the export of capital for railways was growing and the export trade of other industries such as engineering was also on the increase, cotton provided 32.7 per cent of total exports. Not until 1933 did Britain lose its position as the world's primary exporter when Japan overtook it.

There seems little doubt that the existence of these export markets was crucial to the profitability of industry and its social stability. In the first half of the century British industry as a whole was subject to violent cyclical economic fluctuations which in turn were clearly related to social unrest (see Hobsbawm 1964). The cotton industry gradually began to move out of this situation because of the development of growing export markets which at first acted as a counter-cyclical force and later provided the basis for mid-Victorian economic stability. Thus Farnie wrote:

> Foreign demand expanded markedly after 1815 in reaction to the unbalanced extension of the industry's spinning power beyond the immediate absorptive capacity of the internal market and under the pressure of five successive slumps in the home trade, in 1819–20, 1826–32, 1837–42, 1847–50 and 1855. The export trade proved buoyant beyond all precedent and expanded in volume between 1834 and 1873 three times as fast as the home trade . . . the secular expansion of demand compensated abundantly for short-term fluctuations (Farnie, 1979, pp. 84–8).

Of all the foreign markets which were important to cotton, it was India above all that stood out:

> Exports to India were invariably expanded during a general boom in trade and very often increased in years of widespread economic depression so that Indian demand became an important counter-cyclical influence. Thus the Indian market cushioned the cotton industry against the full effects of the depression of 1837–42 . . . . The same counter-cyclical function was fulfilled during 1854 and helped to rescue the industry from the depression induced by the outbreak of the Crimean war. A shrinkage in Indian demand was primarily responsible for only two major depressions suffered by the industry in 1847–8 and 1891–3 but also proved an ancillary in ten recessions experienced between 1829 and 1897 (Farnie, 1979, p. 105).

The point that is being made here is that whatever the social structure that developed in Britain (and Lancashire in particular) whether it can be best understood in the labour aristocracy model or not, its existence was crucially dependent on foreign markets. To this extent, Engels and Lenin were right; if the British working class was reformist, one of the factors that made the cotton section of its reformist was the relative stability of employment and wages resulting from the existence of extensive foreign markets. Without such markets, the trade cycles of the early nineteenth century might never have been overcome and the political agitation that accompanied them might have continued to who knows what end. In no way is this meant to imply that the roots of the class structure have no indigenous soil. On the other hand, whilst it would be wrong to argue that the class structure of Lancashire was determined somehow by its overseas markets, it would be equally wrong to ignore the effects of those markets on Lancashire.

It is in fact possible to probe this interrelationship somewhat further. Foremost amongst the markets for British cotton goods was, as has already been seen, India. To sell cotton goods to India in the nineteenth century was the equivalent of 'sending coals to Newcastle'. India grew cotton; it had a long-established cotton industry based on a domestic handicraft system. In the eighteenth century it was the greatest producer, consumer and exporter of calico (the plain white unprinted cotton cloth which was the base for the more sophisticated designs) in the world, supplying the markets of Asia as well as those of Europe. India was a huge market for cotton goods given the nature of its climate and its socio-cultural traditions. Unlike other people from areas with a hot climate, Indians did not have to be subjected to the missionary propaganda that linked clothes and Christianity – the so-called cult of 'Christianity and calico', directed at the 'naked savages' of Africa. The way in which Britain reversed the flow of calico goods has been told often. The first step was to exclude Indian textiles from Britain by increasing duties on them. Between 1797 and 1819, duties on Indian textiles were increased on twelve separate occasions. The effect of these increases was to kill off any export potential of the Indian cotton industry and to protect the infant indigenous cotton industry. Imports from India reached their peak value in 1800 and their peak quantity in 1802. Thereafter they declined rapidly.

Soon after this, in the wake of the Luddite uprisings and the search for new markets to counteract the cycles generated by production being dependent on low internal demand, the London-based East India Company lost its monopoly of the India trade in the Charter Act of 1813. Merchants were allowed to export to India unhindered by the Company. The privileges of the Company were further eroded in 1823 and totally abolished in 1833. As a result exports of cotton to India increased rapidly. By 1828 they were 50 per cent of all Britain's exports to the sub-continent, continuing to increase until 1871 when they reached their all-time peak of 73 per cent. In 1839 India became the primary market for British cotton goods in terms of volume; in 1843 it became the primary market in value terms and remained Britain's main market for cotton goods until 1943.

It should be clear from what has already been said that what occurred was not a simple process of free international trade. Instead, India's cotton industry was undermined by the effect of tariff barriers put up in England and then, when the British cotton industry had developed its technology sufficiently behind these protectionist barriers by the free trade imposed on it by its colonial masters. As Alavi wrote:

> It was the wall of protection that made possible the survival and growth of British cotton textile industry in the face of Indian competition and facilitated large capital investments in the industry. Without it the English industry would have found it impossible to get a foothold in the home market, let alone abroad, and would not have got off the ground (Alavi, 1980, p. 381).

Alavi went on to quote H. H. Wilson the historian of India, who wrote:

> Had not such prohibitory duties and decrees existed, the mills of Paisley and Manchester would have stopped in their onset and could scarcely have been again set into motion even by the power of steam. They were created by the sacrifice of Indian manufacture. Had India been independent, she could have retaliated, would have imposed prohibitive duties on British goods and would thus have preserved her own productive industry from annihilation. This act of self-defence was not permitted her (Alavi, 1980, p. 385).

The importance of the Indian market and the necessity for imperial power to maintain it meant that in Lancashire, free traders who might previously have supported Cobden's anti-imperialism became the firmest upholders of military expenditure in India and the opium trade in China. (See Harnetty, 1972, and Klein, 1971, for a full discussion of this.)

Lancashire then was probably more dependent than any other area of Britain on the existence of the empire. Without the power of the East India Company and later the Raj to maintain the openness of the Indian market, the ability of Lancashire capitalists to incorporate and control key elements of the working-class in the mid-Victorian period (as described in Foster, 1974, and Joyce, 1980,) would have been severely weakened.

It is possible however to suggest another fundamental way in which this affected Lancashire in terms of the division of labour within the cotton factory. Demand in India was primarily for plain calico cloth, which could be dyed and finished by Indian craftsmen in ways acceptable to Indian taste. As a result, the export trade to India became dominated by plain unfinished cloth. The effect of demand on the industrial structure and the labour process can be significant as previous research on the steel and engineering industries amongst others has shown – see for example, Elbaum and Wilkinson, 1979; Zeitlin, 1979, and the articles in Wood, 1982. Where demand is for standardized products that can be made on a large scale, this research suggests, then there will be a tendency for the industry to be more rapidly mechanized (and de-skilled) than in situations of unstable demand. It can be argued that this is one of the factors that contributed to the growing mechanization and concentration of the cotton industry in the mid-century period. The comparison becomes particularly clear when the woollen and worsted industry of West Yorkshire is brought into the picture. In this area, demand was never so standardized: there was a greater variety of cloth within the woollen/worsted industry which had to be prepared in a variety of different ways and finished and dyed in diverse ways.

In spite of the existence of a few large-scale integrated firms such as that run by Sir Titus Salt in Bradford, the industry in the nineteenth century and to a large extent still (see Morgan and Hooper, 1982) has consisted mainly of small companies operating in specialized sectors of the market. As a result of this, mechanization proceeded slowly in West Yorkshire;

conflicts over the restructuring of craft skills continued late into the nineteenth century. In the cotton industry on the other hand a relatively stable division of labour developed. In spinning, skilled male mule spinners developed trade union agreements with employers based on the exclusion of both management and the piecer assistants, from control over the labour process. In weaving, the level of skill necessary was never sufficiently complex to promote the possibility of exclusionary trade union-ism, and instead the Weavers' Amalgamation was 'a non-sec-tional union, concerned predominantly with the primary problem of direct wage determination' (see also Penn, 1983, and Lazo-nick, 1979). Nevertheless, in all areas of the cotton industry, the labour process was reorganized as the production of cloth for the Indian market became more mechanized and on the basis of these markets, the new labour process and new trade unions, a relatively peaceful system of industrial relations was developed in the second half of the nineteenth century with employers and workers coming together to agree piece lists such as the Blackburn list of 1855. Between 1850 and the mid-1870s, when competition from Bombay and Japan began to be felt in British cotton's traditional export markets, Lanca-shire cotton went through a period of boom, with increased wages, prosperity and quiescent labour relations based on institutionalized conciliation procedures and agreed price lists (though see Kirk, 1981, for a challenge to this view). Joyce drew together the significance of these phenomena compared with an area such as West Yorkshire with its woollen and worsted industry:

The great variety of specialist processes in woollen and worsted were diversified in terms both of ownership and geographical fluctuation. The small firm was more prevalent than in Lancashire . . . The structural unemployment en-demic in a situation of small, often commission-working firms was intensified by trade fluctuations over and above the market fluctuations experienced in cotton. Season, fashion, foreign tariffs all compounded to depress the condition of the operative and sever the link between master and man which continuous dependable work created . . . Thus the history and internal organisation of West Riding textiles meant that only the most primitive system of industrial relations developed. Unlike Lancashire class tension was unmodified by trade union organisation and received much more directly political expression in a continuously lively popular radical tradition and the early receptivity to Labour and socialist politics (Joyce, 1980, pp. 74–6).

To conclude this section of the paper then we can summarize the interrelationship between the class structure of the Lancashire cotton industry and India in the following ways:

1. The existence of the Indian market acted as a strong counter-cyclical force in the first half of the nineteenth century when class tensions in Lancashire cotton industry were at their height.
2. In the mid-century, India provided the stable and profitable market upon which stable class relations were based in Lancashire.
3. The nature of the demand in India for a standardized calico cloth was crucial for allowing the early standardization of the labour process in the cotton industry and the consequent early destruction of craft skills. This is not to say that new forms of segmentation did not arise. On the contrary, they certainly did but in contrast to earlier forms of opposition to the new order *in toto* based on pre-industrial craft and communal solidarities, the new forms of segmentation were often built on the exclusionary power of trade unions and were thus directed as much against other workers (often, in the case of cotton, female workers) as against employers, and hardly at all against the factory system as a whole (cf. Calhoun, 1982, on the different types of radicalism; and Penn, 1983, and Turner, 1962, on trade unionism in the cotton industry.)

By the middle of the nineteenth century, the fate of all cotton workers and capitalists in Lancashire was intimately connected with the India trade which in turn was dependent on continued British rule in the Indian subcontinent.

CHINA TRADE AND INDIA

This dependence itself however was not self-sufficient. Rather it in turn was dependent on a further set of relationships, this time connecting the Indian subcontinent with China. In this section I will show how Britain's India trade was dependent on China and how this dependence in turn caused changes in the social structure of China with consequences that were to result in the interpenetration of class relations between the Canton area of China and the California area of the USA.

Nineteenth-century trade in India cannot be understood without reference to the East India Company. The East India Company had been set up by Royal Charter in 1600 by Elizabeth I. The Company had been given a monopoly on all trade between Britain and all the areas between the Cape of Good Hope and Cape Horn. During the seventeenth and eighteenth centuries, the company increasingly concentrated on trade with India, importing a variety of goods into Britain including cotton piece goods (until their exclusion in the late eighteenth century), raw silk, saltpetre (used for making glass and gunpowder) and pepper. In order to pay for these imports, the Company exported as much as it could to India – mostly woollen cloth and metals. This left a substantial gap between imports and exports in the eighteenth-century India trade which was balanced by large shipments of bullion to India – shipments which were opposed by many British merchants who accepted mercantilist arguments that countries should hoard their bullion. This process was somewhat altered by the acquisition in 1765 of the *diwani* of Bengal. At first the Company had concentrated on trade alone but it had quickly developed forts and depots in India from the security of which its agents could go out into the countryside and trade. However, the Mogul empire was already in decay and with the British, French and Portuguese all seeking rights and privileges to trade, as well as powerful princes seeking their independence, India became increasingly unstable. The British, seeking to protect their trade, began to expand outwards, conquering Indian princedoms and acquiring territorial responsibility. The Mogul responded by seeking to collaborate with the British; in return for the British administering Bengal on behalf of the Emperor, they were given the right to collect taxes from the area. As Moore said:

As they acquired greater territorial responsibilities, they [i.e. the Company] gradually transformed themselves from commercial plunderers to more pacific rulers seeking to establish peace and order with the very small forces at their disposal (Moore, 1966, p. 342).

Whilst this was the first major settlement, it was the start of a process which continued until India became formally part of the Empire in 1858 and saw a marked change in the role of the Company. It created a source of revenue in India separate from commercial profits. Out of this revenue however had to be met the costs of administering India – costs which could certainly be very high during times of war with native princes. However, it was likely that there was the potential for a surplus – a potential which had nevertheless to be carefully nurtured. As Lord North explained to the Commons in 1769:

> If it is asked why do not the Company send all their surplus revenues to England, the answer is, India may be compared to a hen which lays a golden egg a day; if you draw off in bullion the revenues of that country you kill the hen to get all the eggs at once . . . To draw off, therefore, the wealth of that country without ruining it, must be by investments in the growth and manufacture of those countries, which investments must be sold in Europe (quoted in Marshall, 1971, p. 83).

As a result then, the trade balance began to shift in Britain's favour. A proportion of the goods imported into Britain had been received by the Company as payment in kind for their territorial revenues. Britain no longer needed to export so much to India – bullion exports in particular were no longer so necessary. From the turn of the nineteenth century in fact, as British exports of cotton to India really got under way, bullion shipments began to occur in the other direction, with India sending some of her already scarce specie to Britain in exchange for cotton goods. As the demands for the remittance of the obligatory 'home charges' of the Company and the accumulation of private fortunes to Britain from India also began to rise in the age of the nabobs in the late eighteenth and early nineteenth centuries, the prospects for India and its currency appeared serious. It would not have taken long at this rate for the country to have lost a significant amount of its specie

resulting in an artificial price inflation and a consequent decline
of trade with Britain. In order to maintain and even increase
this trade, an alternative means of remitting its profits had to
be found to bullion export.

This means was on hand in the shape of the Company's
China trade. China was the second most profitable part of the
Company's trade monopoly and during the nineteenth century,
trade with China had considerably expanded in one particular
item – tea. Tea-drinking had grown in popularity in Britain
during the eighteenth century in spite of being relatively expensive because of high customs duties. In 1783 however, in
order to undermine tea smuggling which was reducing customs
revenue, the duties were cut from 119 per cent to 12.5 per cent.
The result was a rapid expansion of the China tea trade.
Unfortunately the imports of tea into Britain were not matched
by any expansion of British exports to China. The commodities
of the West were of little interest to the Chinese mandarins
who controlled their foreign trade tightly, only allowing foreign-
ers to trade at designated factories in Canton with a designated group of Chinese merchants known as the *Cohong*. As a
result a trade imbalance in China's favour developed. According to Greenberg:

> From 1792 to 1807, the Company's shipments to England
> from Canton were worth £27 157 000 whereas the English
> exports to Canton came to only £16 602 338 (Greenberg,
> 1949, p. 8).

Once again the use of bullion to finance trade was considered
unsatisfactory and instead merchants sought for commodities
that the Chinese would buy. Greenberg wrote:

> The solution was finally found in India. It was discovered
> that while the Chinese had little taste for British goods, they
> were eager to accept the produce of British India, particu-
> larly raw cotton and opium, though China itself produced
> the one and prohibited the other. The resources of India
> could be used to finance the China investment . . . The
> effect of this can be seen in the changing balance of the
> China trade. After 1804, very little or no silver had to be sent
> from Europe to China by the Company. On the contrary a

rapid increase of Indian imports into Canton soon reversed the flow of treasure (Greenberg, 1949, p. 9).

The result then was that during the first half of the nineteenth century a triangular system of trade developed: Britain sent cotton goods to India; India sent raw cotton and opium to China and China sent tea to Britain. One commentator, T. C. Melville, the Company's auditor general, declared in 1830: 'I am prepared to say that India does entirely depend upon the profits of the China trade' (Greenberg, 1949, pp. 14–15). As Richards said:

> The structure of trade balances and supporting credit and exchange mechanisms between Calcutta, Bombay, Canton and London afforded a convenient, possibly even essential, method of transferring from India to London each year approximately two million pounds sterling (ten million silver rupees) in imperial tribute (Richards, 1981, pp. 66–7).

The thorn in the crown of this imperial trading system was the main commodity exported to China – opium. The Chinese Empire since the early eighteenth century had prohibited the use of opium; as a result the opium trade was a smugglers' trade. As a result of this it was a bullion trade – there were none of the niceties of bartering goods for goods as occurred in the officially regulated Factories at Canton. Instead the smugglers would sell the opium for silver. The smugglers were in fact ships belonging to respectable British merchant houses based in Canton – the East India Company itself kept out of the actual business of selling opium to the Chinese. Instead the sale was left to what was known as 'the country trade'. Although the Company had a monopoly on all trade to and from Britain in the area between the two Capes, it allowed private British merchants to operate within the area. These merchants conducted their business along the coasts of South Asia and China becoming known as the country trade. In the early nineteenth century, opium became one of their main trading commodities.

The Company benefitted from the trade in a number of ways: first, in 1772 Warren Hastings, the new Governor-General of Bengal, had imposed a state monopoly on the production and sale of opium. Although the Act was modified during the nineteenth century the basic structure of the opium monopoly was retained. (For a detailed discussion see Richards, 1981.) Under these rules, private cultivation of poppy was prohibited. Instead, peasants in the opium-producing areas of Bihar and West Bengal were contracted by the Company and later the Opium Agencies run by the Raj to cultivate a specified plot of land and to deliver its entire production, unadulterated, at the fixed government price to the agent. The Company through its opium agents at Patna and Benares supervised the drying, processing and packing into wooden chests of the opium destined for the Company warehouses at Calcutta. A limited amount went to specified outlets for legal sale in British India, much of the rest was purchased by the country traders for sale in China. The second way in which the Company benefitted was that the country traders paid much of their earnings from the opium trade into the Company's treasury at Canton, thus giving the Company specie for its tea purchases (on which it had a monopoly) until 1834. Greenberg says that the Company's Treasury at Canton accepted:

> Specie from country merchants which their Indian produce yielded, in return for Bills on the Court of Directors in London or on the Government of Bengal. These Bills were eagerly sought by the country merchants, whose imports from India far exceeded their exports from China, as a means of remittance of their funds to England and they had difficulty in securing profitable return cargoes from China. Country ships often returned from Canton to India in ballast, carrying the Company's China Bills, which could easily be marketed in Calcutta (Greenberg, 1942, p. 29).

By the 1820s then, the structure of triangular trade between Britain, India and China was established. The structure was however fundamentally unstable. First, the East India Company's monopoly was under threat from the merchants in the Country Trade and their free-trade allies in London. The Company's monopoly of the India trade had been withdrawn in 1813 and as its Charter came up again for renewal in 1833, there was growing opposition to its monopoly on the China trade.

In Canton, merchants were keen to get in on the lucrative tea trade which the Company controlled. In Britain itself, free traders believed that the Company was not promoting exports of British textiles to China. In 1829, an East India Trade Committee was set up in Manchester which demanded the ending of the tea monopoly and full freedom of trade to China. This was the start of a three-year campaign which eventually saw the end of the Company's monopoly in China. As a result the 1830s saw a more vigorous prosecution of the China trade by the private merchants. The basic structure of the triangular trade was retained, though with private companies taking a more prominent part. Contrary to the expectations of the Lancashire textile producers however there was no rapid boom in sales to China. In fact in the ensuing speculation, there were a number of spectacular bankruptcies amongst the *Cohong* merchants. The result however was not an abandonment of the Chinese trade but a growing feeling that now British traders were being hampered by the Chinese refusing to allow free trade and restricting access to their internal market which the merchants still believed had huge potential. Pressure began to build up in Britain and Canton for an opening up of the China trade.

The second factor causing instability was the effect of the opium trade on China itself. As has already been stated, the Chinese Empire had for a long time banned the sale of opium but nevertheless the drug had spread, partly through the corruption of the mandarins as well as the efforts of the smugglers. The area around Canton was gradually disintegrating into social chaos. The effects of opium on the area were multiple; first, there were the effects of addiction on the morale of the peasants in the area; second, there were the effects on lawlessness and criminality – as in Prohibition America, demand for the illegal commodity could only be satisfied by illegal means – gangs of Chinese would bring the drugs ashore and distribute it in the area, often after violent clashes with Imperial forces but sometimes in conjunction with bribed mandarins; third, there was the increasing inability of the Empire to uphold its own laws causing the cycle of criminality to increase even further as people took the law into their own hands. By the late 1830s, then, China around Canton was beginning to resemble those states in India which the Company was increasingly taking into its own control on account of the 'disruption caused to trade' by the venality, corruption and violence of the areas which the native authority was incapable of checking.

The Chinese bureaucracy, however, was not yet as ineffectual as its Mogul counterpart had become. During the late 1830s it launched a strong campaign against opium smuggling, guarding the coastline around Canton with large numbers of ships. At first the Imperial ships attacked only Chinese opium junks but as the merchants sought to get round this by using European boats, knowing that the Viceroy of Canton would be more reluctant to attack these, tension heightened. Eventually Lin Tse-hsu, appointed as Special Imperial Commissioner to stop the opium trade, directly attacked the foreign source of the drug, ordering the merchants at the Canton factories to surrender all their opium. Until they did so, they were to be confined to their factories. So began the first Opium War. There is little doubt that it was a war between an expanding capitalist power and a strong but pre-capitalist empire which was being eroded by the growth of cash relations at its periphery. For Britain, it was a war about the right to free trade; for China, the consequences were the further erosion of the social structure of the Empire. Whilst it took some time for the British to mobilize their forces, with hindsight, the result looks a foregone conclusion. The Chinese fleet was faced with one of the earliest technological innovations that was to industrialize warfare – the flat-bottomed steamboat which had the ability to navigate up-river and attack inland towns. The British sent one of their first steamers – the *Nemesis* – packed with guns, some of them powerful enough to blast a hole in a fortress wall. Although it took the *Nemesis* almost eight months to reach the Chinese Seas from Portsmouth, when she eventually launched her attack in January 1841, the Chinese ships guarding the entry to Canton were routed and forts and junks destroyed at will as the steamboat approached Canton.

Nemesis was reinforced in the following year by more steamers and the British won a decisive naval battle on the Yangtze river, after which the Chinese sued for peace. British technology overcame the Imperial power with ease – the futility of the warfare conducted by this, the most organized of the pre-industrial civilizations, is illustrated by the Chinese secret weapon developed to combat the British steamers – a paddlewheeler armed with brass guns and propelled by men inside the hull operating treadles! (See Headrick, 1981; also Kiernan, 1982).

On 29 August 1842, the Chinese signed the Treaty of Nanking and agreed to the terms of the merchants – the *Cohong* was abolished, four new ports to the north were opened to foreign trade, duties were limited to 5 per cent (except on tea), British consuls were to be admitted to the new ports and Hong Kong was to become a British colony. Opium was not mentioned, but as Alexander Matteson, head of the largest British merchant house in Canton, said in 1843:

> The new tariff and port regulations are really moderate and favourable and, if strictly adhered to by the Chinese, our trade with England is sure to increase very much. The drug trade continues to prosper (quoted in Greenberg, 1949, p. 214).

The British had not conquered China, nor were they ever to do so. What they had done was to set under way changes in Chinese social structure which helped to give rise rapidly to a major peasant revolt – the Taiping rebellion which lasted for almost twenty years from 1850 and involved millions of peasants. As Chesnaux wrote:

> It is no mere coincidence that this powerful peasant outburst occurred in the period of the Opium Wars and the 'opening' of China by the Western powers. The age-old contradictions between the peasants and the feudal holders of power, land and learning were deepened and brought to a climax by a combination of exceptional circumstances. The political and social crisis, which had been fermenting in the Chinese countryside since the beginning of the nineteenth century was brutally exacerbated by the First Opium War and the Treaty of Nanking. The Manchus dynasty was discredited by its readiness to give in to Western demands. The opium traffic, illicit before the war and then legalized, drained China of a large part of her resources of silver, and changed, to the disadvantage of the peasants, the exchange rate, between silver and copper. The opening of other ports in the east of the country deprived Canton of much of the

commerce which had been concentrated there when it had been the only port open to foreign trade. Hundreds of thousands of boatmen and porters in central and southern China were thrown out of work and it was from among this army of unemployed that several of the leaders of the Taiping rebellion emerged (Chesneaux, 1973, pp. 24–5).

In the area around Canton, peasant lives were threatened by competing war-lords, gang-leaders and the imperial army. Their ability to grow rice in the area was hampered by the violence and the effects of opium. The social structure was disintegrating. In these circumstances, many of the Chinese sought to salvage what they could in a manner which they had done for some generations. They would emigrate from the Pearl River delta; as Barth explained it:

> When he found it economically impossible to maintain a large family, the rustic continued to pay tribute to the ideal. Deprived of his resources by the existing disorder, he aimed to support wife, children and dependent parents by emigrating into the Chinese overseas communities . . . The social conditions of the Pearl River delta at the middle of the nineteenth century compelled the Cantonese to test the value of the emigration system as defence of their way of life. Engulfed by political and economic disorder the villagers chose to emigrate to protect the foundation of their world. The rumour of easy riches in California determined their route. The story of the Golden Hills of America reached Hong Kong in the spring of 1848 (Barth, 1964, pp. 28–31).

THE CHINESE IN CALIFORNIA

Even this however does not exhaust our catalogue of interdependencies for the transformation set under way in China by the penetration of British industrial, commercial and political power had implications for a new power arising in the West, the United States of America. The Opium Wars and the Taiping rebellion created large numbers of potential Chinese migrants and the land to which they looked for work was California.

California had only become part of the USA in the 1840s when it was taken from Mexico under Treaty. In these early days there was no rail link across the continent and yet the potential of the area was recognized early on. It was the discovery of gold in 1849 and the gold rush which followed that really placed California on the map. As prospectors set up their camps, demand for industrial and agricultural produce increased. The main problems in satisfying demand were first, the lack of labour to work in the factories and on the land and second the lack of a railroad to bring products from the East to satisfy demand. It was the Chinese who were to be the key in solving these problems.

As the social fabric of the Pearl River delta had deteriorated consequent on the opium trade and British intervention, Chinese men looked to safeguard their families and their land by migrating abroad. The Gold Mountains of California promised wealth in abundance and so in the period after the initial Gold Rush of 1849, the migration began. However, it was not a matter of the geographical transfer of free labour. For Chinese peasants to pay the fare for the journey across the Pacific was out of the question. Instead, the peasants sold themselves into indenture with a Chinese merchant who would arrange for their passage. Once they arrived in San Francisco, they were obliged to work where the merchant or his American contacts wished. If they tried to escape or renege on their obligations, they could expect their family in China to suffer the consequences. Theoretically, they could expect eventually to pay off their debt, but in practical terms they would often remain dependent on the patronage of the rich Chinese merchants and their gangs of hired thugs, the 'tongs'. As Chinamen, they were easily visible once they left Chinatown or the Chinese encampments and as such were easy prey to white racists or to the *tongs* who sought to bring them back to serve their indenture.

For most of the 1850s and early 1860s, the Chinese worked in the gold-mines of the Sierra Nevada. According to Barth, 30 000 of the 48 391 Chinese in California at this time worked in the gold region. This was the period after the initial gold rush. The easy pickings which had existed in 1849 were no more. The original 'Forty-niners' were small prospectors who looked for gold near the surface or by the river-bed in small individual plots. As their success diminished, they moved on to pastures new, selling their stakes at rock-bottom prices. It was at this stage that American and Chinese merchants moved in, using Chinese labour to search for gold in a much more systematic way. Saxton said:

> If the claim had remained in the hands of the original owner, it would probably never have been worked. But the Chinese would do well: 'They appear to have reduced this kind of mining to a science. Old abandoned claims that nobody thought had enough gold in them to buy salt have been purchased by Chinamen and worked with profit'. Through the sixties, Chinese in California were replacing Americans in surface mines and river-bed operations (Saxton, 1971, p. 57).

As mining began to go underground and necessitate larger amounts of capital, the old prospectors drifted away. What was required now to make the mines profitable was wage-labour – this the Chinese provided. Whilst some of the whites got jobs supervising the Chinese, others resented the entry of the Chinese and this competition between large-scale mining operations manned by Chinese and the small-scale prospecting of the whites led to the first violent clashes between the whites and the Chinese in California. The Chinese indentured to the merchants had no choice but to accept the low pay offered to them by the mine-owners. For the whites, however, the Chinese were lowering the pay for all workers and thus destroying the chance for them to move from prospecting to wage-labour in the gold-mines.

The main influx of Chinese however came in the mid- to late-1860s as the effort to complete the intercontinental rail link speeded up. The rail link which eventually joined up at Promontory Point in 1869 was being built from the West by the Central Pacific and from the East by the Union Pacific. As the railroads received a strip of land each side of every section of rail they completed, there was intense rivalry between the railroads to get as far as possible as quickly as possible.

During the early 1860s, however, the Central Pacific made painfully slow progress through the mud-flats and oak thickets of the lower foothills of California. After two years of effort, the railhead was only fifty miles on. One of the main problems was that of getting sufficient numbers of workers for the terribly hard conditions in which the railroad building went on. The Union Pacific, coming from the East, not only had the advantages of building across the prairies of the mid-West; they were also able to recruit a continuous supply of labourers, mostly immigrants from Ireland and Germany. In the West, there was no equivalent surplus of labour until 1865 when the railroad began first to employ Chinese men out of the failing gold-mines but also, with the co-operation of the merchants, importing them in vast quantities from China itself. By the end of 1865 over 3000 Chinese were working on the railroad at a cost of approximately two-thirds that of the white labourer. In the years that followed, more and more Chinese came to work on the railroad; one Dutch merchant, quoted by Saxton, estimated that he had brought into California 30 000 Chinese for the railway. Since at any one time only about 10–11 000 worked on the railroad, it is clear that there must have been a high mortality rate.

Certainly the conditions under which the Chinese worked were unacceptable to the whites. The only whites on the railroad acted as supervisors or engineers. Nearly all the labourers were Chinese. Saxton described their conditions as they worked their way through the Sierra Nevada during the winter:

> The portals of the summit tunnel were buried under fantastic drifts; the Chinese encampments were snowed under. The Chinese dug chimneys and air shafts, lived by lantern light. They tunnelled in from the camps to reach the bore of the tunnel itself and the work continued although materials now had to be lowered 40 ft. or more by steam hoist from the surface of the snow and the waste from the digging taken out in the same way (Saxton, 1971, p. 64).

For a long period, the Chinese were tunnelling through granite, using only sledge-hammers and brute strength. Maxine Hong Kingston in her book *China Man* has reconstructed this time in a fictional form:

> Beneath the soil, they hit granite. Ah Goong struck it with his pickaxe and it jarred his bones, chattered his teeth. He swung his sledge-hammer against it, and the impact rang in the dome of his skull. The mountain that was millions of

years old was locked against them and was not to be broken
into . . . Nothing happened to that grey wall; he had to slam
with strength and will. He hit at the same spot over and over
again, the same rock . . . When the foreman measured at
the end of twenty-four hours of pounding, the rock had
given a foot . . . After tunnelling into granite for about three
years, Ah Goong understood the immovability of the
earth . . . In the third year of pounding granite by hand, a
demon invented dynamite (Kingston, 1981, pp. 133–5).

Dynamite and its seemingly uncontrollable blasts brought
new risks and new dangers to the Chinese labourers but at least
it speeded up the progress. There were many ways to die
building the railway – falling into one of the deep ravines of the
Sierras, being blasted to pieces by dynamite, being crushed to
death beneath a rockfall in a tunnel, or an avalanche on the
side of the mountain, freezing to death in the snow, or just
simply dying of fatigue. The railroad was profligate with the
lives of the China men or the 'heathen Chinese' as they were
known.

As Miller has shown, the image of the Chinese in America
was negative from a very early stage (Miller, 1969; see also
Takaki, 1980). American visitors to China between 1750 and
1850, whether they were missionaries, traders or diplomats,
shared a general view of Chinese civilization as being in a state
of decline caused by inherent racial weaknesses. Missionaries
emphasized the worst aspects of Chinese life as a lesson as to
the effects of heathenism. The Chinese were portrayed as
unfeeling towards their children (infanticide, particularly of
girls, was portrayed as common), addicted to opium and the
slothful habits that entailed, sexually perverse (enjoying young
children), and beneath it all, cunning and deceitful. Stories
circulated of the use of cats, dogs and rats in the cooking, as
well as their propensity to cut up young girls in order to drink
certain fluids from their bodies for medicinal purposes. Inci-
dents such as the massacre at Tsientsin in 1870 when French
priests and nuns were murdered by a Chinese mob furthered
the perception which was also being developed by the 'scientific racists' of the time who sought to place the Chinese in their
hierarchy of races. One author wrote in 1866:

As the type of the Negro is foetal, that of the Mongol is infantile. And in strict accordance with this we find their government, literature and art are infantile also. They are beardless children whose life is a task and whose chief virtue consists in unquestioning obedience (quoted in Miller, 1969, p. 145).

China was seen as full of diseases such as leprosy, syphilis and cholera which in themselves were seen as a reflection of the moral character of the Chinese. Migrants from China were suspect as representatives of this degraded race and possible carriers of these pernicious diseases.

The 1860s, then, saw the formation of social relationships which have a familiar ring. Desperate for labour, white entrepreneurs looked beyond their existing borders to an area of overpopulation where peasants were willing to emigrate for the hope of a better life. Once they came to the new land, the migrants found their opportunities strictly limited and their rewards small. Furthermore as the initial labour shortage was overcome and the railroad completed, the reaction against the Chinese migrants – known as the 'Driving Out' – was rapid and violent. While some of the Chinese continued building railroads across the country, many others found themselves driven out of their settlements. Maxine Hong Kingston reconstructs the 'Drivings Out' from the viewpoint of her grandfather, Ah Goong:

Good at hiding . . . he was not working in a mine when 40 000 Chinamen were driven out of mining. He was not killed or kidnapped in the Los Angeles massacre, though he gave money towards ransoming those whose toes and fingers, a digit per week, and ears grotesquely rotting or pickled and scalped queues were displayed in Chinatowns . . . He was lucky not to be in Colorado when the Denver demons burned all Chinamen's homes and businesses, nor in Rock Springs, Wyoming when the miner demons killed twenty-eight or fifty Chinamen . . . Ah Goong was running elsewhere during the Drivings Out of Tacoma, Seattle, Oregan City, Albania and Marysville (Kingston, 1981, p. 147).

Chinese labour had, in the main, served its purpose once the railroad was completed. Some were able to find sanctuary and work in the larger Chinatowns such as those of San Francisco and Stockton. There they would be employed in domestic service or laundries or sweated trades such as the textile and clothing industry. Their wages would be low and conditions hard. No white would take these jobs, preferring to work in all-white strongholds such as building and printing where wages and conditions were much better. Many of the Chinese, however, were driven out of America altogether, or killed in the process.

The Government too, collaborated with this process. In 1868, the Fourteenth Amendment had given naturalized Americans the same rights as nature-born Americans, but in 1870 the Nationality Act specified that only 'free whites' and 'African aliens' were allowed to apply for naturalization, thus excluding the Chinese. In 1878, California went further and a coalition of working-class, anti-Chinese elements and small shop-keepers and farmers drew up a constitution which prohibited Chinese from entering California. New state laws also empowered cities and countries to confine them within specified areas or to throw them out completely. The Chinese were barred from attending state schools, owning land, or applying for business licences. Whilst some of these laws were later declared unconstitutional by federal courts, they reflected the coalition of class interests that had built up against the Chinese. Two years later, in 1882, the US congress, under pressure from California, passed the first Chinese Exclusion Act. It banned the entrance of Chinese labourers, both skilled and unskilled, for ten years. Anyone unqualified for citizenship could not come in – and by the terms of the 1870 Nationality Act, the Chinese were not qualified for citizenship. The Exclusion Act which was renewed in 1892 and made permanent in 1904, was the first act of exclusion in the history of the US and preceded by some period of years, the first acts directed against stemming the tide of migrants from Southern and Eastern Europe. Those Chinese left after the 'Driving Out' and the Exclusion Act were now safely herded into the Chinatowns of the Californian cities where they performed various menial service tasks and sweated-labour rejected by the whites under the continual threat of harassment and violence from the whites of California. Their key-role in building up the economy of the Western state was now over – the gold-mines were finished and the railroads laid – those Chinese left were now peripheral to the main dynamic of the economy; they were an internal colony marginalized by processes of capitalist expansion in which they themselves had been the unwitting tools of forces crossing over land and ocean for thousands of miles.

The history of the USA has often been written in terms of a melting-pot, but such inexact concepts are of little use in understanding the real process of class formation. In California, the basis of the economy – the railway and the gold-mines – was built by the Chinese. Whilst their role declines from this point in the history of the US, the interdependence that briefly brought together Britain, India, China and the USA is important, as upon it was developed the power of Britain and the USA.

CONCLUSION

In many ways, the object of this study is to show that there are no conclusions in the process of capitalist expansion. We have followed a chain of causation that moulded the social structure of Lancashire and with it the relative industrial and political peace of mid-Victorian England, that locked India and China into an imperial economic and political system that in India's case rapidly, and in China's more slowly, disintegrated the existing social structure, that set under way processes of racial and ethnic stratification in California. These societies at such different levels of development were brought together then in ways that were to have permanent effects on their social structures. One of the few authors to attempt to theorize these linkages is Giddens; he has proposed the concept of a 'time–space edge' to refer to the form of contact and interdependence between different structural types of society:

> these are edges of potential or actual social transformation, the often unstable intersections between different modes of societal organisation (Giddens, 1981, p. 23).

The time–space edge in turn generates what Giddens has referred to as 'episodes', 'processes of social change that have a definite direction and form and in which definite structural transformations occur' (Giddens, 1981, p. 23). Both episodic change and time–space edges served to link Britain with India, China, and the USA in the ways outlined here. To say this is not to propose a new sort of functionalism where capitalist development 'required' these markets and these labourers and ensured these 'effects', but to recognize that this was how things occurred at this particular time. As the century developed, interdependence declined but for a time, the link was crucial. Once again, to use another of Gidden's somewhat grating neologisms, what was crucial at one stage of 'world-time' becomes less significant at a later stage of 'world-time' (see Giddens, 1981, p. 167). Just because there was such a strong link at one time does not mean there must be such a strong link at another time. Nevertheless, this relatively brief period of interdependence had permanent effects on the future of all four of these areas. To study processes of class formation and class struggle within nation–state boundaries is to ignore this fundamental process of interdependence which has been fostered and developed in the era of capitalist expansion. Whilst in this paper our panoramic gaze has undoubtedly concealed some of the detail of the landscapes under review, it nonetheless shows us that these landscapes are connected. Like the great continental plates on which these social dramas are played out, each one connects beneath the surface; movement in one is related to movement in another. That processes of class formation and class struggle are international in capitalism is a Marxist truism with which sociology (and Marxism for that matter) has barely begun to come to terms.

In an age of nuclear weapons, when any recognizable form of social structure may be destroyed within minutes, it ill behoves sociology as a discipline to ignore the many ways in which this interrelationship between states has developed. We are now at the stage where decisions made in one or two power-centres can not just 'affect' the social structure of many areas but destroy it altogether. Now more than ever, therefore, we need to reject old conventions of narrowly focussing on 'society' as though it were contiguous with the boundaries of particular states; our economic well-being, our peaceful coexistence depend upon others. It is up to sociology to start exploring the multiple impact of this dependence over many centuries upon our own social structure rather than treating these exogenous forces as either irrelevant or best left to the analysis of others.

REFERENCES

Alavi, H. (1980) 'India: Transition from Feudalism to Colonial Capitalism', in *Journal of Contemporary Asia*, vol. 10, no. 4.

Barth, G. (1964) *Bitter Strength: A History of the Chinese in the United States 1850–1870* (Cambridge, Mass: Harvard University Press).

Brenner, R. (1977) 'Origins of Capitalist Development', in *New Left Review*, no. 104.

Burgess, K. (1975) *The Origins of British Industrial Relations* (London: Cocom Helm).

Calhoun, C. (1982) *The Question of Class Struggle* (Oxford: Blackwell).

Charlesworth, N. (1982) *British Rule and the Indian Economy 1800–1914* (London: Macmillan).

Chesneaux, J. (1973) *Peasant Revolts in China 1840–1949* (London: Thames and Hudson).

Elbaum, B. and Wilkinson, F. (1979) 'Industrial Relations and Uneven Development: A Comparative Study of the American and British Steel Industries', in *Cambridge Journal of Economics*, 3.

Farnie, D. A. (1979) *The English Cotton Industry and the World Market 1815–1896* (Oxford: Clarendon Press).

Foster, J. (1974) *Class Struggle and the Industrial Revolution* (London: Weidenfeld & Nicolson).

Frank, A. G. (1977) 'Multilateral Merchandise Trade Imbalances and Uneven Economic Development', in *Journal of European Economic History*, vol. 6.

Giddens, A. (1981) *A Contemporary Critique of Historical Materialism* (London: Macmillan).

Gordon, D. M., Edwards, R. and Reich, M. (1982) *Segmented Work: Divided Workers*, (Cambridge: Cambridge University Press).

Gray, R. (1975) 'The Labour Aristocracy in the Victorian Class Structure', in F. Parkin (ed.) *The Social Analysis of Class Structure* (London: Tavistock).

Gray, R. (1981) *The Aristocracy of Labour in Nineteenth Century Britain c.1850–1914* (London: Macmillan).

Greenberg, M. (1949) *British Trade and the Opening of China*, New York: Monthly Review Press.

Harnetty, P. (1972) *Imperialism and Free Trade: Lancashire and India in the mid-19th century* (Manchester: Manchester University Press).

Headrick, M. (1981) *The Tools of Empire: Technology and European Imperialism in the Nineteenth Century* (Oxford: Oxford University Press).

Hobsbawm, E. J. (1964) *Labouring Men* (London: Weidenfeld & Nicolson).

Jones, G. S. (1975) 'Class Struggle and the Industrial Revolution', in *New Left Review*, 90.

Joyce, P. (1980) *Work, Society and Politics* (London: Methuen).

Kiernan, V. G. (1980) *Marxism and Imperialism* (London: Edward Arnold).

Kiernan, V. G. (1982) *European Empires from Conquest to Collapse 1815–1960* (London: Fontana).

Kingston, M. H. (1981) *China Men* (London: Picador).

Kirk, N. (1981) 'Cotton Workers and Deference', in *Bulletin of the Society for the Study of Labour History*.

Klein, I. (1971) 'English Free Traders and Indian Tariffs, 1874–1896', in *Modern Asian Studies*, 5, 3.

Latham, A. J. H. (1977) 'Merchandise Trade Imbalances and Uneven Economic Development in India and China', in *Journal of European Economic History*, vol. 6.

Lazonick, W. (1979) 'Industrial Relations and Technological Change: The Case of the Self-acting Mule', in *Cambridge Journal of Economics*, vol. 3, no. 3.

Lenin, V. I. (1969) *Selected Works* (London: Lawrence & Wishart).

McLennan, G. (1981) 'The "Labour Aristocracy" and "Incorporation" ', in *Social History*, vol. 6, no. 1, January.

Marshall, P. J. (1968) *Problems of Empire: Britain and India 1756–1813* (London: Allen & Unwin).

Marx, K. and Engels, F. (1975) *Selected Correspondence* (London: Lawrence & Wishart).

Miller, S. C. (1969) *The Unwelcome Immigrant: The American Image of the Chinese 1785–1882* (Berkeley, California:).

Moore, B. (1966) *Social Origins of Dictatorship and Democracy* (Harmondsworth: Penguin).

Moorhouse, H. (1979) 'History, Sociology and the Quiescence of the British Working Class', in *Social History*, vol. 4, no. 3, October.

Moorhouse, H. (1981) 'The Marxist Theory of the Labour Aristocracy', in *Social History*, vol. 3, no. 1, January.

Moorhouse, H. (1981) 'The Significance of the Labour Aristocracy', in *Social History*, vol. 6, no. 2, May.

Morgan, G. and Hooper, D. (1982) 'Labour in the Woollen and Worsted Industry: A Critical Analysis of Dual Labour Market Theory' in G. Day, *et al.*, *Diversity and Decomposition in the Labour Market* (London: Gower).

Musson, A. (1976) 'Class Struggle and the Labour Aristocracy', in *Social History*, vol. 1, no. 3, October.

Pelling, H. (1968) *Popular Politics in Late Victorian Britain* (London: Macmillan).

Penn, R. (1983) 'Trade Union Organisation and Skill in the Cotton and Engineering Industries in Britain 1850–1960', in *Social History*, vol. 8, no. 1, January.

Reid, A. (1978) 'Politics and Economics in the Formation of the British Working Class', in *Social History*, vol. 3, no. 3, October.

Rex, J. (1980) 'A Working Paradigm for Race Relations Research', in *Ethnic and Racial Studies*, January.

Richards, J. F. (1981) 'The Indian Empire and Peasant Production of Opium in the 19th Century', in *Modern Asian Studies*, vol. 15, no. 1.

Saxton, A. (1971) *The Indispensable Enemy: Labour and the Anti-Chinese Movement in California* (Berkeley: University of California Press).

Takaki, R. (1980) *Iron Cages: Race and Culture in 19th Century America* (London: Abhlone Press).

Turner, H. (1962) *Trade Union Growth, Structure and Policy* (London: Allen & Unwin).

Urry, J. (1981) 'Localities, Regions and Social Class', in *International Journal of Urban and Regional Research*, vol. 5, no. 4.

Wallerstein, I. (1979) *The Capitalist World Economy* (Cambridge: Cambridge University Press).

Wood, S. (ed.) (1982) *The Degradation of Work?* (London: Hutchinson).

Zeitlin, J. (1979) 'Craft Control and the Division of Labour: Engineers and Compositions in Britain 1890–1930', in *Cambridge Journal of Economics*, vol. 3, no. 3.

7 Racism and Cheap Labour in UK Wool Textiles[1]

RALPH FEVRE

Several industries in the UK displayed symptoms associated with falling demand long before the general recession produced mass redundancies throughout manufacturing industry. Most of the industries which had been shedding labour over a much longer period had faced increased international competition but in some cases the demand for labour fell much more sharply than output. This pattern has become more familiar since 1980, but in earlier years it received little attention, perhaps because the industries concerned were seen as 'traditional' and 'declining'. They were to be allowed to disappear while new jobs would be provided by growth in other sectors. One such 'traditional' industry was wool textiles. Here postwar difficulties with markets led to substantial change. The industry was reorganized through takeovers and closures and there were changes in the labour process in most sectors.

As industrial change proceeded the proportion of wool textile workers who were *Asians* steadily increased. By 1979 (the last year for which figures are available) over 13 per cent of direct production workers in wool textiles were Asian. This chapter will show that industrial change, particularly change in the labour process, may be dependent on the recruitment of workers who are denied access to alternative sources of employment. It will be suggested that many wool textile firms were dependent on the persistence of *racial discrimination* to allow them to put their plans for modernization into practice. Of course the increase in the general level of unemployment in the later 1970s reduced the number of alternative employment opportunities available to most workers, not simply those who

156

suffered discrimination. Employers in many industries have made changes in the labour process in the knowledge that they would not be hindered by a shortage of willing workers. The product of these changes has usually been the same as in wool textiles in earlier periods: a reduction in total demand for labour following increases in output per head. However the wool textile industry does not simply provide an early example of a now familiar pattern. The wool textile industry was also affected by the present recession, and unemployment in areas with a high proportion of wool textile employees rose sharply. How did this affect the Asian workforce? Furthermore, how did rising unemployment affect the practice of discrimination? Does discrimination persist even though it no longer serves the interests of capital – that is, if discrimination produces advantages for some employers when labour is in short supply, does it persist when labour is plentiful?

It is clear that much of this chapter is concerned, of necessity, with theoretical considerations. The findings on which it is based are reported in detail elsewhere,[2] and the reader must make do with a simple summary of trends in numbers of Asians employed. Thus the 1971 census showed that wool textiles had the largest absolute concentration of black workers in the UK. The majority of these workers were Asians and a third of the Asians in the industry were employed in wool textile mills *in Bradford*. It is to these workers that this chapter refers. Their numbers grew throughout the 1960s while overall employment in the industry was falling. The proportion of Bradford's wool textile workers who were Asian continued to rise in the 1970s; however, the absolute numbers of Asian wool textile workers in the city fell throughout the decade. By the middle 1970s the rate of increase in the Asian proportion of *direct production* workers had begun to slow down and the Asian percentage of *all employees* had ceased to rise. Furthermore in 1979 there was a fall (from 25.1 per cent to 23.8 per cent) in the Asian proportion of direct production workers in wool textiles in Bradford. Unfortunately, the Wool Industry Bureau of Statistics – which produced these figures – ceased to collect this information in 1980. It is, however, very likely that the Asian proportion of wool textile workers continued to fall after 1979.

It might be assumed that the recent fall in the Asian proportion of wool textile workers can be directly related to the

general rise in unemployment, but – at least in the early stages
– this assumption would be mistaken. Rather, industrial change
reduced the need for Asian labour at this time, just as in early
years it had led to the increased recruitment of Asian workers.
Before we consider the recent fall in the Asian proportion of
wool textile workers, we must first discuss the relationship
between labour supply and demand when the Asians were first
recruited. Second, we will consider how relevant discrimination against Asians is to their employment distribution. We will
then discuss the relationship between the labour market and
the labour process and, finally, the impact of the recession on
Asian wool textile workers.

LABOUR SUPPLY AND DEMAND

Asian wool textile workers have occupied jobs which white
workers have rejected. They have provided *cheap labour*.
While low pay is certainly the most important attribute of an
unattractive job (Castells, 1975, p. 54; Bohning, 1972, p. 56), it
is widely accepted as unwise to define cheap labour simply in
terms of wages (see for example, Bonacich, n.d., p. 12). The
term is therefore used here to refer to *all* aspects of a job which
make it appear unattractive.

Most writers on the employment of blacks in the UK have
found that black workers occupy unattractive jobs. There was
general agreement with Smith's conclusion that most 'immigrants' were employed in jobs which white workers had rejected because of low pay; low levels of training, skill and
interest; poor conditions and unattractive hours of work (Smith,
1976, *passim*). By the time the Unit for Manpower Studies at
the Department of Employment conducted its study (1977) this
might almost have been thought a commonplace observation,
however most commentators went on to conclude that black
workers' occupancy of such jobs could be put down to the
existence of a general labour shortage (see, for example,
Marshall, 1973, p. 71). It was assumed that blacks would be
excluded under normal circumstances but where labour demand exceeded labour supply most workers were able to move
up the job hierarchy leaving vacancies in the least attractive
jobs. Blacks were therefore drafted in at the bottom of the

hierarchy. If it were not for the shortfall in labour supply black workers would not be needed.

This argument takes the abstract idea of the labour market too literally. It may be useful to assume in economic models that labour supply and demand are fixed and independent, but this assumption is not supported by empirical research. Since the supply of labour is not fixed – for example, activity rates may vary, especially amongst women – employers can influence the supply of labour. Labour shortages can be created when employers allow wages and conditions to deteriorate. Employers can alleviate shortages by making jobs more attractive or by abolishing them. In the former case labour supply will be influenced by the level of labour demand. In the latter case, where employers choose to do without labour, labour demand is influenced by the level of labour supply and employers may choose to substitute capital for labour or to reduce output.

Since the creation of labour shortages is not inevitable, it is difficult to accept that the existence of such shortages 'explains' the employment of black workers. In contrast to those who conclude that blacks find work because labour shortages are created in the least attractive jobs, we should agree with Castells that:

> *immigrant workers do not exist because there are 'arduous and badly paid jobs' to be done, but, rather, arduous and badly paid jobs exist because immigrant workers are present or can be sent for to do them* (Castells, 1975, p. 54, emphasis in original).

Yet if the workers who provide cheap labour are available to one group of employers – who therefore decide to create or maintain unattractive jobs – we would expect such workers to be available to others. Why should certain employers choose to employ cheap labour?

It might be thought that the employers' choice is constrained – for example, that wool textile employers did not have the resources to improve unattractive jobs or to substitute capital for labour (cf. Harris, 1980, p. 45), but in the 1950s, when Asian workers began to appear in wool textile mills, the industry was enjoying a boom period and employers would have been able to support such expenses. In the 1960s and 1970s, when product demand was less buoyant, changes in technology, hours of work and work organization demonstrated that any scarcity of funds would not prevent employers from attempting to transform the labour process. Technical change in the 1960s and 1970s also showed that new machinery *was* available (cf. Briscoe, 1971, p. 176). It is often mistakenly assumed that the technology of the industries which employ cheap labour is static. This assumption owes much to the view which equates cheap labour with 'traditional' or 'backward' industries (see, for example, Peach, 1968, p. 94) and to the promotion – for example, by Hagmann (1968) – of a policy of substituting capital export for labour import where the latter is reduced by immigration controls. Certainly the promotion of controls was implicit in Sir Keith Joseph's assertion that immigration had blocked industrial change in the UK (*Guardian* 24 January 1980).

In fact the most important limitation on the choices open to wool textile employers was provided by the history of their industry. Wool textile employers have habitually turned to cheap labour in the past, especially during crises. The industry was the first within which capitalist social relations became general and capital's relationship to labour in wool textiles has been established for many generations. In all industries the relationship between capital and labour is historical but no other industry has been established as long. The ground-rules for the employers' response to threats to its markets in the post-war period were written more than a century earlier when their predecessors, perhaps the founders of modern firms, were winning the lion's share of the international market for wool textiles. Thus the employers 'opted' for cheap labour – for example, when they refused to consider increasing wages – even where this was no longer the most profitable alternative. As Briscoe pointed out, textile employers'

> aim has *always* been to obtain the cheapest form of labour – at first children and juveniles, then women and immigrants – the price reflecting the ease with which these categories can obtain alternative employment (Briscoe, 1971, p. 174, emphasis added).

The Unit for Manpower Studies at the Department of Employment reported that employers would make work more attractive *and* would substitute capital for labour if cheap labour was unavailable. The Unit added that:

> In some instances, greater capital intensity was seen not only as a means of reducing manpower requirements but also of increasing the earnings of the remaining workers and therefore making it easier for the firm to attract and maintain labour. For example, a number of employers and industrial training boards in various branches of textiles suggested that the industry would in any event, have to become more capitally intensive if it were to meet competition from overseas producers and this would in turn make it possible to increase relative earnings. (Department of Employment, 1977, p. 88).

Nevertheless the majority of wool textile employers did not take this route, despite the exhortations of the unions and the organizations (like the training board) which serviced the industry. In consequence, they did not solve their difficulties in the product market. The nineteenth-century solution was no longer useful in the 1960s and 1970s. Indeed it might be pointed out that the difficulties of British industry as whole could be interpreted in this way. Most industries in the UK were established before their overseas competitors and it may be that the long history of British capital has imposed limitations which are largely responsible for its failure to maintain international competitiveness.[3]

If wool textile employers 'opted' for cheap labour because they mistakenly assumed on the basis of established custom and practice that this was the most profitable alternative, then it seems likely that those employers who did not 'choose' cheap labour were adopting a more profitable course of action. In fact some wool textile firms made *no* response to the post-war crisis and *these* were the least profitable companies. It would therefore be a mistake to assume that cheap labour did not produce some benefits for its employers. Most importantly, it allowed them to reap *some* of the benefits of modernization. The Unit for Manpower Studies reported that, if cheap labour were *not* available, employers would resort to:

> increased productivity not only by replacing labour with capital but also by using labour more efficiently where existing plant and machinery was retained (Department of Employment, 1977, p. 87).

In fact this was exactly what wool textile employers did when they recruited cheap labour. The transformation of the labour process was designed to increase the intensity of exploitation but, in accomplishing this, the employers made wool textile work less attractive. The modernization which did take place could not have been undertaken without access to cheap labour. In particular, the *way in which* employers dispensed with labour led to a deterioration in the jobs occupied by the remaining workers. Far from representing an alternative to cheap labour, reduced labour demand was, *in this case*, the *cause* of problems of labour supply rather than an attempt to alleviate labour shortages.

This emphasis on the relationship between modernization and the deterioration of those jobs which remain is absent from most of the established writings on the subject. It is often admitted that industrial change may be stimulated by *abundant* labour (for example, see Bourguignon *et al.*, 1977, p. 73) but this proposition makes little sense without specification of the effects of industrial change on the nature of work, since the employers':

> problem is not to increase the supply of labour but to increase the supply of labour willing to be employed in certain (usually low grade) occupations (Paine, 1974, p. 10)

In wool textiles, 'low grade occupations' were created in the transformation of the labour process which occurred throughout the 1960s and 1970s. Modernization depended on the ease with which workers could be found to fill the unattractive jobs which it created. In other words, certain types of industrial change require the use of *cheap* labour.

DISCRIMINATION

It is, however, clear that industrial change and cheap labour are not always related in this way and we will return to their relationship later. For the moment we must make sure we understand why the workers who provided cheap labour were willing to go along with the deterioration which modernization implied. Some writers, particularly those who have cited evidence interpreted by Butterworth (1964; 1967) and Cohen and

Jenner (1968) from the wool textile industry, have argued that change in the labour process may produce jobs which are *suitable* for cheap labour, first, because of the characteristics of the workers who sell their labour cheaply. Cohen and Jenner pointed to the Asians' lack of custom and practice which might have enabled them to resist change (Cohen and Jenner, 1968, pp. 55–6). Second, a particular group of workers might be suitable because the jobs which were created where the labour process was transformed were fitting to workers with few skills (see for example, Ward, 1975, pp. 29–30). Neither of these arguments is convincing. Indeed they seem to have originated with the employers of cheap labour and can be seen as attempts to justify hiring workers who are assumed to be inferior. In fact the only evidence of the Asian's assumed lack of resistance to change is their refusal to reject the jobs which constitute cheap labour. Similarly they were not particularly *suited* to the de-skilled jobs created in wool textiles but rather unable to reject them. Thus the workers who provided cheap labour went along with modernization because they had no alternative. They were denied access to other sources of employment because most employers discriminated against Asian applicants. Since discrimination in other areas of employment forced Asians to sell their labour cheaply, wool textile employers benefitted from the existence of discrimination. The 'disadvantaged' position of Asian workers produced advantages for their employers.

This furnishes yet another corrective to the view that industrial change encourages the elimination of discrimination,[4] nevertheless some difficulties remain. In large part these problems stem from confusions over the nature of discrimination. Bonacich, for example, denied that employers want to discriminate and gave credence to the employers' claim that they are forced by their employees to discriminate. She is sure that all employers want to use the cheapest labour, regardless of colour, but adds that most incur costs arising from white worker resistance when they hire black workers (for example, see Bonacich, 1976, p. 44). Thus cheap labour will only be used where white worker resistance is minimal.

Certainly there was no vociferous resistance from white workers employed in semi-skilled wool textile jobs and it was to these jobs that Asians were recruited. Furthermore, Asians were not hired where resistance was vocal and organized, for example, in wool-sorting and in skilled occupations in dyeing and finishing. However, even if we admit of a correlation between white-worker resistance and employers' discrimination against black applicants, it does not follow that the former causes the latter, indeed both phenomena can be explained in the same way. Black workers suffer discrimination in *more attractive* jobs and it is here that white-worker resistance is strongest. Resistance is manifested where jobs are thought to be worth holding onto, that is, where employers can, in any case, discriminate against black applicants since this does not leave them short of labour. Where jobs are relatively *unattractive*, resistance is expressed by quitting: the incumbents simply leave for better jobs elsewhere. When white workers leave – because they are not prepared to put up with unattractive jobs – employers are not able to discriminate unless they wish to create a labour shortage. In other words the need for cheap labour and pressure for discrimination against blacks from white employees do not coincide.

Bonacich's explanation of the relationship between cheap labour and discrimination must be rejected because her initial assumption that employers are 'colour blind' is wrong. It makes much more sense to assume that employers want to discriminate and will satisfy this need *as long as this does not involve extra costs*. Thus those employers who do hire blacks consider that discrimination would involve costs in the form of labour shortages or wage increases and other expensive alternatives to cheap labour. Their 'choice' of cheap labour makes it impossible for them to find labour while discriminating.

Discrimination has been used in only one sense in this chapter; to refer to those occasions on which employers exclude black applicants from employment. Some writers have given a different meaning to the term in an effort to make sense of the relationship between discrimination and cheap labour. Thus it is suggested that employers discriminate *between* those blacks and whites workers they have *already* hired in setting wages and work rates. This notion of discrimination is not applicable in UK wool textiles.

It has been proved beyond doubt that black workers are likely to receive lower wages and to work harder than most white workers and there can really be no objection to the statement that blacks suffer 'super exploitation' (cf. Nikolinakos, 1973, pp. 371–2; Roemer, 1978, *passim*). There is no need, however, to explain the 'super exploitation' of black workers by assuming that employers *discriminate between* black and white employees. It is unnecessary to claim that employers 'set' a higher level of exploitation in some jobs because they are performed by blacks. Nor is it necessary to claim that employers give particular jobs to blacks because they know that, once at work, they will be able to extract more surplus value from the labour of these workers. Rather, 'super exploitation' is guaranteed when employers find workers who are willing to perform the jobs which constitute cheap labour.

Once we have dismissed alternative interpretations of discrimination, the relationship between discrimination and cheap labour can be understood. The employment distribution of black workers results from employers' efforts to discriminate against black applicants combined with the inability of *some* employers to exclude blacks. Black workers find that discrimination leaves them no alternative but to sell their labour to those employers who cannot recruit white workers. The jobs which blacks do are peculiar in that their pay seems to be unrelated to the level of labour demand in these occupations. Excess demand is not translated into higher pay. Thus black workers sell their labour as if the labour market did not exist; indeed it does not exist for black workers since they suffer discrimination. There is therefore an excess supply of black workers for the unattractive jobs. In borderline cases, where employers have not yet abandoned attempts to discriminate, this produces the apparent paradox of vacancies and high labour turnover while (black) labour is abundant.

At the beginning of this chapter it was stated that cheap labour was performed by workers who took the jobs which others had rejected. Any group of workers who perform cheap labour must therefore be excluded from alternative employment. By definition, the jobs which constitute cheap labour can only be attractive to those without access to alternatives. There may be any number of reasons for this exclusion. For example, it may be illegal to employ the workers who perform cheap labour in any other kind of work, but in the case we have been considering, exclusion results from racial discrimination.

In spite of the fact that they would prefer to employ only white workers, some employers benefit from employing blacks. Employers do not conspire to make black workers sell their labour cheaply. The employers of cheap labour are not responsible for the exclusion of black workers elsewhere, and it is this which makes blacks available as cheap labour. Furthermore, discrimination does not increase the profitability of those employers who totally exclude black workers. Nevertheless, although the 'disadvantaged' position of the Asians does not result simply from capital's desire to exploit labour, black workers are only employed at all because they sell their labour cheaply. In this sense the employment distribution of black workers *is* dependent on the creation of advantages for employers, but this does not explain how the distribution comes into being. It results, rather, from the accommodation of discrimination in capitalist relations of production.

THE LABOUR MARKET AND THE LABOUR PROCESS

We can now return to the relationship between cheap labour and modernization. Cheap labour will be recruited with change in the labour process where this change creates unattractive jobs, but cheap labour may also be recruited where no change has taken place in the labour process. In wool textiles in the 1950s, change in the labour *market* seems to have been the predominant factor affecting the number of unattractive jobs. At least until 1958, cheap labour was recruited without noticeable change in the labour *process*. Some jobs became undesireable because their occupants found that better jobs were available elsewhere – that is, labour *market* conditions changed. Employers chose not to improve these jobs because they found they could recruit from alternative sources of labour. This was the case in wool-combing and, periodically in later years, in other sections as well.

By 1964, the employers' organizations were deeply concerned with problems of labour supply: the first industrial training board in the UK was created out of the industry's own recruitment and training organization and the board's first reports emphasized the large number of vacancies in the industry (Wool ITB, 1966, p. 10). Nevertheless, change in the labour process was also occurring, *and in a way which actually made problems of labour supply more acute.*

Change in the labour process is not a result of the technical requirements of production (Castells, 1975, p. 44) but a matter of cash flow, competition, the size of the market and so on, as well as technology. The calculation of the most profitable way in which to change the labour process may not involve pressure from the labour market but it can do so (in the form of labour shortages or rising labour costs). Nevertheless, if, after considering all the available labour supply, employers decide the profitable alternative is to create jobs which will probably be unattractive to the majority of workers *but will nevertheless be filled*, they will take it. Thus wool textile employers degraded labour in the 1960s in the knowledge that these jobs would be filled, as had increasingly unattractive jobs in the 1950s, no matter that the workers who filled them would be Asians. They could therefore ignore the growth of attractive alternatives in the labour market. In the middle 1970s this pattern was repeated in respect of skilled jobs. Better opportunities were available for skilled workers and wool textiles suffered selective labour shortages as a result, but instead of making those jobs more attractive wool textile employers degraded them still further. The semi-skilled jobs for which there was no shortage of labour, on the other hand, were *eliminated*!

Even if black workers are available, unattractive jobs may disappear and employers will have more opportunity to discriminate, thus the percentage of Asian workers in wool textiles began to fall in the late 1970s. Unattractive jobs can be eliminated by structural change or by the loss of alternative opportunities elsewhere in the labour market, but in wool textiles unattractive jobs have also been eliminated by change in the labour process. The gap between wool textile work and its alternatives has been too wide to be affected by all but the most severe rise in unemployment and fall in vacancies. As the recession began, white workers found they had fewer alternatives to unattractive jobs, but these jobs had themselves been casualties of the recession and some undesirable jobs were completely eliminated. Employers knew that suitable recruits (black or white) would be available to take on the remaining or replacement jobs but they now found they could afford to discriminate. They did not change the labour process in order to change the composition of the labour force. Employers might have expected to be short of white labour but nevertheless further degraded *skilled* jobs. Thus more jobs would have been put in the borderline category where employers would have difficulty in discriminating against black workers.

To summarize, the desirability of all jobs will be affected by changes in the labour process and the labour market but the former seems to predominate. It is not simply that the labour process can be changed independently of conditions in the labour market. In fact it should be explained that conditions in the labour market are dependent on change in the labour process. Although there was no premeditation of its effects, change in the labour process in wool textiles in the early 1960s reduced the labour force so that numbers of Asian workers were displaced from wool-combing and made available for other industries and wool textile sections. In the next decade redundant workers provided a pool of ready trained labour. These were mostly Asians since white workers were more likely to leave the industry permanently, perhaps after a number of redundancies, because they could find better alternative jobs (the same was true of skilled white workers). However, labour supply was affected by other factors than redundancy: wool textile employers reduced training, and hence *effective* labour supply, to a minimum. They therefore increased their demand for trained workers.

It seems that employers will put their requirements of the labour process above any consideration of labour market conditions, at least in so far as these conditions affect their ability to discriminate. This led to dissatisfaction amongst junior managers in wool textile mills. They wished that senior managers and employers would put 'racial' considerations before production and profit. It has been a constant theme of the discussion of the interaction between the labour process and the labour market that change in either can reduce or increase the employers' opportunities for discrimination *but* that employers' decisions on change in the labour process take the labour market into account only to the extent that it is assumed that workers will be available, even if they have to be imported, to satisfy labour requirements. They do not take into account whether they will thereby be creating relatively unattractive jobs. All employers would prefer to remain profitable *and* discriminate but the former undoubtedly takes precedence.

In the 1950s wool textile employers may not have known that their refusal to respond to changed labour market conditions would force them to hire black workers. They may have been surprised when they found they could not discriminate (when white workers left or did not apply for work). But in the 1960s they knew a great deal more about the labour market and the jobs they were creating. Employers at least suspected they were going to have to take on black workers but they did not change the labour process in order to discriminate 'in advance' because this would override their primary motive, profit-making. Employers may be aware of the effects of planned labour process change on the composition of the labour force but they do not take these effects into account. In the later 1970s, as in the 1950s, employers may not have had all the information which would allow them to anticipate changes in their labour force. They may not have realized the potential fall in alternative job opportunities in the 1970s and so may have been pleasantly surprised when white people 'returned' to wool textiles – in fact, this means only that the net decline for white workers was less than the net decline in the numbers of black workers – and that they now had an opportunity to discriminate against blacks. Nevertheless, even if this had been anticipated it would not have been taken into account in decisions on the labour process.

RISING UNEMPLOYMENT

Unemployment in Bradford rose for quite some time without wool textile jobs becoming noticeably more attractive to the majority of the population. This apparent paradox has been noted in other industries (for example, see Wright, 1968, p. 213) and in regard to the UK economy as a whole (Bohning, 1972, p. 36). Harris concluded that, 'the demand for cheap labour does not disappear in slump. On the contrary, it can increase' (Harris, 1980, p. 5) and Castells pointed out that, in the UK, permanent settlement of migrants has coincided with *increased* unemployment and increased emigration (Castells, 1975, p. 44; see also Shanin, 1978, p. 284).

Some writers attempt to solve this problem by proposing that the labour market is 'segmented'. Since it is difficult for workers to transfer from one market to the other, cheap labour can go straight into employment in the 'secondary sector' while other workers are unemployed in the 'primary sector' (cf. Tabb, 1970, p. 110), but segmented labour market theory explains the existence of separate labour markets in terms of the culture of the workforce and the worker characteristics required by employers. It recalls the argument developed by Cohen and Jenner and criticized in the foregoing discussion of discrimination. Other writers have attempted to explain the paradox in terms of Marx's theory of the reserve army of labour (see, for example, Marshall, 1973, p. 17).

It has been suggested that some groups of workers may have a smaller reserve army, thus a given level of (national) unemployment will be less likely to make some workers accept unattractive jobs than others (cf. Friedman, 1978, pp. 113, 270; see also Beechey, 1978, *passim*). There is some doubt as to whether the reserve army of labour can be differentiated in this way (Anthias, 1980, p. 53) and in any event this explanation begs the question: why *should* some groups of workers have a larger reserve army? The answer is, at least in the case we have been studying, that they suffer *discrimination* and are excluded from most jobs. The existence of discrimination also explains why black workers may actually suffer *less* unemployment – as they did in some years in the 1960s – and yet still find unattractive jobs acceptable. While unemployed whites might expect to find better jobs (than textiles, for example) in time, blacks did not have such expectations. Nevertheless, unemployment amongst blacks began to rise – and at a greater rate than all unemployment – in the 1970s.

Employers are more likely to have unattractive jobs – and therefore to employ cheap labour – when their industry is undergoing change, but employers may also be more likely to *dispense* with cheap labour when industrial change occurs. The outcome of such change is dependent on the interaction of labour process and labour market. In any event, their location in those parts of the labour process most subject to transformation makes the workers who perform cheap labour especially vulnerable to change.[5] First, part of the reason for their jobs being unattractive to other workers may be that they are insecure (cf. Anthias, 1980, p. 53). Second, the very fact that cheap labour may allow industrial change to proceed may make it vulnerable. Since the organization of work structures labour demand, increased exploitation may lead to rising unemployment. In the 1970s this meant that Asians in employment worked harder while the numbers of Asians employed in wool textiles fell. By the end of the decade, however, the *proportion* of Asians began to fall, that is the level of exploitation of *white* workers was increasing. In part this was accomplished through de-skilling. As in other industries, skilled workers suffered de-skilling while the less skilled (in this case, black) workers lost their jobs. In sum, rising unemployment amongst black workers in Bradford was by no means contingent on the appearance of a general recession.

Nevertheless, it may be that in the 1980s unemployment had reached the level at which those workers who did not suffer discrimination were prepared to take low-grade jobs in the wool textile industry. It is likely that unemployment amongst white workers had risen to a level at which these jobs had ceased to be unattractive to may workers. The recession had put them in the same position that blacks had occupied in earlier years: they had no alternative sources of employment. In this event, wool textile jobs ceased, by definition, to require cheap labour and black workers were no longer needed. While we are unable to monitor this trend in published statistics we can assume that it will continue throughout the remaining life of wool textiles as a significant employer in Bradford and the UK.

CONCLUSIONS

The jobs which constitute cheap labour exist because black workers are there, or can be imported, to do them. Employers want to discriminate against black applicants but for some employers the cost of excluding black workers is too much to bear. They would be forced to make employment in their companies more attractive – and they expect that this would decrease profits – if they were to discriminate against black workers. Nevertheless, the desire of capital to exploit labour cannot explain the advantages (to employers) which arise from the 'disadvantaged' position of black workers. Blacks are made available as cheap labour by the prior existence of racial categorization and discrimination. The roots of discrimination cannot be found in the capitalist labour process.

Since we know that racial discrimination arises independently of any advantages which might accrue to employers, it is no surprise that discrimination persists even after it has ceased to be 'useful' in this way. Discrimination does not produce advantages for those employers who practise it.

Similarly, discrimination does not increase profits for those employers who *begin* to practise it when unemployment rises. Discrimination continues even though it is no longer required in order to allow some employers to fill unattractive jobs. Blacks remain in a 'disadvantaged' position even where this no longer produces advantages for employers. Thus a disproportionately large number of blacks may suffer unemployment even though there are sufficient unemployed white workers to satisfy *all* employers' needs (without the persistence of discrimination). Recession does not lead to the elimination of discrimination, in fact rising unemployment gives employers the opportunity to exclude black workers from an even wider range of jobs. It seems that with mass unemployment blacks increasingly find that they are denied acess to *any* jobs, even the most menial.

NOTES

1. I would like to thank the editors of this volume and Professor Michael Banton for their helpful comments on earlier drafts of this paper. However, the responsibility for any errors or ommissions rests with the author. The paper represents an amended version of a chapter in the author's *Cheap Labour and Racial Discrimination*, published by Gower Press, 1984.
2. Fevre, R. W. 1984.
3. I am indebted to Huw Beynon for this insight.
4. This view stems from the assumption that advanced capitalism is incompatible with ascription. This assumption has received substantial criticism elsewhere, an early example being given by Wolpe (1970) especially p. 152).
5. This was also true of the white women workers who preceded the Asians in wool textile jobs although the women found more attractive alternatives to wool textile work.

REFERENCES

Anthias, F. (1980) 'Women and the Reserve Army of Labour: a Critique of Veronica Beechey', in *Capital and Class*, X (Spring) pp. 50–63.
Beechey, V. (1978) 'Women and Production: a Critical Analysis of Some Sociological Theories of Women's Work' in Kuhn, A. and Wolpe, A. (eds) *Feminism and Materialism* (London: Routledge & Kegan Paul).

Blauner, R. (1972) *Racial oppression in America*, (New York: Harper & Row).

Blumer, H. (1965) 'Industrialisation and Race Relations' in Hunter, G. (ed.) *Industrialisation and Race Relations* (Oxford: Oxford University Press for the Institute of Race Relations).

Bohning, W. R. (1972) *The Migration of Workers in the UK and the European Community* (Oxford: Oxford University Press for the Institute of Race Relations).

Bohning, W. R. and Maillat, D. (1974) *Effects of the Employment of Foreign Workers*, (Paris: Organization for Economic Co-operation and Development).

Bonacich, E. (n.d.) *US Capitalism and Korean Immigrant Small Business*, University of California Riverside, Mimeo.

Bonacich, E. (1976) 'Advanced Capitalism and Black/White Race Relations in the United States: a Split Labour Market Interpretation', in *American Sociological Review*, 41/ (February) pp. 34–51.

Bourguignon, F., *et al*, (1977) *International Labour Migrations and Economic Choices, the European Case* (Paris: Organization for Economic Co-operation and Development).

Briscoe, L. (1971) *The Textile and Clothing Industries of the United Kingdom*, (Manchester: Manchester University Press).

Burawoy, M. (1976) 'The Functions and Reproduction of Migrant Labour: Comparative Material from South Africa and US', in *American Journal of Sociology*, 81(5) (March) pp. 1050–87.

Butterworth, E. (1964) 'Aspects of Race Relations in Bradford', in *Race*, 6 (October) pp. 129–41.

Butterworth, E. (ed.) (1967) *Immigrants in West Yorkshire: Social Conditions and the Lives of Pakistanis, Indians and West Indians* (London: Institute of Race Relations) Special Series.

Castells, M. (1975) 'Immigrant Workers and Class Struggle in Advanced Capitalism', in *Politics and Society*, 5(1) pp. 33–66.

Castles, S. and Kosack, G. (1973) *Immigrant Workers and Class Struggle in Advanced Capitalism* (London: Oxford University Press and the Institute of Race Relations).

Cohen, B. G. and Jenner, P. J. (1968) 'The Employment of Immigrants: A Case Study within the Wool Industry', in *Race*, X(1) pp. 41–56.

Collard, D. (1970) 'Immigration and Discrimination: Some Economic Aspects', in Wilson, C. (ed.) *Economic Issues in Immigration* (London: Institute of Economic Affairs).

Community Development Project (CDP) (1977) *The Costs of Industrial Change* (London: CDP).

Corrigan, P. R. D. C. 'Feudal Relics or Capitalist Monuments', in *Sociology*, II, pp. 435–63.

Counter Information Services (CIS) (n.d.) *Racism – Who Profits* (CIS).

Department of Employment (1977) *Unit for Manpower Studies Project Report: the Role of Immigrants in the Labour Market* (London: DE,).

Fevre, R. W. (1984) *Cheap Labour and Racial Discrimination* (Aldershot: Gower).

Franklin, R. S. and Resnick, S. (1973) *The Political Economy of Racism*, (New York: Holt, Rinehart & Winston).

174   *Racism and Cheap Labour in UK Wool Textiles*

Freeman, M. D. A. and Spencer, S. (1979) 'Immigration Control, Black Workers and the Economy', in *British Journal of Law and Society*, 6(1) pp. 1–29.

Friedman, A. (1978) *Industry and Labour* (London: Macmillan).

Hagmann, H. M. (1968) 'Capital to Men or Men to Capital', in *Migration Today*, pp. 5–11.

Hallet, G. (1970) 'The Political Economy of Immigration Control', in Wilson, C. (ed.) *Economic Issues in Immigration* (London: Institute of Economic Affairs).

Harris, N. (1980) 'The New Untouchables: the International Migration of Labour', in *International Socialism*, 2(8) pp. 37–63.

Hepple, B. (1970) *Race, Jobs and the Law in Britain* (Harmondsworth: Penguin).

Kennedy-Brenner, C. (1979) *Foreign Workers and Immigration Policy*, (Paris: Development Centre of the Organisation for Economic Co-operation and Development).

Kindleberger, C. P. (1965) 'Mass Migration, Then and Now', in *Foreign Affairs*, 43(4) (July).

Lewis, W. A. (1954) *Economic Development with Unlimited Supplies of Labour* (Manchester: The Manchester School of Economics and Statistics).

Marshall, A. (1973) *The Import of Labour* (Rotterdam: Rotterdam University Press).

Nikolinakos, M. (1973) 'Notes on an Economic Theory of Racism', in *Race*, XIV(4) (April).

Paine, S. (1974) *Exporting Workers: the Turkish Case* (Cambridge: Cambridge University Press).

Peach, C. (1968) *West Indian Migration to Britain* (Oxford: Oxford University Press for the Institute of Race Relations).

Preston, A. (1969) 'Effects on the Economy', in Rose, E. J. B. (ed.) *Colour and Citizenship* (Oxford: Oxford University Press for the Institute of Race Relations).

Roemer, J. E. (1978) 'Differentially Exploited Labour: a Marxian Theory of Discrimination', in *Review of Radical Political Economics*, 10(2) pp. 43–53.

Shanin, T. (1978) 'The Peasants are Coming: Migrants who Labour, Peasants who Travel and Marxists who Write', in *Race and Class* XIX(3) (Winter).

Smith, D. J. (1976) *The Facts of Racial Disadvantage: a National Survey* (London: PEP, 1976).

Stokes, R. (1975) 'How Long is the Long Run: Race and Industrialisation', in *International Review of Community Development*, 4 (Winter) pp. 123–36.

Tabb, W. K. (1970) *Political Economy of the Black Ghetto* (New York: W. W. Norton).

Wainwright, H. (1978) 'Women and the Division of Labour', in P. Abrams (ed.) *Work, Urbanism and Inequality* (London: Weidenfeld & Nicolson).

Ward, A. (1975) 'European Capitalism's Reserve Army', in *Monthly Review* 27(6) (November) pp. 17–32.

Wilson, C. (ed.) (1970) *Economic Issues in Immigration* (London: Institute of Economic Affairs).

Wolpe, H. (1970) 'Industrialism and Race in South Africa', in S. Zubaida (ed.) *Race and Racialism* (London: Tavistock/British Sociological Association).

Wolpe, H. (1976) 'The "White Working Class" in South Africa', in *Economy and Society*, 5(2) (May).

Wool Industry Training Board (Wool ITB, later the Wool Jute and Flax Industrial Training Board) *Annual Reports* (1966–1980).

Wright, P. (1968) *The Coloured Worker in British Industry*, (Oxford: Oxford University Press for the Institute of Race Relations).

Part III
The Restructuring of Capital and the Sexual Division of Labour

Part III

8 Women Workers and Bureaucratic Control in Irish Electronics Factories

PETER MURRAY
JAMES WICKHAM

This chapter analyzes the relationships between management and employees in the Irish electronics industry. It is based on case-studies of two electronics factories, both of which are wholly-owned subsidiaries of US corporations and both of which employ predominantly female assembly workers.[1]

The first part of the chapter outlines the starting-point of our approach, the concept of 'bureaucratic control'. After a description of the case-study plants, subsequent sections examine the relationship between bureaucratic control and the labour process, the internal labour market and industrial relations. Ireland is often considered part of the 'periphery' of Europe, and women are often held to be 'peripheral' members of the workforce. Nonetheless, our argument is that the form of managerial control in these plants is 'bureaucratic control' – a form of control usually associated with male workers in primary labour markets of core economies.

BUREAUCRATIC CONTROL AND THE INTERNATIONAL DIVISION OF LABOUR

In the Irish electronics industry most workers are employed in subsidiaries of US-owned companies (Table 8.1); over half are semi-skilled assemblers (Table 8.2); nearly three quarters are

TABLE 8.1   *Electronics manufacturing plants in the Republic of Ireland: size by nationality of parent corporation*

Number of Employees	Irish	US	Other	Row Total
Less than 25	17	2	10	29
26–50	7	2	2	11
51–100	3	12	4	19
101–250	2	14	3	19
More than 251	2	9	4	15
Column Total	31	39	23	93

SOURCE   Postal survey.

TABLE 8.2   *Occupational structure of US electronics industry, Irish electronics industry, all Irish industry (various years)*

	US electronics (1980) (%)	Irish electronics (1981) (%)	All Irish industry (1976) (%)
Managers	11	6.4	6.5
Professionals	17	5.3	1.3
Administrators	na	3.9	5.2
Technicians	11	7.8	1.6
Supervisors	na	5.1	4.7
Sales	1	na	na
Clerical	12	7.5	7.7
Craft Workers	10	3.1	12.6
Apprentices	na	—	4.2
Operatives, etc.[1]	32	57.4	56.3
Labourers, etc.[2]	4	3.2	na
Total	100	99.7	100.1
N	1 572 800	11 338	220 500

[1] 'Operatives' (USA); 'Non-Craft Production Workers' (Irish electronics); Other Workers (all Irish industry)
[2] 'Labourers' (USA); 'Others' (Irish electronics)

SOURCE   US Electronics: *Global Electronics Information Newsletter*, September 1982; Irish Electronics: Postal Survey, 1981; All Irish Industry: AnCo, Research and Planning Division, *Manpower Survey 1976*.

women.[2] Yet such figures by themselves do not justify seeing the industry simply in terms of the literature on the new international division of labour (Froebel *et al.*, 1980) or on women semi-skilled assembly workers (Cavendish, 1980; Herzog, 1980; Pollert, 1981).

First, multinational production in 'peripheral' areas involves other issues than simply the 'decomposition of the labour process' to utilize low-wage areas for low-skill mass assembly. While Irish wages are certainly lower than US ones, the location in Ireland of particular operations of US multinational companies has also depended on the accessibility of the EEC market by the size and nature of the financial incentives offered by the Irish state. Most foreign-owned electronics plants in Ireland involve batch production rather than mass assembly, while the *raison d'être* of the industry is the supply of finished products to the European market, so that final-stage testing as well as assembly occurs within Ireland.

These two factors produce a skill structure which is very different from that of the offshore assembly plants of southeast Asia, where a much higher proportion of employees are female assemblers (Cogan and O'Brien, 1983; Murray and Wickham, 1983). While the Irish electronics industry has a less skilled workforce (with, in particular, a higher proportion of production workers) than the US industry, it also has a greater proportion of technical and professional workers than Irish industry as a whole (Table 8.3).

Second, not all the features of women's semi-skilled assembly work described in recent studies appear to apply to such workers in Irish electronics factories. For example, Harris (1983) characterizes the situation of women working in an Irish-owned factory in North Mayo in terms of (i) extensive piece-work combined with machine-pacing by the assembly line; (ii) close supervision by immediate supervisors who impose discipline in an often arbitrary fashion; (iii) extreme sexual segregation, so that women are concentrated in lower grades than men; (iv) a shop-floor culture which provides solidarity and informal resistance; (v) a trade union organization that is dominated by men, whose sexist behaviour ensures that most opposition to management also involves opposition to the formal trade union organization in the factory.

By contrast, in the two case-study factories, production is

batch production not mass assembly; detailed task times are not determined by work study or formal output norms; the large number of individual production lines means that there is little constant repetition of minutely detailed task sequences. Finally there is considerable variation in production volume over the year. Hence management has to put a premium on worker flexibility, responsibility and co-operativeness, and cannot rely on direct methods of control.

Clearly then there are important variations in the situation of semi-skilled women workers. Indeed, in some respects, the workers in the case study plants formed an élite within this general category. The case-study plants offer higher pay and better job security than other semi-skilled jobs open to women;[3] the firms make more use of educational qualifications and formal selection procedures to recruit their workers than do employers such as the factory in a 'traditional' sector of Irish industry described by Harris.

The most useful approach to the form of control exercised in this situation would appear to be the concept of 'bureaucratic control' (Edwards, 1979). Under bureaucratic control company rules define the duties of employees within a multiplicity of jobs, each of which in turn is divided into grades. Workers comply with company rules because of the possibility of promotion through this finely-graded job structure. Promotion procedures are highly formalized, with the criteria known to workers. As such promotion, like day-to-day supervision, appears 'objective', the result of the even-handed application of bureaucratic rules.[4] Such a system rewards the 'good worker', rather than merely the individual worker's output, and so creates an identity between the worker and the firm: 'The soulful corporation demands the worker's soul, or at least the worker's identity' (Edwards, 1979, p. 152).

According to Edwards, bureaucratic control produces the 'independent primary' labour market, within which jobs with large corporations situated at the 'core' of advanced capitalist economies are secure, relatively well-paid, and have established promotion possibilities for their male occupants. This would appear to make the concept irrelevant for the analysis of sexually and spatially 'peripheral' female Irish assembly workers. However, as we shall now argue, women semi-skilled workers can remain in a different segment of the labour market from men, but nonetheless be subjected to a form of control that in Edwards' schema is only meaningfully associated with the 'primary' labour market.

THE PLANTS

The case-study plants are referred to throughout the paper by the pseudonyms 'Hightech' and 'Miltech'. Hightech is owned by one of the new wave of electronics corporations which have emerged on the US west coast. Although in the USA it comprises only two factories with little over a thousand employees, it can claim to be one of the largest world manufacturers of its main product. By contrast, Miltech is part of a much older and larger corporation, for which electronics is only a part of its total manufacturing operations.

Hightech's Irish plant is on a new industrial estate in Dublin and is mainly involved in the assembly and final testing of the firm's chief product, a minicomputer, for the European Original Equipment Manufacturer (OEM) market. The Miltech plant is in Ireland's mid-west region near Shannon Airport. It assembles printed circuit boards for military contractors which are flown back to the USA for testing according to US military specifications (MILSPEC). Both plants are purely manufacturing plants with no current involvement in either product design or development.[5] In both, manufacturing operations had started just over two years before our research in the plant began, by which time each was employing about 125 employees.

As appears to be the case in most foreign-owned manufacturing plants in Ireland, each plant has a closed-shop agreement for its hourly-paid workers with the Irish Transport and General Workers' Union (ITGWU) – the largest union in the Republic. In neither case is there any union representation or collective bargaining for any of the salaried grades not covered by the agreement with the ITGWU. In both factories the unionized grades make up about 45 per cent of the total workforce excluding senior management, and include assemblers, quality control inspectors, storekeepers and ancillary workers.

In both firms there is a clear sexual hierarchy. Women are concentrated in the assembly and clerical grades, while nearly all managers, professionals and technical workers are male. The greater number of intermediary grades at Hightech means that its workforce is 60 per cent male, while at Miltech the proportion is only 40 per cent. The differences in workforce structure and in the union agreements in the two factories mean that, although in both women are 'over-represented' in union membership, at Hightech they are a minority of the union membership, whereas at Miltech they form a 90 per cent majority.

In both plants the manufacturing process begins with the preparation of components which are then inserted onto print-ed circuit boards. These are then passed through an automatic soldering machine. The next stage is 'touch-up', where ma-chine-soldering faults are removed and any components which cannot be machine-soldered are soldered by hand. The final assembly stage is rework, where faults subsequently discovered by quality-control inspection (visual quality-control inspections take place after each stage of assembly) or test procedures are removed. At Miltech the boards are then flown back to the USA to be tested, but at Hightech the assembled boards are then tested automatically to identify mechanical faults arising from incorrect assembly. They are subsequently tested by technicians using diagnostic programs to identify electronic system faults, and then placed in an environmental test cham-ber. Finally the boards are configured, mounted in chassis, equipped with power supply and consoles, tested again and given a final quality-control inspection before being shipped to customers.

BUREAUCRATIC CONTROL AND THE LABOUR PROCESS

According to Edwards, control over the labour process necess-arily has three elements: direction, discipline and evaluation. Whereas in earlier forms of control only the first is formalized, in bureaucratic control all three functions are carried out according to explicit rules. This section shows how this occurs in the case-study plants, and in particular how indirect control through the evaluation of workers' performance takes priority over more direct control through discipline. While the overall form of control is thus clearly 'bureaucratic', we also suggest that this form of control can create problems for management which were not noticed by Edwards.

In both plants the work of supervision is divided among different departments. Production supervisors direct and discipline production workers, whose performance is evaluated by the test and above all the quality-control departments. The sheer extent of supervisory labour (as Table 8.4 shows, between a quarter and a third of all *hourly-paid* employees have some supervisory function) creates the hierarchical differentiation of posts necessary for the operation of an internal labour market. While Edwards and other radical accounts of internal labour markets (for example, Stone, 1974) have suggested that internal labour markets stem from an essentially arbitrary hierarchy of jobs, in both plants the division of supervisory labour is built into the sequential organization of the production process. Such jobs, and the internal labour market to

TABLE 8.3   *Hourly-paid grades by sex*

	Male	Female
Hightech		
General worker	1	—
Electronic assembly	5	12
Electro-mechanical assembly	3	—
Rework	1	4
Stores	6	—
Quality control in process	1	3
Test operative	10	—
Quality control receiving and final	2	1
	29	20
Miltech (50% sample)		
Assembly	2	14
Line leader	—	1
Group leader	—	1
Stores	1	—
Tester	1	—
Quality control	—	3
	4	19

SOURCE   Workforce surveys.

which they give rise, thus appear not as an arbitrary management creation, but as the necessary result of the organization of production, and the hierarchy which they involve can appear as a hierarchy of merit.

As boards progress through the production process they pass through a series of inspections and tests. These yield statistics which are collated by the Quality-control department to provide management with its principal indices for the assessment of current manufacturing performance. Control over production workers thus stems initially from the plethora of inspectors and testers who are assessing output according to 'technical' criteria, and not from those charged with maintaining discipline itself:

> We'd have seen the work going to inspection and if it's not up to scratch then we generate what's called a Corrective Action Notice – the following person has been causing problems in all these areas, what are you [the production supervisors] going to do about it? (Miltech quality-control supervisor).

Adequate performance is clearly specified by an elaborate system of formal rules, whether of a technical (test) or procedural quality-control kind. Equally, infringement of the rules has to be formally documented, in particular by the quality-control inspectors.

> There's constant bickering and everything [with the production department] but if you show them the line in the book and say 'It's not me it's coming from, it's coming from page ten, process spec so and so', they can't argue with the book. It's like going into a court case. You have to have documented evidence (Miltech quality-control supervisor).

In this bureaucratic control sytem, the greater the division of assembly labour, the more loosely are individuals controlled. At Miltech the high MILSPEC quality standards mean work has been organized so that each job comes onto the shop-floor in kits which contain printed circuit boards together with all the necessary parts and drawings needed for their assembly. One operator is responsible for all manual work on the batch of boards contained in the kit:

> The individuals are isolated you see. The in-process inspectors basically inspect everything that's built and they know of course the particular operator that's built it so there's no way that the operator can escape. It's an excellent control mechanism (Miltech Training Officer).

By contrast in Hightech's 'commercial' environment assembly work is decomposed: different workers are assigned to assembly, touch-up and rework areas and component insertion is organized on a line basis. In such a situation quality-control statistics can only identify collective responsibility for unacceptable work. The contrast is confirmed by Miltech's experience with a minicomputer for the European commercial market which is no longer manufactured in the plant:

> I'm glad that's gone. Everybody was handling all the boards and nobody knew who'd done anything. At the end of the day they didn't care because nobody had to answer, you see, they answered as a group. But when you're talking to one person in particular about their boards they get embarrassed and they take more care (Miltech Production Supervisor).

Testing and inspection necessarily locate faults after they have been created (and the later they are located, the more expensive they are to rectify). Consequently, management also undertakes 'communication initiatives' to foster the 'right attitude' on the shop-floor. Particular quality-control statistics are highlighted and targets set for their immediate improvement. Regular 'pep talks' and slide-shows on good workmanship are given by management and supervisors. A group of assemblers is selected and their work intensively reviewed and discussed over several weeks; the members of the group are then dispersed around the plant in the hope that their increased awareness will filter through to their colleagues. Senior assembler categories ('lead hands' or 'line leaders') are created and charged, among other things, with the encouragement of self-inspection in their area, and finally 'quality circles' are set up.

However, the very complexity of overall supervision creates its own problems. The different departments have their own interests which are not easily woven together by the seamless web of management communication. As Hightech's Quality-control Manager ruefully noted:

> We have get-together and talks on what's going on and try to get them [the quality-control inspectors] to start trying to change attitudes. The communications side of it is our biggest stumbling block and it's traditional that Quality Control have always been hated by Production because they think they're there to pick holes in their work.

The interest of the Quality-control department in quality conflicts with that of production in quantity. Rigorous quality-control inspection reduces output by increasing rework time and delays shipments. Thus Hightech's Quality Control Manager wished to extend from one to three days the period which boards spent in the 'burn-in' test to increase their reliability, but found himself under great pressure from Production to relax this so that shipments could be met. Similarly, Miltech's production supervisors also found it necessary continually to question quality-control decisions:

> We do it very often, if we can, just to let them know that we're watching what they're writing up you know, because you have to because they get carried away (Miltech Production Supervisor).

And production supervisors are not above maintaining their authority and the morale of 'their' workers by occasionally 'having a go' at the Quality Control Department.

For the assemblers, such contradictory demands undermine the impersonal authority of production rules and legitimize the informal sanctioning of over-zealous quality-control inspectors. While management can present problems as failures in 'communication' between different *functions*, its own communication initiatives can end up emphasizing and destabilizing the factual *authority* structure. Responding to bad quality-control figures from the assembly area, Hightech's Production Manager launched what he termed 'a communications programme':

> I decided I would go in there [the assembly area] with an

engineer and actually work in the area, sit down with the people, find out what the problems were, why the hell the product was so slow.

While the quality acceptance rate rose, the production super-visor however 'became very depressed, very defensive, and I had all sorts of problems' (Production Manager). Indeed, she ended up on extended sick leave and in her (temporary) absence the immediate organization of the lines was handled by the lead hands with an improvement in output and quality. Despite strong criticism from his fellow-managers for under-mining his supervisor's authority, the Production Manager himself doubted whether supervisors had any useful function.

This episode illustrates the relatively peripheral role of the supervisor and of immediate discipline within bureaucratic control. However, as the next section shows, supervisors are central to the internal labour market through which the 'good worker' can expect to be promoted. Thus short-term improve-ments in quality-consciousness can be counter-productive if the longer-term reward structure is jeopardized. Such tensions can hardly be termed 'resistance', but they do indicate how, like many other writers in the 'labour process' tradition, Edwards failed to recognize conflicts *within management*. These ensure that bureaucratic control can never be completely accepted by workers as a unitary system of impersonal and objective rules.

BUREAUCRATIC CONTROL AND THE INTERNAL LABOUR MARKET

According to Edwards, workers comply with bureaucratic control because it promises promotion through the finely-graded hierarchy of jobs. However, this internal labour market must also be insulated from the wider labour market by the selection of 'suitable' workers, who – once within the firm – must somehow develop the necessary ideology so that they actually *want* promotion.

In both plants the most important screening device is formal industrial training. At Miltech all applicants for assembly posts have to attend a two-week training school taught by company instructors. Here work-tests are set and examined and those who fail (estimated to be about one third at the time of our fieldwork) are let go at the end of the training period. Those who pass are awarded a soldering 'certificate' and required to undergo recertification every eighteen months.

This training was experienced by Miltech assemblers as directly relevant to the work they performed.[6] However, job applicants are screened not just for 'technical' competence, but also for 'character':

> They try to be very selective about the people they pick. There's a fine bunch of people working here, they're nice and refined and you don't have any hassles. We try and keep it that way – that's why it's hard to get in here (Miltech Production Supervisor).

Hightech provides virtually no formal training. However, over a third of the assemblers have attended a six-week course in electronics assembly run by AnCO (the Irish Industrial Training Authority) and, in all, three-quarters have had some form of training since leaving full-time education. The great majority of those with training considered that such qualifications had been important in *acquiring* their jobs. A much smaller proportion considered that it helped them to *do* their job – this applied as much to those who had done electronics assembly as to those with apparently irrelevant secretarial or nursing qualifications. Nearly all assemblers had either been placed in their jobs by the training authority at the end of their electronics courses, or had gained them by being spoken for by friends or relatives already working in the factory. Thus, while training may not provide skills used *in* work, it is a crucial mode of access *to* work.

Assembly jobs at Hightech are designed to require as little skill as possible, but the firm attempts to recruit people with above-average educational qualifications. Whereas of all 1980 school-leavers who were employed in skilled or semi-skilled work in 1981 only 4 per cent of girls and 30 per cent of boys had passed the Leaving Certificate (National Manpower Service, 1982),[7] at Hightech the proportions among the young assemblers were 21 per cent and 42 per cent respectively:

I try to employ somebody who is what I call reasonably

intelligent. You might say more intelligent than necessary. I do like to employ people in the assembly area just putting ICs into boards who have Leaving Certificate. It means they have a potential to develop within the company and I can probably get more mileage out of them by allowing them to progress – let them channel their way through a career path (Hightech Production Manager).

In both factories management exercises such selectivity because of its need for worker co-operation and self-inspection. But what of the other side of the bureaucratic control 'bargain' – the career-mobility incentive?

Batch production, particularly where, as at Hightech, it incorporates final-product testing, increases the proportion of administrative, technical and clerical personnel within the workforce. Despite the barrier of educational requirements, some of these positions, particularly the lower ones, are open to entry from the shop-floor. In addition, in start-up situations an entirely new workforce is being recruited and a complete hierarchy of jobs is created *ex nihilo* in a relatively short space of time. Where (as in both factories) management gives priority to filling new positions and vacancies by internal promotion, this creates a 'hothouse' internal labour market.

Hardly surprisingly therefore, in both factories one third of hourly-paid workers reported having been promoted from the basic assembly grade (Table 8.4). There was also noticeable promotion from hourly-paid to 'staff' grades at both Hightech and Miltech. In both plants two mobility routes exist across this divide: (i) into area supervisor jobs quality-control supervisor, production supervisor, training instructor) or (ii) into junior materials management and production control jobs (expeditor, buyer, stock control clerk). Within the hourly grades there is a sexual hierarchy, with men overrepresented in the higher posts (Table 8.3 above). Women are promoted into direct production-supervision jobs – line-leader, group leader, quality-control inspector, supervisor. As such they are restricted to jobs where, as has traditionally been the case, they are supervising other women. Men tend to move along one of two routes, each of which can lead rather further. Some enter junior materials and production management via storekeeping. Here opportunities for promotion off the shop-floor without formal education are

TABLE 8.4   *Hourly-paid workers reporting experience of promotion*

Present Post	Hightech	Miltech
Reworker	4	na
Lead hand/line leader	3	1
Group leader	na	1
Storekeeper	—	1
Quality-control inspector	4	3
Test operative/tester	5	1
Total promoted	16	7
Total hourly-paid	49	23

Hightech figures are based on complete coverage of all hourly-paid workers; Miltech figures are a 50% sample.

SOURCE   Workforce surveys.

greatest. Others study part-time and enter lower-level testing jobs, which they see as the way to a full technician's qualification (Murray and Wickham, 1983).

However, for *some* women assemblers promotion was discredited by the cul-de-sac jobs it led to; for *some* the quasi-supervisory work it involved was not worth the extra 'hassle':

[In quality control] you're responsible for the work that goes out, it's your stamp that's on it . . . Once you've got there that's full stop. If you stayed possibly you could eventually get Line Leader maybe and possibly Supervisor if they expanded but that's about it . . . Quality Control is about ten pounds [a week] extra (Miltech assembler).

Yet a majority of women assemblers in both plants expected to be working in the electronics industry in three years' time, and of those who expected to stay with their respective employers, about half expected to be promoted during this period. Despite such relatively high identification with particular firms, many women were clearly leaving their jobs when they had their first or in particular their second child.[8] Paradoxically, this turnover enables bureaucratic control to work more effectively, for it creates flexibility in the internal labour market after the initial start-up period. As a result the 'hot house' internal labour market is not as transitory as it first appears. In addition, the commitment to their work which is demanded of assemblers hardly means a *lifetime* commitment: for the women assemblers there is no contradiction between intending eventually to leave wage-work and aspiring to promotion in the meantime.

Such aspirations rest on the assumption that the firm will be able to provide secure employment in the future. This derives not just from workers' experience in the factories, but also from the more general image they have of 'their' industry. Since the mid-1970s in Ireland massive publicity has been given to the opening of new electronics plants; the Irish media has wrapped the green flag around the 'Irish' electronics industry and has depicted the Republic as riding to prosperity on the irresistible wave of 'microchip' technology and as being the 'Silicon Valley of Europe'.

Workers' positive expectations of the electronics industry also derive from participation in an industry sub-culture in which:

> Shop-floor workers [in electronics plants] do not, despite the industry's advanced technology, receive much formal training . . . yet those who work in the industry are very conscious of their connections with science and scientific research (Curran and Stanworth, 1979).

Radical accounts (cf. CSE Microelectronics Group, 1980) assume that the glamour of high technology is reserved for men in the upper ranks of the electronics workforce. In fact it is crucial to an all-pervasive industry ideology reaching down to the shop-floor. It provides men *and women* assemblers with the motivation to comply with day-to-day bureaucratic supervision and with the aspiration for promotion without which the entire control system could not function.

TRADE UNION ORGANIZATION WITHIN BUREAUCRATIC CONTROL

Edwards argued that bureaucratic control is primarily a management strategy to pre-empt trade union organization; where trade unions do already exist, they become incorporated in the administration of the internal labour market. In fact neither alternative describes the situation in the two case-study factories, while the different level of trade-union involvement in each plant suggests the limitations of bureaucratic control.

Trade union organization in both plants is typical of foreign-owned industry in the Republic, and as such is neither the result of bureaucratic control nor of the gender composition of the workforce. There is closed shop, single-union representation on a 'green-field' site with the union organization established before any workers have been hired. Such agreements (to their critics, 'sweetheart deals') insulate the foreign-owned sector from the 'British situation' of industrial relations in many Irish-owned firms and much public-sector employment: multiple union organization, strict job-demarcation, relatively effective rank-and-file organization. Thus in both factories the union agreement explicitly affirms management's absolute discretion to allocate workers' tasks and to define promotion criteria. Apart from the right to collective wage bargaining, the agreements confer no absolute rights on workers which they do not already have under state employment legislation.

In neither plant do union members identify strongly with the official aims and aspirations of the trade union movement. As the shop stewards remarked:

> I suppose a younger generation here, they don't accept it at face value the way it's put . . . They aren't fully in favour of this brothers and comradeship and all this type of phraseology and the clichés that the unions throw out (Hightech Shop Steward).

> They don't bother . . . I think all that sort of interest is gone. People have got very hard . . . It's just themselves. In a couple of years you can see the difference and I suppose that's the way the world has us made (Miltech Shop Steward).

Within this common restricted framework the union operates differently in each plant. At Miltech the shop steward and the two other members of the union committee were women. Although a sizeable minority of the hourly-paid workers seemed oblivious even of their union membership, there was also a minority who did put forward demands through the union, especially for higher wages. There was also a greater tendency than at Hightech for workers to see the union as shielding them from continuous management pressure. At Hightech the shop steward and two other members of the five-person committee were male (reflecting both an actual male majority amongst union members and the sex hierarchy within the hourly-paid grades) and commitment to the union was low.

Two factors largely explain this difference. First, at Hightech the full-time trade union official 'servicing' the factory was seen as ineffectual and badly informed, while at Miltech there was a high opinion of the negotiating skills of his local counterpart. Second, divisions of class and gender were less pronounced at Hightech. Test technicians with higher educational qualifications worked on the shop-floor, so the distinction between white-collar and blue-collar workers was blurred; routine testing and extensive storekeeping ensured that the hourly-paid grades were sexually mixed; management policy deliberately minimized status divisions by imposing the same working hours on all employees. Al Miltech there were no intermediate groups such as technicians on the shop-floor; office and shop-floor employees had different working hours and break times, so that contact between the two groups was minimal. The result was an almost complete polarization between 'the girls on the floor' and the other employees.

These differences are illustrated by the question of extending trade-union membership to the salaried grades. At Hightech the issue had been much discussed but nothing had been done, largely because union membership was not seen as particularly beneficial by those who already had it. At Miltech the lack of contact between the two groups meant that the question was hardly meaningful – indeed the shop steward was under the illusion that clerical and professional employees had their own unions!

At Hightech bureaucratic control interacted with the existence of a formal union structure to produce the demand for the *extension* of bureaucratic control. At the revision of the plant agreement the union proposed the introduction of an annual review, similar to that undergone by salaried employees, in which each individual hourly-paid worker and his/her supervisor would participate. Another proposal was for what amounted to a job evaluation survey of the plant:

> We felt we could make a valuable contribution to the run-
> ning of the company in that way. If everything is going more
> streamlined and the company is making more money, then
> there's no reason why we can't do better as individuals out of
> it because we're helping to make the money (Hightech Shop
> Steward).

Such proposals may seem surprising – even Hightech's management was said to be 'very amazed' by the last one. However, they are a rational choice of means to increased rewards
in a situation where the option of union bargaining has been
largely foregone, but expectations of employment stability are
high. Shortly after completion of our main fieldwork at Hightech, about one in six of the workforce was suddenly declared
redundant. The union was able to ensure that amongst the
hourly-paid workers redundancies were on a 'last in, first out'
basis (as did not occur amongst the salaried grades). For the first
time since the firm opened, the union was suddenly seen to
have some daily relevance to its members and the union
committee vowed to be more wary in future of co-operating
with management.

At Miltech by contrast, production workers had always
tended to act in a more 'class' fashion, despite the constraints
of a 'sweetheart' deal and the more developed bureaucratic
control mechanisms. By itself therefore bureaucratic control
cannot completely marginalize trade union organization.

CONCLUSION

Bureaucratic control has been taken by Edwards to be a
feature of the 'core' enterprises of 'core' economies: indeed he
suggested (Edwards, 1979, p. 178) that one reason why US
corporations move production abroad is to avoid the high costs
of applying bureaucratic control to their entire labour force.
Why then is it applied to branch plants in Ireland?

First, we have argued that batch production in electronics
places a premium on quality standards being internalized by
the workforce; bureaucratic control promises a workforce that

is 'reliable' in these terms. This applies as much to Miltech, which (unusually for an 'Irish' electronics factory, is re-exporting to the USA) as to Hightech, supplying the European market with finished products.

Second, categorizing both Ireland and an area such as southeast Asia as 'peripheral' (with all the expected consequences for the form of management control) is simplistic. For example, in the Republic of Ireland as a whole the proportion of employees who are members of trade unions is higher even than in Britain, let alone than in the USA. In such a situation the necessity for foreign firms to find some 'progressive' way of heading-off effective union organization is crucial.

One aspect of the appealing 'modernity' of bureaucratic control is that it appears not to discriminate between men and women: all are subjected to the same 'unbiassed' company rules. In the two plants women are concentrated in the lower hourly-paid grades and have different and less extensive mobility routes from those of men, but this derives from features of the wider society which are external to the particular form of control in the factories. Nonetheless, this different labour market situation outside the factory relates to the operation of bureaucratic control within the factory in two ways. First, within the Irish context, management in particular industries may well opt for the 'expensive' strategy of bureaucratic control because of the low level of wages in international terms. Second, the internal labour market which is central to bureaucratic control can only continue to promise promotion because of the relatively high turnover of the women workers. In this respect then, bureaucratic control in Irish electronics plants operates not despite the high proportion of women in the workforces, but because of it.

NOTES

1. Fieldwork was carried out in 1981–2 as part of a wider project on the electronics industry in the Republic of Ireland, on which we are currently engaged. The project is funded by the National Board for Science and Technology and the Employment Equality Agency. Each case study involved a survey of all employees with the exception of senior management, detailed observation of the main jobs and extended tape-recorded interviews with management and trade union representatives. We would

like to thank all who participated in the study for their co-operation.

2. The overall structure of the industry workforce is discussed in more detail in Murray and Wickham (1982). This reports the results of a postal survey which we carried out early in 1981 in which 93 of the 110 manufacturing firms in the industry at that time participated.

3. Information from trade union officials and workforce surveys.

4. Edwards' account of the impact of bureaucratic control is in these terms strikingly similar to Offe's (1976) discussion of the growing importance of 'normative orientations' for control, selection, promotion and reward in·industrial work.

5. Miltech also carries out various forms of design work in the same plant. However, these are part of a separate division of the corporation and involve only technical and other white-collar employees who have no connection with the assembly operation.

6. Information from workforce survey.

7. The Leaving Certificate is the final Irish school examination and is normally considered to be between the British 'O'- and 'A'-level examinations.

8. Although both workforces were relatively youthful, there was a higher proportion of women assemblers with more than one child at Miltech. Some of these women were interviewed shortly after giving up their jobs. They explained their decision in financial terms: the high costs of child-minding, combined with the high level of tax and social insurance contributions.

REFERENCES

Cavendish, R. (1980) *Women on the Line* (London: Routledge & Kegan Paul).

Cogan, D. and O'Brien, R. (1983) 'The Irish Electronics Sector: Technical Manpower as an Indicator of Structure and Sophistication', in *Journal of Irish Business and Administrative Research* (IBAR) 5.1 (April) pp. 3–11.

CSE Microelectronics Group (1980) *Micro-Electronics: Capitalist Technology and the Working Class* (London: CSE).

Curran, J. and Stanworth, J. (1979) 'Worker Involvement and Social Relations in the Small Firm' in *Sociological Review* 27, 2 (May) pp. 317–42.

Edwards, R. (1979) *Contested Terrain: The Tranformation of the Workplace in the Twentieth Century* (London: Heinemann).

Froebel, V. *et al.* (1980) *The New International Division of Labour* (Cambridge: Cambridge University Press).

Harris, L. (1983) 'Industry, Women and Working Class Politics in the West of Ireland', in *Capital and Class*, 19 (Spring) pp. 100–17.

Herzog, M. (1980) *From Hand to Mouth: Women and Piecework* (Harmondsworth: Penguin).

Murray, P. and Wickham, J. (1982) 'Technocratic Ideology and the Reproduction of Inequality: The Case of the Electronics Industry in the Republic of Ireland', in Day G. *et al.* (eds) *Diversity and Decomposition in the*

Labour Market (Aldershot: Gower).
Murray, P. and Wickham J. (1983) "Technical Training and Technical Knowledge in an Irish Electronics Factory', in Winch, G. (ed.) *Information Technology in Manufacturing Processes: Case Studies in Technological Change* (London: Rossendale).
National Manpower Service (1982) *School Leavers 1980: Results of a Survey carried out in May 1981* (Dublin: Department of Labour).
Offe, C. (1976) *Industry and Inequality* (London: Edward Arnold).
Pollert, A. (1981) *Girls, Wives, Factory Lives* (London: Macmillan).
Stone, K. (1974) 'The Origins of Job Structures in the Steel Industry', in *Review of Radical Political Economics* 6, pp. 113–73.

9 Tertiarization and Feminization at the Periphery: The Case of Wales[1]

VICTORIA WINCKLER

There has been a rapid growth in the size of both service – or tertiary – sector and female employment in Britain since 1960. This increase has been especially significant in peripheral areas such as Wales. In part this is because the rise in both service sector and female employment has been coupled with a decline in employment in traditional industries and hence in male employment. However it is also due to a very substantial increase in the absolute numbers of female and service workers. Almost all of Wales' service sector expansion has been concentrated in the 1970s, as opposed to the steady British growth throughout the past twenty years; whilst the increase in female employment of some 20 per cent, 1970–80, has been the most rapid in Britain. As a result employment in the service sector and female employment have become increasingly prominent. In 1980 women were 40 per cent of the workforce and the service sector accounted for 56 per cent of all employment.

The expansion of state services has played a particularly important role in the tertiarization and feminization of the Welsh economy. Between 1971 and 1977 education, medical, and national and local government services provided 37 000 additional jobs in Wales, many of which were taken by women. The importance of state service employment to female employment is such that 37 per cent of all working women in Wales are found there. Many state services have developed *in situ* to serve local needs – for example, primary schools and hospitals. However one state service, namely headquarters work of the civil service, has been deliberately located in Wales as a result of successive governments' policies to disperse civil service work away from London.

Dispersal policy was formally introduced in 1962 as part of a package of measures designed to reduce congestion in London (Hansard, 18 July 1963). By the mid-1960s it had acquired a more regional dimension, and the policy continued to run throughout the 1960s and 1970s although with varying intensity, until it was cancelled in July 1979 (Hansard, 26 July 1979).

Civil service dispersal has brought large numbers of jobs to peripheral regions. Altogether 65 000 civil service jobs were established away from London, with some 70 per cent going to the assisted areas. Wales did exceptionally well in the dispersal programme, receiving over 9 000 non-industrial civil service jobs between 1962 and 1980, a figure equalled only by Scotland and far greater than any other British region.

In this paper I will argue that the policy of dispersing the civil service was less about reducing congestion in London and providing employment in the regions (which was the official rationale) than it was about resolving some of the problems faced by the civil service and the state during the 1960s and 1970s. In particular it seems that the introduction of office technology to the civil service made dispersal to areas with large reserves of female labour very attractive. I will begin by looking at recent work on the relocation of certain industries and changes in the labour process, and then go on to look at pressures on the state and the civil service. I will then look at the impact of office technology on the office labour process in four major offices dispersed to south Wales, and its relationship to the availability of female labour. Finally I will assess the implications of civil service dispersal for the regional development of south Wales.

INDUSTRIAL RESTRUCTURING AND THE LABOUR PROCESS

Recent work on changes in the structure and location of industry has tended to concentrate on certain sectors of manufacturing industry, such as electrical engineering (Massey and

Meegan, 1979). It seems that this kind of analysis is also relevant to understanding some of the changes occurring in office work, though there are some problems.

The argument is essentially that some manufacturing industries have responded to problems in production by changing their production techniques – for example, by introducing new technology. This tends to reduce the skill levels required in production, thus freeing a firm from dependence on its former, skilled, workforce. Instead the firm can locate wherever conditions are most attractive. Often this is where an unskilled, cheap and docile workforce is available. In many peripheral regions there are large reserves of female labour, lacking work and trade union experience. Eager to take advantage of this and often with the aid of Government grants, some firms have relocated automated production processes in such regions (see, for example, Massey, 1979; Massey and Meegan, 1979; Carney, 1980; and Rees, 1980).

Many of the processes found in the restructuring of manufacturing industry seem to be present in the service sector also. The labour process in the office has not changed fundamentally since the nineteenth century, and in the past twenty years it has come under increasing pressure as the costs of office work have risen (CSE Microelectronics Group, 1980). The introduction of office technology, particularly computers, has offered some solution to this problem. Computers can handle huge amounts of simple data and greatly increase the productivity of office workers. At the same time, they may create many very routine clerical jobs to process the computer data (Department of Employment, 1972). It is possible therefore that this kind of routine office work may be relocated away from the head office, as with some manufacturing industries, wherever conditions are most attractive.

At the heart of this argument is the concept of de-skilling, that is that changes in the division of labour, especially when associated with technological change, result in a reduction of the skill content of a job (see Braverman, 1974). There are however two major difficulties with this. First, the meaning of the term 'skill' is not clearly spelt out. Beechey (1982) has identified three separate uses of the term: as an occupational label, to denote 'complex competencies', and as control over the labour process. The conceptualization of skill as control

over the labour process seems to be particularly useful since it
is control which is central to the utilization of labour power
(Littler and Salaman, 1982). In addition it also transcends any
tendency towards sexual bias in occupational labels, for example a female clerk is just a clerk but a male clerk may be called
'a trainee manager' (Phillips and Taylor, 1980; Crompton,
Jones and Reid, 1982).

Second, de-skilling is not the inevitable consequence of
technological change and changes in the division of labour.
Other factors, most notably class struggle, are of vital importance in determining the outcome of any attempts to change
the labour process. Elger (1982) argued that de-skilling should
be seen simply as one factor, albeit a very powerful one,
among others which affect the organization of work.

Despite these problems the approach to industrial change
and relocation in manufacturing industry has been very useful
in pinpointing key processes involved. Similar processes appear to have been operating in office work in general and in the
civil service in particular in the guise of dispersal policy.

DISPERSAL POLICY

The period during which dispersal policy operated saw considerable pressures being exerted on governments and on the civil
service itself. Basically these pressures arose from the complex
changes occurring within British capitalism and the way in
which the state responded to them. The civil service was in a
unique position, since on the one hand as the apparatus of the
state it was directly responsive to changes in the state's role,
but on the other it was limited by the demands of capital to
minimize its cost.

The economic problems of the late 1950s and early 1960s led
to both Conservative and Labour administrations taking positive steps to encourage economic growth (Budd, 1979). The
1964 Labour government claimed to have the most radical
strategy. It aimed to modernize the economy through technological progress and change, and though it now seems that this
was largely rhetorical (Morgan, 1980) the emphasis on modernization and technological change nevertheless coloured the
way in which Labour responded to various pressures.

First, the strategy of economic regeneration adopted in the 1960s and to a lesser extent in the 1970s involved substantial regional growth and diversification, in particular 'to make use of the reserves of unused labour' in the regions (Department of Economic Affairs, 1965, p. 84). Regional policies aimed to bring new industries to regions dominated by traditional activities and the dispersal of civil service office work was clearly in accordance with this aim.

Accompanying the emphasis on regional development was the desire to reduce what was termed the congestion in London (Hansard, 10 November 1964; Cmnd 4506, 1970). This seems to have been largely a euphemism for reducing office rents during the property booms of the time. Certainly dispersal itself had little effect on the numbers of civil servants in London, which were the same in 1980 as in the mid-1960s (Hammond, 1967; Civil Service Department, 1980).

Second, Labour's plans to modernize the economy also included the rationalization of many traditional industries in the regions, which resulted in large job losses in the coal industry in Wales. Later rationalization plans for steel saw further large redundancies. Labour administrations were understandably sensitive to mounting criticism and demands for new jobs from Welsh MPs and the wider Labour movement in a traditional Labour constituency. The civil service was a visible and ready-made palliative. Referring to the cancellation of the dispersal of 5 000 Ministry of Defence jobs to Cardiff in 1979, James Callaghan said:

> When the East Moors Steelworks was closed down last year, nearly 4000 jobs were lost. It was said frequently that this would be made up . . . by the transfer of the . . . jobs (Hansard, 26 July 1979).

Third, the government's concern with modernization was extended to the civil service itself. An efficient administration was essential for a strategy which depended so heavily on controlling the economy (Warde, 1982). Harold Wilson made this clear when he referred to:

> the modernisation of the institution on whose efficiency, [and] expertise . . . the success of almost every effort in our

modernisation depends to so great an extent (Hansard, 21 November 1968).

In 1966 an investigative committee, the Fulton committee, was established to 'ensure that the Service was properly equipped for its role in the modern state' (Fulton Report, 1968a, p. 107). Although its recommendations were limited to the structure and management of the civil service, it nevertheless introduced into the civil service a sense of progress, efficiency and change.

Fourth, Conservative and Labour governments alike adopted economic and social policies based on increased state intervention. Many new state activities were introduced or existing functions expanded – for example, the collection and dissemination of business statistics was greatly increased in 1966. The civil service quite simply had more work to do. The size of the civil service increased very rapidly during these years. Between 1965 and 1970 over 34 000 extra staff were recruited, whilst the increase between 1974 and 1977 was even more rapid with 59 000 additional staff in just three years (Civil Service Department, 1975, 1981).

The increased workload and size of the civil service created a number of serious problems however. In the first place the civil service was unable to recruit sufficient staff especially in London and the south east. It was specifically a shortage of female labour for clerical and secretarial posts. The annual reports on staffing in the civil service repeatedly stressed the problem of staff shortages:

the special problem of recruitment for posts in the London area has not by any means been solved (Civil Service Commission, 1966, p. 12).

clerical recruitment . . . in the London area . . . continues to be very difficult (Civil Service Commission, 1969, p. 21).

recruitment particularly to . . . clerical posts in London became noticeably more difficult (Civil Service Commission, 1972, p. 7).

Indeed in order to recruit sufficient staff the civil service had to resort to increasingly drastic measures, such as raising the age limit for entry and waiving formal entry qualifications in London. Even so, in 1973 there were almost 6 000 unfilled clerical posts in London.

Fifth, as the civil service increased in size so did its cost. There was growing pressure on the Government to attempt to limit it. On several occasions the size of the civil service was frozen and 1970–4 saw explicit steps to reduce its numbers. However these measures were rarely accompanied by cuts in the workload of the civil service. If anything, it continued to increase; in other words the Civil Service had to become more productive.

The Government's response to this was as that of any other employer. On being asked what efforts were being made to improve the efficiency of the civil service 'with a view to more work being done by fewer people' the Government replied:

> Modern management techniques, including automatic data processing, clerical work measurement, management reviews, management by objectives, management accounting, work study and operational research (Hansard, 27 February 1968, vol 759).

The civil service was therefore under great pressure during these years. It was one management technique, automatic data processing, which appeared to offer a radical solution to the civil service's problems.

OFFICE TECHNOLOGY AND THE LABOUR PROCESS

Automatic data processing (ADP) was introduced into the civil service rapidly and enthusiastically. The rate of investment in computers doubled every two to three years (Civil Service Department, 1971) so that by the mid-1970s the civil service was Britain's largest user of computers and employer of computer staff (Owen, 1974).

ADP was undoubtedly introduced because of its potential for increasing productivity and reducing costs. The Treasury analyzed the likely return on investment in ADP (Fulton Report, 1968b) and referred to its 'profitability' (Civil Service

Department, 1971). ADP's ability to handle large amounts of data meant either that staff were saved or, more significantly when Government functions were expanding, that vastly increased output with the same number of staff could be achieved. As the Treasury itself noted:

> We are now rapidly moving into an era when the sheer volume of work . . . could not be performed within the available time by manual means and . . . the question of staff savings becomes academic (Fulton Report, 1968b, p. 635).

The official view of the impact of technological change on the labour process tends to support the idea of de-skilling. ADP was seen to have a polarizing effect on staff, eliminating middle level posts and replacing them with large numbers of routine and lower grade staff and a few senior posts (Fulton Report, 1968c; Civil Service Department, 1971).

This view is borne out in the four major dispersed offices in south Wales – the Driver and Vehicle Licensing Centre (DVLC), the Companies Registration Office (CRO), the Business Statistics Office (BSO), and the Export Credit Guarantees Department (ECGD). All use some kind of office technology although it

TABLE 9.1   *The percentage of clerical and other low grades in four dispersed offices and Great Britain as a whole*

Grade	DVLC	CRO	BSO	ECGD	GB
Clerical assistants	37.7	28.6	6.1	9.9	12.9
Clerical officers	20.2	31.6	32.9	24.9	15.6
Data processors	19.7			2.8	1.6
Messengers, office keepers etc	6.3	12.2	17.3	12.2	7.1
Photoprinters etc	0.5	14.7	0.9	0.5	1.2
Percentage of total staff:	84.4	87.2	57.2	50.3	38.4

NOTE   data for individual offices are for 1982, Great Britain data are for 1981.

SOURCE   Individual offices derived from personal communications, Great Britain figures derived from Civil Service Department, 1981.

differs in both type and extent of use. The grade structure of the offices (see Table 9.1) does suggest that the extensive use of technology is associated with large numbers of low-grade jobs. The two offices with very high percentages of their staff in low grades – the DVLC and CRO – both use office technology extensively. The other two, the BSO and ECGD, make less use of office technology but still have far higher proportions of their staff in low grades than the British average.

However occupational labels such as the grades in the civil service do not really indicate the skill content of a job, especially the amount of control which workers have over the labour process. It is therefore necessary to look at the labour process in these dispersed offices in more detail. Because relocation in Wales involved changes in the activities of offices, either through expansion (at the BSO), centralization (at the DVLC), or fragmentation of functions, a 'before and after' comparison is not possible. Instead I have concentrated on the nature of the office jobs as they are at present.

Semi-structured interviews were carried out with trade union officials of the clerical union, the Civil and Public Services Association (CPSA), in the four offices in summer 1982. Although there was considerable variation both within and between each individual office, the basic function of each office was the same: the receipt, processing and despatch of information. Indeed the sheer volume of the work handled by the offices is staggering. The DVLC issues one million vehicle registration forms a month, the CRO handles 40 000 company files a week and the BSO processes nearly half a million statistical returns a year. This handling of vast quantities of information resulted in some of the offices being characterized as 'paper factories' by union officials (cf. Lipietz's (1980) 'office factories'):

> It's very much a paper factory – you think of it as simply a process of mail coming in, it gets sorted out, checked, edited, coded and keyed into the computer, then onto the printer and then to outward despatch.

> In some respects it's a massive clerical process of getting 40 000 documents onto the files each week.

The large quantities of work coupled with an extensive use

of technology were associated with a considerable division of labour and structuration of the total office process. I will attempt to assess the impact of office technology on the labour process by following the flow of information through, looking at (i) Mail reception (ii) Data checking (iii) Data processing (iv) Data retrieval and despatch and (v) Peripheral areas of work.

Mail Reception

The quantity of incoming mail in each office meant that its reception generally occurred separately from its processing. In one office, mail arrived ready-sorted by post-codes and clerical staff were just required to check it off and transfer it to a conveyor belt to the rest of the building. Then clerical workers open and sort or check the mail. The procedure for this at one office until very recently was:

> The post opening section . . . had about 200 people in teams of about ten. In the middle there was a conveyor belt and you'd get an envelope . . . and you'd open it up, make sure everything was there, staple it together, date it with a receipt stamp, and it goes off and drops into this little box and goes on. You had people doing this all day

Although that particular procedure has since been abandoned, partly because of the pressure and boredom experienced by workers, similar procedures were present in other offices. In one for example, a worker's sole task was to open envelopes and put them in the correct pigeon-hole above their desks.

It is clear that this kind of work offers very little individual autonomy or control over the labour process; the work came in a continuous flow, and any discretion extended only to the simple choice of the destination of the letter. The work must therefore be seen as essentially manual work; work which was also very routine and very boring. However workers had sometimes been granted some degree of autonomy, such as being able to get up and walk around or talk. As well as minimizing the likelihood of any disruption, this also made working conditions more bearable:

Although the job is boring, they can chat to their neighbours and have quite a pleasant time doing the work.

Data Checking

In all the offices the largest area of work came in the checking and preparation of information for storage on computer, microfiche or microfilm. The work essentially involves checking incoming information for its accuracy, completeness and compatibility with the computer, microfiche or film. In one office a union official summed up the work:

> Who wants to do a job that just involves saying: 'that block has (a) got writing in it, and (b) that writing is saying what needs to be said'. That's basically the job.

In another office the checking process had been highly fragmented until its recent integration. Nevertheless it was still felt to be the same chain of 'boring little jobs':

> [they] unclip [the mail], look at it, check it – was the form signed, was the cheque signed – and if it is, pass it on to the next line. There were two or three hundred people doing that on one floor. Then it was passed on to the next floor [where] they edit it and code it. If it didn't [have a postcode] they used to have to find a postcode. And then you had people checking it.

Again this kind of work was characterized by workers' lack of control over the labour process. Although they have some discretion in deciding whether a form is adequately completed, that discretion is often strictly confined to a very few alternatives. The extent of discretion did however vary between offices, with checking certain types of form being said to be more interesting than others.

Data Processing

The actual storage of prepared data saw some of the most dramatic effects of technological change. Where data was stored on computer large numbers of data processors – 'the key punch girls' – were employed. Their task was to transfer paper-based information to magnetic or paper tape by 'typing' as fast as possible onto a small keyboard with a visual display unit attached. This area of work highlights the importance of distinguishing different elements in the term skill. Data processing required considerable technical ability, and workers were trained by the civil service and paid a skill bonus. However these workers have virtually no control over the labour process whatsoever. At times key depressions have been monitored:

> They used to record how many key depressions were made a minute and if your key depressions were down, you'd have a letter saying 'what the hell's going on here? You can't have a pixie in the works'

That this practice has now ceased as a result of union pressure and higher speeds being obtained without monitoring emphasizes that the impact of technological change is not predetermined and that the organization of work can be altered, albeit in a fairly minor way, by the actions of workers.

The work involved in storing information on microfiche and microfilm was similar to that of computerized systems. Clerical staff or the photoprinting grades fed documents into the microfilming machines. Here too there was very little worker autonomy or discretion in the labour process; workers had to be at their places, and sometimes a tally would be kept of their output. The little discretion they did have came in checking the quality of the microfilm produced on their machine.

Information Retrieval and Despatch

The retrieval of information from computer storage provided little employment as most information was printed out automatically by the computers. However where microfilm or microfiche was used, large numbers of clerical staff were required. Essentially their job was to find and sometimes copy a microfiche or microfilm in response to a request for information and to despatch it. The mental content of the work was small, with little scope for individual autonomy. The task was closely defined and work came in a continuous flow. Again the work bore more resemblance to manual work. As in other kinds of routine work however, the conditions of work were very important, and in several cases managerial control was not fully enforced. For example, workers were able to have the radio on in one office and could get up and move around.

Last, even the despatch of mail was automated in several offices. Machines folded and inserted computer printout into envelopes, then sealed them. The task of machine operators was simply to mind the machine, and to feed in and remove envelopes as necessary. Not only did this work lack any autonomy or discretion whatsoever, but it was also paced by the machine. This kind of work is closest to Braverman's (1974) picture of operative work.

Peripheral Areas of Work

The peripheral areas of work were not usually related to office technology. Either office technology played only a minor role in the office anyway or office technology had marginalized these areas bacause they dealt with non-standard cases.

Almost by definition therefore this work required considerable responsibility and discretion. Clerical workers would be able to take decisions on whether to grant an insurance claim, whether to allow a company name, or whether to issue a driving licence. This involved a substantial amount of control over the labour process: clerks would pursue their cases, contacting individuals and organizations, and gathering information as necessary. One union official noted:

> We tend to find that our clerical officers deal at a very high level with people in outside business . . . Although they're not supposed to give company law advice . . . they often [do].

In one case the organization of a section had been altered to increase this autonomy, to provide a better service to the public and as a response to workers' dissatisfaction with the previously highly-fragmented system. Again it is clear that the division of labour is not fixed.

The bulk of the work dispersed to south Wales is therefore

very routine, very monotonous and very boring. There was little worker autonomy or control over the labour process, and it was this which distinguished clerical work in these offices from other routine civil service clerical work. This is seen in the way in which the work was generally described as being 'boring' with only minimum training being required:

> I would say that the bulk of the jobs in the major areas need very little training, I mean I think you could train a monkey to do half of them.

> Perhaps 80 per cent of the clerical jobs [here] are extremely boring. The job I'm doing now . . . [is] an incredibly tedious job which takes no intellectual ability whatsoever.

The reorganization of working practices and the concessions to workers, such as having the radio on, seemed to be of great importance in making such routine work bearable. However although this kind of work was predominant in three of the four offices, there were some areas of work which were very different. This kind of work required considerable training and experience, said to be up to two years in one section. In addition, the clear distinctions between grades which were found in other areas became blurred because of the high levels of responsibility.

It would seem therefore that the impact of technological change is not necessarily to de-skill the labour process. Though much of the work is very routine there is evidence of some changes in work organization, and in addition there are small areas of relatively skilled work. Even so, de-skilling has been a very powerful tendency in the organization of the civil service work dispersed to south Wales, with by far the majority of jobs being extremely routine, repetitive and boring.

DISPERSAL AND FEMALE LABOUR

It is argued that unskilled work is often located in peripheral areas such as Wales because these areas have reserves of female labour which is supposedly cheap, inexperienced and docile.

In Wales in the 1960s and 1970s there were large numbers of women not in waged work. Welsh female activity rates have been consistently below the British average and well below those for the south-east of England. In 1966 nearly three quarters of Welsh women were *not* in paid employment or registered as seeking it. Even by 1971 this figure was nearly two-thirds.

In part, the low female activity rate in Wales reflects the absence of work considered suitable for women. One third of all women work in offices (Bird, 1980) but only 19 per cent of total employment in Wales was in office occupations in 1971, compared with 38 per cent in London (Goddard, 1979). However it also reflects the sexual division of labour in the home in which men are the primary wage-earners and women are housewives and child-rearers, thus limiting women's access to waged work.

Governments and the civil service were well aware of the presence of large numbers of potential women workers in Wales. As early as 1962 the Civil Service Commissioners noted that 'posts . . . in South Wales could be filled many times over' (Civil Service Commissioners, 1962, p. 3) and that in the long run the solution to recruitment problems in London would be 'to reduce *demand* in London by moving clerical work out to areas where recruitment is easier' (*ibid.*, emphasis in original). A decade later the Hardman Report (1973) on dispersal examined regional variations in office and female employment to determine the capacity of different locations for receiving civil service work: Wales had a high capacity.

Not only were women in large numbers available for work but it seems that they were also very anxious and willing to work. The desire of many married women to work seems to have been increased in the 1960s and 1970s by the decline in male-employing industries, especially coal and steel, and by the high incidence of industrial disease in south Wales. By the time of this research many women civil servants were said to have become the family breadwinners.

With few alternative sources of employment, work in the civil service was an attractive proposition for many women. Clerical work has long been sex-typed as 'women's work' (Davies, 1979) and also enjoys a higher status than, say, factory work. In addition the civil service is a 'good' employer, with nationally-agreed rates of pay, job security, pension rights, flexible hours and so on. The civil service had no difficulty in filling posts in the newly-dispersed offices, often with staff with well above the minimum educational requirements:

> There never has been [any recruitment problem] for the simple reason . . . that it was one of the few decent jobs that were about.

> since this office opened there's been no difficulty in getting not just the calibre, but a higher level of calibre than perhaps we would've got in London.

The nationally-agreed conditions of service also meant that there was no special advantage to the civil service in relocating in an area of plentiful female labour in terms of lowering wage rates. What dispersal does seem to have achieved for the civil service is a reduction of overall costs through the creation of a large number of low-grade jobs, as well as reduced office rents.

Although many of the women recruited to the offices had previously been without waged work experience, their inexperience did not make them a docile workforce. Rates of union membership were high amongst the clerical grades at over 90 per cent, and though this is not necessarily indicative of militancy it does point to the workforce at least being organized. Second and more important, in three out of the four offices women were relatively active in their union, certainly more so than their male or London counterparts. The 1981 pay dispute saw many women union members taking organized and militant action, such as walk-outs, 'sit-rounds', and picketing, which earned them the praise of their union officials:

> when the strike came along there were one or two little sparks and that was it! . . . When it came to walkouts we had about 95 per cent support.

> The women were marvellous, on all-night strike, leaving their families and children at home, but they never wavered. It takes a lot of doing.

In locating in south Wales, it seems that the civil service was able to offset some of the employment consequences of introducing office technology at a time when there was a severe shortage of clerical labour in London and the south east. The civil service was able to take advantage of the large reserve of female labour in Wales by filling relatively unattractive jobs with willing and well-qualified workers. This is not to say that the civil service found a cheap or docile workforce however, women workers were generally loyal and sometimes active members of their union.

DISPERSAL AND REGIONAL CHANGE

The dispersal of the civil service to south Wales has had a profound effect on the region's economic and social character. At a very general level dispersal has contributed to the tertiarization and feminization of employment by bringing over 9000 office jobs, many of which were taken by women, to an area traditionally dominated by extractive and basic manufacturing industries with a largely male workforce. Both service sector and female employment increased by almost 20 per cent in the 1970s with dispersal accounting for one fifth of the growth.

However, although dispersal provided many additional jobs in south Wales, it does not seem to have reduced regional inequalities. If anything it has increased and reinforced them. Whilst conventional indicators of regional disparities, such as unemployment, have showed convergence, new dimensions of inequality have opened up.

This is because of the *kind* of employment brought by the new civil service offices. Dispersal has helped to create a new spatial division of labour in the civil service, in which large, routine clerical operations have been relocated to peripheral areas and higher order decision-making functions have remained, on the whole, in London. Over half of all the jobs dispersed to Wales were in the two clerical grades alone. The Welsh civil service now has the highest proportion in Britain of its administrative staff in the lowest clerical grade: 40 per cent, compared with only 25 per cent in the south-east region (Civil Service Department, 1977). As we have seen, the majority of these jobs are of low skill and require very little training. Workers in these jobs become confined to low skill occupations, and Wales itself develops a relatively unskilled labour market, which in turns attracts more unskilled employment. In addition the dispersed jobs are characterized by low pay. A new clerical assistant can expect only £48 per week gross, rising to £83 after eight years service. This is well below the Welsh average for both men and women. The influx of a large number of low-paying jobs further reinforces Wales' poverty and inequality.

Dispersal has also increased the dependence of Wales on the state for its employment, extending it from basic industries (see Cooke and Rees, 1981) to the service sector and women also. This dependence makes employment very vulnerable to changes in government policy. As well as bearing their share of the current 14 per cent reduction in the size of the civil service, these offices are also likely to lose jobs with cuts in specific services, for example reductions in the collection and provision of business statistics. Routine office jobs are also vulnerable to the introduction of further new technology – for example, data-checking jobs are threatened by the introduction of optical character recognition which can 'read' and check simple forms. Although the implications in terms of skill content are as yet unclear, it seems certain that in the long run jobs will be lost.

Dispersal has not had any great impact on the reduction of sexual inequalities in Wales either. Although dispersal has provided many women with paid work (one office employs over 3000 women) women in Wales are still less likely to be in paid work than are women in any other region in Britain, and far less likely to be in employment than men. Those women who are in work are also likely to be in a worse position than men. Existing sexual inequalities are reproduced within the civil service. Women comprise the overwhelming majority of clerks and machine operators, with their attendant low pay and prospects. Their bosses in the executive and managerial grades are almost invariably men.

The effects of the dispersal of the civil service go far beyond a simple increase in employment opportunities. The composition of the Welsh workforce has been substantially changed, and though some existing inequalities have declined, the emerging spatial and sexual division of labour have created new and deeply entrenched differences both between Wales and the rest of Britain, and between men and women.

CONCLUSION

The dispersal of the civil service has been less of an attempt to reduce congestion in London and create regional balance than it has been a means of easing some of the pressures experienced by governments and the civil service in the 1960s and 1970s, especially pressures created by mounting economic problems and exacerbated by the state's response to them.

Dispersal and the introduction of office technology were two solutions which were also complementary. Office technology has tended to create routine and relatively unskilled jobs; dispersal to areas with plentiful female labour meant that they were easily filled. However, female labour in this case was not cheap or docile labour, and nor was the nature of the work totally immutable. It is ironic that in bringing this kind of office work to Wales, dispersal seems to have reinforced regional inequalities, and has not substantially reduced sexual inequalities.

Regional recomposition also has considerable political implications for the future. The grounds on which previous class struggles and sexual politics took place have shifted. There are now more civil servants than miners in a region which has traditionally looked to the miners as the vanguard of class action. Women are almost half the workforce in an area where trades unions are still highly male-oriented. This does not mean an end to active trades unionism or sexual antagonism however, but a change in both the form and the arena of politics.

It is clear that the processes of industrial restructuring, regional recomposition and the creation of a new spatial division of labour are not confined to private sector manufacturing industries, but are also occurring in the service sector and in state employment. The restructuring of these sectors is likely to increase as pressures on them grow and new technology becomes more widespread.

NOTE

1. This paper is based on research financed by an ESRC postgraduate training award. I would like to thank Gareth Rees for his helpful comments.

REFERENCES

Beechey, V. (1982) 'The Sexual Division of Labour and the Labour Process: a Critical Assessment of Braverman', in Wood, S., *The Degradation of Work? Skill, Deskilling and the Labour Process* (London: Hutchinson).

Bird, E. (1980) *Information Technology in the Office: the Impact on Women's Jobs* (Manchester: Equal Opportunities Commission).

Braverman, H. (1974) *Labor and Monopoly Capital* (New York: Monthly Review Press).

Budd, A. (1979) *The Politics of Economic Planning* (London: Fontana).

CSE Microelectronics Group (1980) *Microelectronics, Capitalist Technology and the Working Class* (London: Conference of Socialist Economists).

Cmnd 4506 (1970) *The Reorganisation of Central Government* (London: HMSO).

Carney, J. (1980) 'Regions in Crisis: Accumulation, Regional Problems, and Crisis Formation', in Carney, J.; Hudson, R., and Lewis, J., *Regions in Crisis* (London: Croom Helm).

Civil Service Commission (1966) *Annual Report* (London: HMSO).

Civil Service Commission (1969) *Annual Report* (London: HMSO).

Civil Service Commission (1972) *Annual Report* (London: HMSO).

Civil Service Commission (1962) *Annual Report* (London: HMSO).

Civil Service Department (1971) *Computers in Central Government. Ten Years Ahead* (London: HMSO) Management Studies 2.

Civil Service Department (1975) *Civil Service Statistics* (London: HMSO).

Civil Service Department (1980) *Civil Service Statistics* (London: HMSO).

Civil Service Department (1981) *Civil Service Statistics* (London: HMSO).

Cooke, P. and Rees, G. (1981) 'The Industrial Restructuring of South Wales: the Career of a State-managed Region', in *Policy Studies Journal*, vol. 10, no. 2, pp. 128–44.

Crompton, R., Jones, G. and Reid, S. (1982) 'Contemporary Clerical Work: A Case Study of Local Government', in West, J., *Work, Women and the Labour Market* (London: Routledge & Kegan Paul).

Davies, M. (1979) 'Woman's Place is at the Typewriter: the Feminisation of the Clerical Labour Force', in Eisenstein, Z., *Capitalist Patriarchy and the Case for Socialist Feminism* (New York: Monthly Review Press).

Department of Economic Affairs (1965) *The National Plan* (London: HMSO) Cmnd 2764.

Department of Employment (1972) *Computers in Offices* (London: HMSO) Manpower Studies no. 12.

Elger, T. (1982) 'Braverman, Capital Accumulation and Deskilling', in Wood, S., *The Degradation of Work? Skill, Deskilling and the Labour Process* (London: Hutchinson).

Fulton Report (1968a) *The Civil Service* (London: HMSO) vol. 1.

Fulton Report (1968b) *The Civil Service* (London: HMSO) vol. 4.

Fulton Report (1968c) *The Civil Service* (London: HMSO) vol. 2.

Goddard, J. (1979) 'Office Development and Urban and Regional Development in Britain', in Daniels, P., *Spatial Patterns of Office Growth and Location* (London: Wiley & Sons).

Hammond, E. (1967) 'Dispersal of Government Offices: a Survey', in *Urban Studies* vol. 4, no. 3, pp. 258–75.

Hansard, 18 July 1963, vol. 681, Written Answers, col. 82–6.

Hansard, 27 February 1968, vol. 759, Written Answers, col. 310.

Hansard, 10 November 1964, vol. 701, col. 710.

Hansard, 21 November 1968, vol. 773, col. 1542–680.

Hansard, 26 July 1979, vol. 971, col. 902–22.

Hardman Report (1973) *The Dispersal of Government Work from London* (London: HMSO) Cmnd 5322.

Lipietz, A. (1980) 'Inter-regional polarisation and the Tertiarisation of Society', in *Papers of the Regional Science Association*, no. 44, pp. 3–17.

Littler, C. R. and Salaman, G. (1982) 'Bravermania and Beyond: Recent Theories of the Labour Process', in *Sociology*, vol. 16, no. 2, pp. 251–69.

Massey, D. (1979) 'In What Sense a Regional Problem?' *Regional Studies*, vol. 13, no. 2, pp. 233–43.

Massey, D. and Meegan, R. (1979) 'The Geography of Industrial Reorganisation: The Spatial Effects of the Restructuring of the Electrical Engineering Sector under the Industrial Reorganisation Corporation', in *Progress in Planning*, vol. 10, no. 3.

Morgan, K. (1980) *The Reformulation of the Regional Question: Regional Policy and the British State* (University of Sussex: Urban and Regional Studies Working Paper 18).

Owen, K. (1974) *Computing in Government* (London: Central Computer Agency and Civil Service Department).

Phillips, A. and Taylor, B. (1980) 'Sex and Skill: Notes towards a Feminist Economics', in *Feminist Review*, no. 6, pp. 79–88.

Rees, G. (1980) 'Uneven Development, State Intervention and the Generation of Inequality: The Case of Industrial South Wales', in Rees, G., and Rees, T., *Poverty and Social Inequality in Wales* (London: Croom Helm).

Warde, A. (1982) *Consensus and Beyond: The Development of Labour Party Strategy since the Second World War* (Manchester: Manchester University Press).

10 Renegotiation of the Domestic Division of Labour in the Context of Male Redundancy

LYDIA D. MORRIS

INTRODUCTION

One aspect of post-war change in the UK economy which is increasingly attracting the attention of social scientists is the contraction of employment opportunities in the traditionally masculine occupations associated with heavy industry, co-inciding with the expansion of the service sector and con-sumer-based light industries employing a large proportion of women.

It seems reasonable to assume, as do a number of writers (for example, Urry, 1981; Massey, 1982; Morgan, 1983) that such changes 'will significantly alter the nature and compo-sition of the local working class, and can lead to important conflicts of interest between men and women' (Bowlby *et al.*, 1983).

South Wales provides us with a prime example of an area which has recently seen increased participation by women in the waged labour force, alongside the shedding of a predomi-nantly male work force by heavy industry.[2]

In this chapter I seek to demonstrate, with reference to a sample of forty redundant male steelworkers, all married, that redundancy, in the context of a wider economic recession, is unlikely to produce a reversal of pre-existing patterns of sex-role behaviour. I go on to argue, with specific reference to male *unemployment*, that there are powerful social forces at work which militate against, though without necessarily prohibiting, a renegotiation of the domestic division of labour.

Although I found some evidence of a blurring of boundaries between the sexes in the division of domestic tasks, I consider it in no way sufficiently extensive as to constitute a strong challenge to the established division of labour within the household.[3]

Whether the changes which *have* occurred represent a minor adaptation permitting the maintenance of pre-existing sex roles, or are rather the first step in a long process of renegotiation in the domestic division of labour, prompted by a restructuring of the economy, is still open to speculation and debate.

FEMALE ECONOMIC ACTIVITY

Before reporting in detail on the selection of my sample, and the characteristics of domestic organization in the context of male redundancy, it may be useful to examine some background information concerning the recent trends in participation in the waged labour force by married women. In contrast to a falling economic activity rate among single women,[4] the trend throughout the 1970s for married women was towards rising participation in the waged labour force, producing an increase which stabilized between 1978 and 1980 (General Household Survey, 1980, Table 5.1). For the 16–59 age group the rate of economic activity rose from 52 per cent to 62 per cent – a rise substantially accounted for by an increase in part-time working.[5]

The greatest differences between rates of female employment are found when the age of the youngest child is taken into account. Women are increasingly likely to work as the youngest child gets older, though where there are more than one child in the household the increase is concentrated in part-time employment.[6]

The implications for a renegotiation of the domestic division of labour are obvious. A woman with a very young child is likely to be inhibited from taking on paid employment, be it full-time or part-time, unless there is readily available childcare. Although one might expect male unemployment to facilitate an arrangement whereby a husband cares for children while his wife is gainfully employed, the General Household Survey for 1980 (Table 5.10) reports rather the opposite tendency. Amongst couples of working age (that is, husband aged 16–64, wife aged 16–59) 57 per cent were both employed in 1980. However, only 35 per cent of wives of unemployed men worked outside the home, in contrast to 62 per cent of wives of men in employment. A number of informants explained their reluctance to consider a change in traditional roles by the conviction that a women would be unable to earn as much as a man could claim in benefit.

METHODOLOGY

It is in the context of these general, complex trends in the employment pattern of married women that I wish to present my data. My sample of forty redundant male steelworkers, resident in and around Port Talbot, was selected from a larger random sample of 750, made redundant from BSC's Port Talbot plant in the summer of 1980.[7] Given my particular interest in the potential for flexibility in domestic organization as a result of redundancy for a male main earner, I decided to contact only households of married men likely to expect to continue to be economically active (that is, aged 20–55). This meant that the households concerned would also be likely to be involved in some stage of child-rearing. Indeed, the vast majority of my sample have pre-school children (19 cases) or school-age children (14 cases). The critical test of whether or not there is any fundamental renegotiation of the domestic division of labour in the context of male redundancy will be in households containing young children, and in this respect my sample is ideal. This does not of course mean that we learn nothing from those homes without children, but simply that in such cases the test is less rigorous.

In another respect the sample is less than ideal. Most of my interviewing was carried out in the summer of 1982, just two years after the redundancies were announced – sufficient time for changes in domestic organization to have manifested themselves. However, various factors dependent on the availability of funds from the European Coal and Steel Community,[8] whose influence was felt quite some time after the redundancies, have had the effect of softening the blow for many households, and postponing the full financial and psychological impact of the redundancies. Such circumstances may well have assisted what can be seen as a post-redundancy struggle to maintain the old order of gender relations, thus making it difficult to say with any certainty to what extent there will be significant changes now that these special factors are no longer operative.

I would also stress that I am concerned with responses to male *redundancy*, which may or may not be followed by male unemployment. This chapter examines the sexual division of labour inside and outside the home in response to male job loss. It is important that the sample should not be *confined to* the male unemployed – although the resultant variety in the sample means, of course, that my conclusions must be based on rather small numbers.

CENTRAL ISSUES

This paper, then, attempts to trace the complex inter-relations between the labour-market experience of men and women, and the organization of domestic labour in the wake of male redundancy. The central questions, crudely put, must be (i) how is work work outside the household distributed amongst its members; (ii) how is work within the household distributed amongst its members, and (iii) what is the relationship between these two divisions of labour? One must then ask whether or not any non-residents contribute to domestic labour, and what effect their contribution has on the division of labour negotiated within a given household. To address the issues in this way is to distinguish two different aspects of the household's organization. The distribution of paid work *outside* the household, between its members, will be termed 'the domestic division of labour'. The distribution of domestic tasks *within* the household, between its members, will be termed 'the division of domestic labour'. This being said, in examining my data I shall deal firstly with the domestic division of labour (external), that is, the distribution, between household members, of responsibility for the task of providing an income sufficient to meet the collective needs of the household.

The notion of collective needs requires some explication. First, it does not presume that all members have equal access to this income, though the manner in which it is controlled and allocated within a household is too complex to deal with here and will be the subject of another paper. Second, the term does not in any way preclude or ignore the possibility that non-members of a household may contribute to that household's income. Third, needs are not regarded as fixed; indeed, the renegotiation of levels of need is an important element in the response to redundancy, although there is, of course, an extent to which need is socially defined (see Townsend, 1979).

In the context of redundancy for a male main earner we are especially concerned with whether or not there is a change in the domestic division of labour (external) as a result of redundancy, and to what extent this has been dependent on a renegotiation of the divison of domestic labour (internal). I shall also focus attention on the more specific question of male unemployment, examining its effects on both types of labour.

THE DOMESTIC DIVISION OF LABOUR

Out of a total sample of forty households there were only two households in which the woman had become the main earner, and remained so throughout the post-redundancy period, until the time of interviewing. In one case all the children had grown up and moved away, and the women (aged 53) holds a well-paid and responsible position – a job she held at the time of the redundancies. In the other case the couple have no children and the woman (aged 27) works as an insurance bank clerk, again having held the job for some time prior to her husband's redundancy. In four other homes the women were gainfully employed during their husbands' fairly long spells of unemployment – that is, a period of one month or more without paid work.

Comparing the pre-redundancy employment status of women with their employment status at the time of interview (18 months to 2 years after redundancy) we find:

Pre-redundancy		*Post-redundancy*
23	Not in paid work	24
–	Self-employed with husband	1
12	Employed full-time	7
5	Employed part-time	8

The most marked change is, in fact, a fall in the number of women gainfully employed on a full-time basis. Although the number of women workers employed on a part-time basis has risen since the redundancies, compared with their pre-redundancy counterparts these women are employed on average for fewer hours.[9]

Clearly, any likelihood of a woman taking on the role of main wage earner has been reduced by the impact of the recession on the availability of employment for women. Nevertheless, fifteen women did have some form of paid employment at the time of interviewing, and we must now ask to what extent, if at all, this relates to the employment status of their husbands. The easiest and clearest approach to this question is to look at changes in the employment status of women, comparing pre-redundancy to post-redundancy employment status, and asking why the changes occurred. Let us first examine the cases in which a woman's gainful employment ended at some point after her husband's redundancy:

10 changes were due to redundancy for the woman, coinciding in 4 cases with the husband's redundancy

2 changes were a result of the woman leaving employment because of pregnancy

2 changes were due to the women leaving employment because it was no longer financially worth while (one for tax reasons, one because her husband was claiming supplementary benefit).

A number of women commented that financially it would not be worth their while to work, since their earnings would be deducted from their husband's claim for supplementary benefit. This number is likely to increase as more households move from dependence on unemployment benefit to dependence on supplementary benefit.[10] Other women felt they should nevertheless keep their jobs, on the assumption that their husbands would eventually find work, and that they themselves were by no means sure of finding another job should they leave their present one.

Cases of a woman *taking on* paid work after her husband's redundancy accounted for thirteen changes in employment status, but in only two cases was the man unemployed at the time, and in each case the wife's job was part-time and temporary. The nature of a woman's decision to take on paid employment is in part reflected by the informal and fortuitous way in which the women found their jobs:

9 by chance through information conveyed by friends
2 entered joint ventures with their husbands
1 returned to a previous job
1 applied in response to a newspaper advert.

In summary, then, only four changes in employment status for women were directly related to changes in the employment status of their husbands: the two who gave up work for financial reasons, and the two who took on temporary jobs just before Christmas because their husbands were unemployed.

THE DIVISION OF DOMESTIC LABOUR

We may now turn to the rather more complex issue of the division of domestic labour (internal). As the figures presented at the beginning of the chapter were intended to show, a crucial question influencing a woman's ability to take on paid employment is whether or not she is responsible for the care of young children.

We must therefore ask who provided child-care when necessary in households in which the mother was gainfully employed, and compare the pre-redundancy and post-redundancy periods. Prior to the redundancies, of the twelve women gainfully employed on a full-time basis, seven had no children, and two had only adult children. The other three women had school-age children, in one case old enough to be independent, though under the supervision of a friend in school holidays. One woman's 9-year-old child was cared for by an older sister for a brief period after school, and one woman was able to determine her own hours of work, calling on her mother or sister, both of whom live opposite, should assistance be required. In other words, none of the women relied upon their husbands for child-care.

The number of women gainfully employed full-time had fallen from twelve to seven by the time of my interviews. Two of the husbands had experienced significant periods of unemployment,[11] but arrangements for child-care did not change fundamentally. One man would occasionally cook for himself and his school-age children whilst awaiting his wife's return from work, but this was by no means a regular or even predictable occurrence.

If we look at part-time workers then the pattern is similar. Prior to the redundancies, of the five part-time women workers, two would depend on their own mothers for child care (one of these was relieved by the husband on his return from work), two had children old enough to be independent, and one woman worked an hour a day as a school dinner-lady, her two children having dinner at school.

As I have already noted, part-time women workers increased from five to eight after the redundancies. Two of these have been mentioned and experienced no change in their arrangements. Of the remaining six, one took her pre-school child with her, collecting payments from house to house; one worked school hours only; one woman worked an hour a day (again as a dinner-lady in her children's school); one woman exchanged child-care services with a female friend living nearby (despite her own husband's unemployment); one depended on her mother-in-law; and one paid a baby-sitter, her husband having left her.

In three cases of women taking on short-term, temporary work, one called on her own mother and mother-in-law for child-care, whilst two relied on their unemployed husbands, one of whom simply took the child to his own mother.

As we can see, both before and after the redundancies the participation of men in child-care in order to free their wives to take up paid employment was minimal.

If we look more broadly at the division of domestic labour

(internal), which of course includes child care, then the question to be posed is double-edged:

1. We are interested in how domestic work within the home is distributed, given the fact that the woman, who traditionally performs the vast majority of domestic tasks, may have taken on additional work outside the home. A number of authors have convincingly argued that the minimum cost of waged labour is lowered as a result of the existence of domestic labour, an arrangement which necessarily operates to the advantage of capital. (For a review of the literature see Smith, 1978 and Rushton, 1979.) This does not in any way explain the process by which *women* have become primarily responsible for the domestic sphere, though it does draw attention to their role in reproducing and maintaining the labour force.

2. The question of who performs domestic labour when the main male earner becomes unemployed is of particular interest in this context. It seems clear that the only way in which a previous standard of living can be maintained with falling income is by an intensification of domestic labour (see Gardiner, 1975 and Molyneux, 1979). Where the division of domestic labour is along traditional lines male job-loss may mean an increase in activity and responsibility for the woman, just at a time when the man has been deprived of his major focus of activity. Hence, where redundancy has resulted in long-term male unemployment, we must then ask whether the availability of free time for the man leads to his assuming domestic tasks within the home from which he has traditionally been freed by virtue of his labour outside the home. This question is of interest *whether or not* the woman is gainfully employed.

ROLE REVERSAL?

Bearing in mind the paucity of examples of female main earners in my sample, I shall approach the first part of this question by the use of a brief case study in which I examine the implications of the notion of a 'role-swap', a term usually applied in situations in which the woman rather than the man has become the main wage-earner in a household. The case I have chosen is the one which of all the sample demonstrates the *greatest* degree of flexibility on the part of the man:

Mr and Mrs B. have three children, aged 6, 8 and 10, and live on a large council estate close to Mrs B.'s mother. Mr B.'s parents live on the same estate but rather farther away. After his redundancy Mr B. experienced 10 months of unbroken unemployment. His wife had taken on an evening job as a factory cleaner about a year prior to her husband's redundancy. Despite the fact that her husband's benefit was reduced because she was working Mrs B. decided to keep the job, on the assumption that he would eventually find work (as he did). Later, the couple jointly decided that Mrs B. should take on an additional part-time job as a home help. Mr B. had originally suggested that his wife seek full-time work, thinking she might have a better chance than he had of finding a job. Mrs B. was not enthusiastic: 'Well I wasn't very keen on the idea of him doing the housework because he wouldn't do it properly anyway, and I'd still have the lot to do after work.

During the period in which Mrs B. held two jobs and Mr B. remained unemployed, Mrs B. worked morning until about 2 p.m., and evenings from 5 p.m. until 8 p.m. The children had their midday meal at school and Mrs B. would prepare their tea before leaving for work at 4.45 p.m., leaving the dishes for her husband. She would then return from work to cook an evening meal for herself and Mr B.

Although in theory Mr B. took on the task of keeping the house clean, Mrs B. was far from satisfied with the arrangement:

He doesn't like housework anyway. I suppose he thinks it's not manly. He'd dust and tidy downstairs but he won't do upstairs because no-one sees it, and he won't clean the front windows in case the neighbours see him. I dont' mind housework myself as long as I've got time to do it, but I get irritable at the weekend when there's a backlog of things to do and he won't help. He just tells me to leave it. He doesn't understand that it's got to be done sometime. A full-time job would have been just impossible, but I think we'd have driven each other mad if one of us hadn't been out of the house for a bit in the day.

The couple shopped together while Mr B. was out of work, a change from the previous pattern, because Mr B. was available to drive his wife to the cheaper shops: 'I'd try to get him to come round the shelves with me and I was glad of the chance to show him the prices. I try to tell him now they've gone up but it doesn't sink in.' Nevertheless, Mrs B. had total responsibility for budgeting and for planning and catering for the household's weekly needs.

In principle Mr B. is against the idea that a woman might permanently become the main wage earner, while her husband runs the home:

A 'housewife' means just that. She's supposed to stay at home . . . While I was out of work I felt I wasn't playing a part in things, ashamed that I wasn't keeping my family. I suppose tension would have been worse if the wife hadn't been working, but I'd spend sleepless nights. I'd get up and come downstairs sometimes, at three in the morning, worrying that I'm the man and it's my job to see that everything's right between these four walls. If it's not then it's my fault.

The point to note about this particular case study, then, is that although the couple perceived the situation as a 'role-swap' (albeit one expected to be temporary) the woman in effect continued to run the house, with minimal assistance from her husband. From his point of view, however, he had made a significant shift in the extent to which he participated in domestic labour within the home, in response to his wife's employment. He was also going against a well-established cultural tradition in the area. His comments may be taken as fairly typical, and were echoed by other men in similar situations.

Mr B. however, was more flexible than most. One woman, who had held a full-time job predating her husband's redundancy by about a year, spoke of his six months out of work and the viability of swapping roles:

It wouldn't work. He wouldn't stand it and there'd be more quarrels than it's worth. I'd rather do the work myself . . . His mother used to throw it up at his family that she worked you see, and he'd never let it happen here. Anyway, I couldn't stand the strain. He'd be out with the horses most days (his friend runs a stables) and I'd get home at tea time to find nothing done. He wouldn't do a thing. 'What do you think I am' he'd say, 'some old housewife?' It killed him some days seeing me getting up for work though. I'd like to have dropped the job just to show him, but we just couldn't do without the money.

Another woman in a similar situation expressed her feelings rather differently: 'If there was any way that I thought giving up my own job would help him get one I'd do it like a shot. It's hard on any man to be out of work.'

There is clearly a strong feeling on the part of both men and women that it is the man's place to be the main wage-earner, and that any other arrangement will necessarily be in some sense stressful for one or both partners.

SPHERES OF RESPONSIBILITY

I wish now to consider more specifically the organization of labour within the home. As always, when dealing with case material, and especially from such a varied sample as this, one is faced with the question of the representativeness of the emotions, attitudes and ideologies embodied in particular case studies. As a means of having some measure of this with regard to the division of domestic labour (internal), I examined my data on the division of domestic labour in all the households at the time of interviewing, regardless of employment status for either husband or wife, whilst also noting any changes which had occured *since* redundancy.

It is clear from the data collected that there are culturally-established spheres of responsibility which guide the division of labour within each home, though some men will offer assistance in the 'woman's sphere' more readily than others. All the literature attempting to deal with the division of domestic labour (hereafter DDL (internal)) runs up against the same methodological problems. Normative statements from respondents do not necessarily offer a clear guide to their behaviour. Indeed, the men who most readily identified areas of domestic labour to which they would not contribute were in fact those who in general proved to be most flexible. Those men whose behaviour was most rigid in refusing to contribute to domestic labour often denied that there was any particular task in which they would not participate.

My solution to the problem has been to identify a core domain of female domestic activity and ask to what extent there has been any blurring of the boundaries in terms of actual behaviour. Assistance by men in the 'woman's sphere' was usually in the nature of 'occasional help'. By this I mean reasonably frequent assistance which, though not in any way regularized, is neither so rare as to be insignificant. The areas in which this kind of help is most commonly proffered are preparation of food, transport for shopping, help with the dishes, minding and playing with children (for short periods). In contrast to these areas of activity we find that the woman is responsible for washing and ironing clothes, bathing children, cleaning the house and planning the weekly shopping. There were twenty men who identified areas of domestic labour in which they refused to participate. Among them, these twenty men made thirty objections to activities related to the washing and ironing of clothes, and ten objections to tasks which were specifically seen as 'highly visible'.

I shall refer to the pattern of domestic labour (internal) implied by the above as 'traditional', and go on to identify variations on this arrangement. The incidence of different patterns in my sample is as follows:

1. *Traditional* (as described above) – 16 households.
2. *Traditional-rigid* – 14 households in which there is no evidence of a flexible attitude towards DDL (internal) on the part of the man, nor any actual blurring of boundaries between male and female spheres.
3. *Traditional-flexible* – 6 households in which men have shown a significant degree of adaptability at some point since their redundancy, but in which domestic organization is nevertheless based on the traditional pattern.
4. *Renegotiated* – 4 households in which the man assumes responsibility for a substantial number of tasks traditionally regarded as 'female', although one can still identify a remnant of the traditional division of labour.

We might compare these findings with Oakley's remark (1974,

p. 164) that, 'In only a small number of marriages is the husband notably domesticated, and even where this happens a fundamental separation remains'.

If we examine the six households in which the division of domestic labour (internal) is traditional but flexible then we find no clear association between flexibility and the employment status of either spouse. In the six households in question only one woman was gainfully employed for a period which overlapped with a time of unemployment for her husband. In the remaining five households none of the women are gainfully employed, two of the men had experienced significant periods of unemployment since redundancy, one had been in almost constant employment though by virtue of a series of short-term-jobs, and two men had experienced no unemployment.

Looking at the four households with a 'renegotiated' pattern of DDL (internal) we find that three of the women work full-time, whilst one is in ill health. Three of the men concerned are unemployed and one in full-time employment. This might suggest that full-time female employment, especially in combination with male unemployment, is an important contributory factor in bringing about a renegotiation of the DDL (internal). However, in the remaining six households where the woman is gainfully employed on a full-time basis the situation is somewhat different. Five of the homes are classified as having a traditional-rigid DDL (internal) and one a traditional DDL (internal) despite the fact that five of the men had experienced significant periods of unemployment. This suggests that some other factor must be present in addition to employment status to constitute a sufficient condition of renegotiation. It also suggests that, for at least some men, a response to unemployment, especially if the wife is working, may be to emphasize their traditional role. Let us look, now, at the second part of the question I posed earlier – the effects of unemployment on the DDL (internal).

THE EFFECTS OF MALE UNEMPLOYMENT

In my sample of forty, eleven men experienced no unemployment after redundancy, and three were out of work for periods of less than a month only. Of the remaining twenty six:

6 were unemployed for periods of 1–3 months
8 were unemployed for periods of 3–6 months
6 were unemployed for periods of 6–12 months
6 were unemployed for periods of 12 months or more.

(These figures refer to their longest period out of work, and it may be that some of them experienced more than one period of unemployment.)

The responses of these men to the experience of unemployment were varied, but certain tendencies should be noted. It is clear that a number of men have reacted to unemployment by slightly increasing their contribution to domestic labour but without significantly departing from the traditionally-established pattern described earlier. In other words, there may be an increase in general tidying about the house, help with the dishes, and possibly with food preparation. This seems to have occurred mainly where the woman is gainfully employed, but in no way represents a major assumption of domestic responsibility (internal) on the part of the man, and is in almost all cases viewed as a temporary arrangement. Mr and Mrs B. provide a good example. On the other hand, in certain cases where the wife lost her own job at the same time as her husband's redundancy, there has been a contraction in the man's contribution to domestic labour (internal) because the wife was then considered to be fully available to carry out such labour herself. As Oakley has noted (1974, p. 135): 'Legal definitions current in our culture tie the status of "wife" to the role of unpaid domestic worker.'

However, one may see an increase in male participation in domestic labour (internal), but again within the traditional framework outlined, in cases where the woman is not gainfully employed, and usually as a response to boredom on the part of the man. This pattern is likely to be short-lived for two reasons: on the one hand the woman usually finds interference disruptive of her own routine, and judges the standard of work performed by her husband to be low. On the other hand, often in the face of irritation on the part of their wives, men soon tire of domestic work, and anyway seem reluctant to make a commitment to perform particular tasks regularly.

Of the twenty-six households in which men have experienced significant periods of unemployment,[12] ten fall into one or other of these patterns, and at this point an illustrative case study may be helpful.

Mr and Mrs J. (aged respectively 27 and 25) have an 18-month-old child, and live in Maesteg, some three miles from Mr J.'s parents and five miles from Mrs J.'s parents. Since his redundancy Mr J. has experienced three months' unemployment, followed by one year's retraining, and a further year of unbroken unemployment. Mrs J. took a shop assistant's job towards the end of her husband's retraining course, lasting a month into this second period of unemployment. She left the job because her earnings were deducted from her husband's benefit claim. During the three months she spent in paid employment, Mrs J. continued to have full responsibility for running the home, while her mother-in-law looked after the child. During Mr J.'s time of unemployment and while Mrs J. was employed, he was to have responsibility for the child, but in fact went with her up to this parent's home.

Although Mr J. has difficulty filling the day, he participates very little in the domestic labour of the household. Rather, he gets out of bed as late as possible, reads, gardens, watches TV and spends occasional afternoons watching his father's video. He did some work on the house during his earlier spell of unemployment:

> Then you start slowing down. I'm often not up till eleven because there's nothing to do. At night you can sit up late watching TV and reading. You lose your energy, can't be bothered with anything. The wife thinks I could do more. At first I did but you lose interest in everything. I'd rather go out and dig the garden – anything to get out of the house. She's always on the go and gets on at me to help, but if I try I do it wrong, or she does it again anyway, and gets annoyed at my interfering.

Mrs J. gives much the same account:

> I like to do the housework myself really, because I need something to do, and don't want to be bored. If he does something I just do it again, but I still get cross to see him sitting about doing nothing and getting in the way . . . It disturbs my whole routine, and my friends don't like to pop in any more with him here.

Mrs J.'s comments reflect a feeling I detected in a number of other women, that is, that the home is their personal environment and the running of it something which they simultaneously resent and value. It is their domain, and the location of their identity. The very presence of their husband at home during the day is seen as disruptive.

The third and final pattern of response to unemployment on the part of men takes the form of an extreme reaction against any surrender of the traditional division of labour, which will be maintained by his creating some surrogate form of work. Sixteen of the twenty-six men who experienced significant periods of unemployment may be characterized in this way. Many took on the task of completing major structural alterations to the house – a popular use of redundancy payments (encouraged by the DHSS ruling on supplementary benefit which denies eligibility to anyone with £2000 or over, regardless of source), and/or performing similar tasks for kin and friends. This response shades into a pattern of performing tasks for particular individual clients, for which some form of payment – not necessarily in cash – will be made (see Lee *et al.*, 1983). Alternatively, a man may accept paid employment which is not declared to the DHSS. In most cases such bouts of employment are short-term and unpredictable. In a few rare instances they will be full-time and long-term. Slightly more common is a pattern of fairly regular, though nevertheless insecure and unpredictable odd-jobbing which may be for an employer, or an individual client.

It is interesting to note that of the sixteen men who had had such additional sources of income at some point since their redundancy, only three had done so whilst holding a relatively secure job. Mr and Mrs F. provide a good illustration of this kind of response to male unemployment:

Aged respectively 29 and 27, *Mr and Mrs F.* have two children, aged 4 and 8, and live on a large council estate in the same street of Mr F.'s parents. Mrs F.'s parents live a ten-minute drive away. Apart from one spell of employment lasting two months Mr F. has been unemployed ever since his redundancy. Initially he spent a good deal of time completing alterations to the home. Now he spends as much of his day as possible out of the house – gardening, or welding in a small garden shed, doing odd jobs for kin, neighbours and other contacts, and occasionally taking on a job jointly with an old school friend who lives nearby.

Mr F. has a wide range of contacts within the locality, and a particular crowd of friends whom he sees regularly at a sports club. The only contribution he makes to the day-to-day running of the home is occasionally to prepare food, and to provide transport when his wife goes shopping, although he maintains that if his wife could find a well-paid full-time job he would gladly take over the running of the home. Mrs F., on the other hand, maintains that she could never consider a full-time job:

> He's hopeless. Not domesticated at all. With some it would be all right, but not Jim. He just couldn't manage. My work takes longer now he's home because somehow if he's there he's always in the way and never helps.

Mrs. F. has recently taken on part-time job in her uncle's shop. During these afternoons working she relies on a friend to collect their youngest child from nursery class, along with her own son, and to mind him until tea-time. In return Mrs F. takes her friend's child for the full day each Thursday while his mother works for the day in her grandfather's shop.

What is remarkable about this case is that despite the recent change in the woman's employment status, and the long period of unemployment experienced by Mr F., the division of labour within the home has not been affected in any way, and Mr F. continues to organize his life as far as possible as if he were still in a full-time job.

FACTORS EXTERNAL TO THE HOUSEHOLD

Perhaps I can end this chapter by making some tentative remarks about the possible influence of factors external to the household upon the domestic division of labour.

In an earlier paper (Lee *et al.*, 1983) I documented the mutual aid networks between men which support informal economic activity, and which clearly play a vital role in determining responses to unemployment. The suggestion was that where one finds an extensive local network of acquaintances among whom there is a high degree of mutual trust and regular contact there will be an informal exchange of information and services, producing opportunities for economic activity, whether formal or informal. A typical focus for the development of such a network would be a local sports or social club.

Elizabeth Bott's work (see Bott, 1957) has suggested that there is an association between the nature of a married couple's social networks and their degree of marital role segregation. Role segregation, she maintained, will be most marked where the couple are most deeply embedded in close-knit social networks. Harris (1969) has developed this idea and drawn attention to the vital importance of whether or not spouses after marriage retain membership of a single-sex primary group outside the family. Although there are aspects of Bott's work which are both confused and confusing (for comment see Harris, 1969, pp. 162–75) her central insight has been extremely valuable in orienting more recent writing on similar issues (see, for example, Edgell, 1981). In my own research, and on the very specific issue of the division of domestic labour there are a number of question which arise in connection with Bott's hypothesis and its later development by Harris.

The most obvious concerns the readiness or reluctance of a married man to assume tasks within the home which are culturally defined as 'women's work', and the extent to which his attitude may be reinforced by membership of a predominantly male social network. Quite apart from the pressure towards role conformity which is likely to result from membership of a cohesive, all-male group, it seems also to be the case that membership of such a group can supply an unemployed man with ways of coping which do not require the renegotiation of the domestic division of labour – informal economic activity as a surrogate for paid employment and a source of personal income which would not otherwise be available, given the minimal provision made by supplementary benefit payments.

My data suggest not simply that men with highly developed local social networks are most likely to be presented with opportunities for informal economic activity, but that they are also most likely to maintain a rigid approach to the traditional division of domestic labour within their own homes.

The attitudes of women may, of course, be similarly influenced by the nature of their local social networks, but here the issues are not so clear-cut. On the one hand, a highly-developed network of female friends and/or kin could provide domestic assistance, usually child-care, which would free a woman to take on paid work outside the home, whilst on the other hand, membership of such a network may be the source of social pressure reinforcing her traditional role, and emphasizing her obligations within the home as a wife and mother.

CONCLUSION

The questions raised will be more fully investigated at some future date, and I would like to conclude by referring back to the question originally posed: what is the potential for flexibility in the domestic division of labour (internal and external) in the context of redundancy for a male main earner?

In its broadest sense renegotiation is dependent not on male unemployment but on the availability of employment opportunities for women, which have fallen considerably in Wales as a result of the recession, albeit to a lesser extent than employment opportunities for men. In my sample the number of women working full-time has shrunk in comparison with the situation prior to the BSC redundancies, and though the number employed part-time has increased the average number of hours worked has fallen.

Where paid employment is available to women then there are three options concerning the division of domestic labour:

1. the woman does two jobs – one in the home and one outside the home;
2. the man assumes an increased share of domestic labour (internal);
3. the woman remains responsible for domestic labour (internal) but looks beyond household members for assistance.

Of course some combination of these options will be likely to beadopted in any given case, and I have suggested that the sorts of arrangements arrived at will, in different ways, be influenced by the nature of the local social networks of each member of the couple.

Male unemployment raises further questions related to the

potential for flexibility in the division of domestic labour (internal) whether or not the wife is employed. What I have reported here are a number of variations occurring on the basis of a massively taken-for-granted division of labour. Although there is some evidence of a blurring of the boundaries which segregate male and female labour (both inside and outside the home) there is no evidence of a fundamental shift away from the traditional pattern.

What I suggest is that we are witnessing a renegotiation of certain details of everyday life within the household which is so far distinct from any serious renegotiation of the underlying principles. My respondents appear to be dealing with a period of personal confusion in a context of dramatic social change by endeavouring to maintain some continuity with their past life, and this is, of course, an understandable initial reaction. Whether it will persist, or whether the slight indications of flexibility we have seen represent the first step in some more far-reaching reorganization of domestic labour, it is impossible at this stage to say. One can only remark here that there are powerful social forces at work which will tend to preserve the *status quo*.

NOTES

1. Based on research financed by the Social Science Research Council (SSRC) and first presented at the 1983 British Sociological Association's conference 'Beyond the Fringe'.
2. Between 1971 and 1978 the male waged labour force for Wales as a whole fell by 2.4 per cent and the female waged labour force rose by 20.4 per cent. Between 1978 and 1981 the male waged labour force fell by 11.9 per cent and the female waged labour force by 7 per cent. In 1979 the rate of economically active women (41.2 per cent) was nevertheless low compared with the male rate of 75.8 per cent.
   We should also note, however, that in the league of female employment by region for the UK, Wales in 1979 was lowest with 41.2 per cent female participation as compared with the highest-ranking region, Scotland, with 48.8 per cent and a UK average of 46.6 per cent (Labour Force Survey 1979, Table 4.5, Office of Population Censuses and Surveys).
3. Ann Oakley (1974, p. 136) has suggested that social science has played a part in popularizing an egalitarian image of modern marriage which may be based on false premises.
4. From 72 to 61 between 1973 and 1980 – see General Household Survey, Office of Population Censuses and Surveys, 1980, Table 5.2.
5. Full-time employment rose from 25 per cent to 26 per cent for married

women, 1973–80, whilst part-time employment rose from 28 per cent to 33 per cent (Ibid, Table 5.2).

6. General Household Survey (1980), shows percentages of respectively 30, 62, and 71 as the age of the youngest child increases from 0–4 to 5–9 to over 10 years, as Table 5.7 reproduced below shows:

Age of youngest child	Mother's employment status		
	% Full-time	% Part-time	% Total
0–4	6	23	30
5–9	14	48	62
10 +	28	43	71
TOTAL	16	37	54

7. Each couple was interviewed jointly, and later as individuals in the absence of the other spouse. In contrast to Oakley, (1974, p. 137) I was afraid not only of overestimating the male input to domestic labour but also of collecting distorted data which reflected certain resentments about the content of gender roles.

8. For example, retraining, previous salary, preferential earnings-related benefit, the redundancy payment itself, make-up pay for those in jobs paying less than their BSC wage, etc.

9. Pre-redundancy, 4 worked 15 hours a week and 1 worked 5 hours a week. Post-redundancy, 3 worked 5 hours a week, 1 worked 12 hours a week, and 3 worked 15+ hours a week.

10. The length of time prior to the transition to supplementary benefit was lengthened for many by periods on make-up pay, retraining, or by spells of short-term employment.

11. I use this term throughout to refer to uninterrupted periods of employment lasting 1 month or more. In the 2 cases in question the men had been out of work for periods of 4 and 6 months respectively.

12. See note 11.

REFERENCES

Bott, E. (1957) *Family and Social Network* (London: Tavistock).
Bowlby, S. R. *et al.* (1983) 'Urban Austerity – the Impact on Women', unpublished paper presented at the SSRC Urban Change and Conflict Conference, Clacton, 1983.
Edgell, S. (1981) *Middle Class Couples* (London: Allen & Unwin).
Gardiner, J. (1975) 'Women's Domestic Labour', in *New Left Review*, no. 89. pp. 47–57.
General Household Survey (1980) Office of Population and Census Surveys.
Harris, C. C. (1969) *The Family* (London, Allen & Unwin).

Lee, R. M. *et al.* (1983) 'Aspects of the Everyday Life of the Redundant: The Place of Informal Relations', unpublished paper presented at the SSRC Urban Change and Conflict Conference, Clacton, 1983.

Massey, D. (1982) 'Industrial Restructuring as Class Restructuring', mimeo., London School of Economics.

Molyneux, M. (1979) 'Beyond the Domestic Labour Debate', in *New Left Review*, no. 116, pp. 3–24.

Morgan, K. (1983) 'Restructuring Steel', in *International Journal of Urban and Regional Research*, vol. 7, no. 2.

Oakley, A. (1974) *The Sociology of Housework* (London: Robertson).

Rushton, P. (1979) 'Marxism, Domestic Labour and the Capitalist Economy', in Harris, C. C. (ed.) 'The Sociology of the Family' (Keele: Sociological Review Monograph, no. 28) pp. 32–48.

Smith, P. (1978) 'Domestic Labour and Marx's Theory of Value', in Kuhn, A. and Wolpe, A. M. (eds) *Feminism and Materialism* (London: Routledge & Kegan Paul).

Townsend, P. (1979) *Poverty in the UK* (Harmondsworth: Penguin).

Urry, J. (1981) 'Localities, Regions and Social Class', in *International Journal of Urban and Regional Research* vol. 5, no. 4.

Index

245

Westergaard, J., 117, 123
Whitehead, A., 21, 40
Wickham, J., 14, 179–99
Wiesenthal, H., 36, 37, 40
Wigan, 57, 58, 59
Wilkinson, F., 133, 153
Williams, K., 4, 17
Williamson, J., 43, 62
Wilson, H., 132

Winckler, V., 14–15, 200–20
Wood, S., 133, 155, 219
wool industry, 156–75
Wool Industry Training Board, 166, 175
Wright, P., 169, 175

youth culture, 113

Zeitlin, J., 133, 155